SET THE WORLD ON FIRE

POLITICS AND CULTURE IN MODERN AMERICA

Series Editors:
Margot Canaday, Glenda Gilmore, Michael Kazin, Stephen Pitti, Thomas J. Sugrue

Volumes in the series narrate and analyze political and social change in the
broadest dimensions from 1865 to the present, including ideas about the ways
people have sought and wielded power in the public sphere and the language and
institutions of politics at all levels—local, national, and transnational. The series is
motivated by a desire to reverse the fragmentation of modern U.S. history and to
encourage synthetic perspectives on social movements and the state, on gender,
race, and labor, and on intellectual history and popular culture.

SET THE WORLD ON FIRE

Black Nationalist Women
and the Global Struggle for Freedom

KEISHA N. BLAIN

PENN

UNIVERSITY OF PENNSYLVANIA PRESS

PHILADELPHIA

Published by
University of Pennsylvania Press
Philadelphia, Pennsylvania 19104-4112
www.upenn.edu/pennpress

Printed in the United States of America
on acid-free paper

2 4 6 8 10 9 7 5 3 1

Library of Congress Cataloging-in-Publication Data

Names: Blain, Keisha N., 1985– author.
Title: Set the world on fire : black nationalist women and the
    global struggle for freedom / Keisha N. Blain.
Other titles: Politics and culture in modern America.
Description: 1st edition. | Philadelphia : University of Pennsylvania
    Press, [2018] | Series: Politics and culture in modern America |
    Includes bibliographical references and index.
Identifiers: LCCN 2017026795 | ISBN 9780812249880 (hardcover :
    alk. paper)
Subjects: LCSH: Black nationalism—History—20th century. |
    African diaspora—History—20th century. | Pan-Africanism—
    History—20th century. | African American women—Political
    activity—History—20th century. | African American women
    political activists—History—20th century. | Women in
    politics—United States—History.
Classification: LCC E185.6 .B65 2018 | DDC 320.54/60904—dc23
LC record available at https://lccn.loc.gov/2017026795

FOR MOM, WITH LOVE

CONTENTS

꒰

Introduction

꒦

> We want to set the world on fire, we want freedom and justice and a
> chance to build for ourselves. And if we must set the world on fire . . .
> we will, like other men, die for the realization of our dreams.
>   —Josephine Moody, "We Want to Set the World on Fire,"
>   *New Negro World*, January 1942

SET THE WORLD ON FIRE tells the story of how a cadre of black nationalist
women—Mittie Maude Lena Gordon, Ethel Waddell, Celia Jane Allen,
Ethel Collins, Amy Jacques Garvey, Amy Ashwood Garvey, Maymie Leona
Turpeau De Mena, and several others—vigorously fought to challenge
global white supremacy during the twentieth century. In various locales in
the United States, including Chicago, Harlem, and the Mississippi Delta,
and in other parts of the globe, including Britain and Jamaica, these women
emerged as leaders in national and transnational black political movements,
seeking to advance black nationalist and internationalist politics. At a
moment when people of African descent were being denied full citizenship
and human rights, the women profiled in this book utilized various strategies and tactics, such as letter-writing campaigns, grassroots organizing, and
lobbying, to agitate for the rights and dignity of people of African descent.

Drawing on an array of previously untapped sources, including archival
materials, government records, and unpublished songs and poetry, this
book uncovers the previously hidden voices of black nationalist women
activists and intellectuals whose ideas and activities differed significantly
from their counterparts in well-known organizations such as the National

Association of Colored Women (NACW), the National Association for the Advancement of Colored People (NAACP), and the National Urban League (NUL). While the activists and intellectuals in these prominent organizations were equally committed to ending racism and discrimination and eradicating the global color line, they rejected many of the ideas and strategies black nationalist women endorsed and often exhibited elitist views that caused a rift among activists. Feeling alienated from many of the ideas and political approaches of activists in mainstream civil rights organizations like the NAACP and the NUL and rejecting the Marxist platform of leftist organizations like the Communist Party, the black nationalist women chronicled in this book created spaces of their own in which to experiment with various strategies and ideologies.

Set the World on Fire centers on women leaders who were actively involved in several black political organizations of the period. Many of the women chronicled in this book were active members of Marcus Garvey's Universal Negro Improvement Association (UNIA), the dominant black nationalist organization in the United States and worldwide in the immediate post–World War I era.[1] When the UNIA began to crumble under the weight of factionalism and conflict in the aftermath of Garvey's 1927 deportation, some attempted to keep the UNIA afloat and worked under the auspices of the fragmented organization to keep black nationalist ideas alive and vibrant in political discourse. Others chose to pursue new avenues. In 1932, former UNIA member Mittie Maude Lena Gordon, an activist originally from Louisiana, established the Peace Movement of Ethiopia (PME) at the back of her restaurant in Chicago. In the presence of her husband, William, and twelve other black men and women, Gordon drafted the organization's mission statement, endorsing black emigration to West Africa, black political self-determination, and the "confraternity among all dark races."[2] Within only a matter of months, the PME grew from a small group of black working-class activists in Chicago to become the largest and most influential black nationalist political movement in the United States, attracting an estimated 300,000 supporters in more than a dozen cities across the country.[3]

While the PME and the UNIA represented the two largest black political organizations in which black nationalist women were active, they were by no means the only ones. During the twentieth century, the women profiled in this book were involved in several black political groups, including the Harlem-based Universal Ethiopian Students Association (UESA) and the

Peace Movement of Ethiopia, Inc., an offshoot of Gordon's PME. Regardless of their organizational affiliation, however, all of these women were key proponents of black nationalism—the political view that people of African descent constitute a separate group or nationality on the basis of their distinct culture, shared history, and experiences.[4] As black nationalists, the women profiled in this book advocated Pan-African unity, African redemption from European colonization, racial separatism, black pride, political self-determination, and economic self-sufficiency. With few material resources during a period of much economic and political turmoil, these women asserted their political power in various locales across the United States and in other parts of the African diaspora. This book highlights black nationalist women's political organizing in the U.S. North, Midwest, and Jim Crow South and examines their transnational work and collaborations with activists in North America, Africa, Asia, Europe, Latin America, and the Caribbean.

If, as one historian has argued, the period from 1850 to 1925 was the "golden age of black nationalism," its decline did not occur after Marcus Garvey's deportation.[5] Rather, the collapse of Garvey's UNIA provided opportunities for women activists to engage in nationalist politics in new, idiosyncratic, and innovative ways. While historians generally portray the period between the Garvey movement of the 1920s and Black Power of the 1960s and 1970s as an era of declining black nationalist activism, this book reframes the Great Depression, World War II, and early Cold War as significant eras of black nationalist ferment.[6] During this period, women became central leaders in various black nationalist movements in the United States and other parts of the globe, agitating for racial unity, black political self-determination, and economic self-sufficiency. This is not to suggest that women's engagement in black nationalist politics prior to 1927 was insignificant or that they did not play key roles in earlier black nationalist movements. The post-Garvey moment, however, opened up unique opportunities for women in the movement to refine and redefine black nationalist politics on their own terms.

With the effective collapse of the UNIA during the mid-1920s, a vanguard of nationalist women leaders emerged on the local, national, and international scenes, practicing a pragmatic form of nationalist politics that allowed for greater flexibility, adaptability, and experimentation. The women chronicled in this book employed multiple protest strategies and tactics. They combined numerous religious and political ideologies such as Garveyism, Ethiopianism, Pan-Africanism, and Islam. And they forged unlikely political alliances—with Japanese activists, for instance—in their struggles against racism, sexism, colonialism, and imperialism. As pragmatic activists, black nationalist women were willing to embrace "whatever seemed likely to help blacks live better lives in their half-free environment."[7] Given the shifting political and social terrain on which black nationalist women were fighting to combat racism and discrimination, their methods were diverse and ever-changing. For this reason, the strategies and tactics that appeared likely to help black people at one moment could be easily abandoned the next.

*   *   *

The emergence of this "golden age" of black nationalist women's political activism coincided with the onset of the Great Depression, one of the most catastrophic periods of U.S. and world history. In the United States, the Depression was especially difficult for black Americans, exacerbating already poor socioeconomic conditions that existed long before 1929. Although Franklin D. Roosevelt's New Deal programs promised to improve economic conditions for all, black Americans received a "raw deal," facing rampant discrimination, disenfranchisement, and unrelenting racial violence.[8] The challenges black people faced on the national front were deeply intertwined with the struggles people of African descent experienced in other parts of the globe. As the United States, Britain, and other world powers inched closer to war in the late 1930s, black men and women were engaged in a war of their own. Although the leaders of these world powers claimed to endorse the democratic principles of "freedom and justice for all," people of African descent were fighting for human rights and demanding equal recognition and participation in global civil society.

Across the African and Asian continents and throughout Latin America and the Caribbean, the impact of white imperial control could be felt. Despite the rhetoric of self-determination, global democracy, and freedom, British colonial rule persisted well into the twentieth century while the United States continued to exercise territorial, economic, and political control over people of color.[9] In parts of Africa and Asia, Britain controlled a vast empire, encompassing diverse territories such as Nigeria, Sierra Leone, and India. Throughout the Anglophone Caribbean, the lives of people of color were circumscribed by a racial hierarchy in which British imperialists controlled the domestic economies.[10] Similarly, the United States was in the business of "empire making"—culturally, politically, economically, and even territorially.[11] The significant U.S. presence in Haiti, Cuba, Nicaragua, and elsewhere helped to "internationalize U.S. culture," providing an opening for U.S. policy makers to formally institute a system of imperial domination and exploitation.[12] These two world powers played crucial roles in maintaining the global color line, which placed people of color at the bottom of the social, economic, and political hierarchy.

The desperate conditions under which black men and women were living during this period often called for desperate measures. Not surprisingly, the women chronicled in this book were willing to explore all avenues, no matter how controversial or seemingly unusual in hindsight, in hopes that they might accomplish their political goals. Rather than assessing these women's ideas and activism solely based on the tangible outcomes of their political struggles, this book examines the principles and the philosophies that undergirded black nationalist women's actions. Moreover, it pays close attention to how black nationalist women, especially working-class and impoverished women, sought to achieve their political goals and explains why they pursued certain strategies, tactics, and methods.

* * *

The key figures in this book expressed distinct concerns and interests, as well as utilized diverse political approaches that were influenced by various factors, including their socioeconomic backgrounds, their personal upbringings, their specific locales, and their organizational affiliations. Regardless of these distinctions, however, they were all black nationalists—a term they often used to describe themselves. Similar to other ideologies, black nationalism is neither static nor monolithic. Indeed, it has taken on several different forms and manifestations—such as cultural nationalism, economic nationalism, and religious nationalism—at various historical moments. Notwithstanding its complexity, the term provides a relevant theoretical framework and a crucial starting point for understanding the political ideas and activism of the women chronicled here. Indeed, the black women activists in this book embraced racial separatism, black pride and unity, political self-determination, and economic self-sufficiency. These core tenets, with varying degrees of emphasis at certain historical moments, have been fundamental to understanding black nationalism since its earliest articulations.[13]

From Maria Stewart's and David Walker's writings and speeches in the 1830s to the political work and expressions of Audley "Queen Mother" Moore, Malcolm X, and other black activists and intellectuals during the Black Power era, what has distinguished black nationalist thought in the United States from other political ideologies is a militant response to white supremacy, a recognition of the distinctiveness of black culture and history, and an emphasis on how people who represent a "nation within a nation" ought to create for themselves autonomous spaces in which to advance their own social, political, and economic goals. At the heart of black nationalism is a recognition that integration, were it ever to be realized, cannot fully address the persistent challenges of people of African descent in the United States and other parts of the diaspora. To view black nationalism as an oppositional stance in relation to integration does not imply that activists operated within a rigid ideological binary. Indeed, as history has repeatedly shown us, political ideas and activities are contingent, fluid, and disorderly.[14] To that end, the women in this book often pushed beyond the perceived boundaries of black nationalism to craft an idiosyncratic political praxis born out of necessity.

Many of the women in this book were, in varying ways, drawn to black nationalism through Garveyism—the teachings and principles of Marcus Garvey. In addition to Mittie Maude Lena Gordon and Ethel Waddell, other women, such as UNIA cofounder Amy Ashwood (Garvey's first wife), UNIA national organizer Maymie De Mena, and Pan-Africanist feminist Amy Jacques Garvey (Garvey's second wife), were active in the Garvey movement during the 1920s. In the post-Garvey era, some remained involved in the fragmented UNIA, whereas others moved in different directions. For this reason, all of the black nationalist women in this book should not be classified *solely* as "Garveyites"—a term that reinforces the ideological ties to Garvey yet does not account for the diverse political and religious traditions on which black nationalist women drew.

Indeed, while this book joins an ongoing scholarly effort to assess the global impact and enduring legacies of Garveyism—as an ideology and political organizing tool—it moves beyond Garveyism as the sole or even primary prism through which women leaders crafted a political response to global white supremacy.[15] *Set the World on Fire* highlights women's efforts to formulate a black nationalist politics that often took on new shapes and meanings during the post-Garvey era. Black nationalist women's political ideas and activities were not simply efforts to maintain or even to extend Garveyism but often to depart from it entirely. In the absence of Garvey's direct leadership and influence, the expressions of black nationalism that emerged during the post-1927 era sometimes resembled Garveyism but at other times did not.

Similar to many of the black nationalists who preceded them, the women in this book drew on both radical and conservative traditions to formulate their political ideas and praxis. On one hand, black nationalist women embraced heteronormative gender politics and generally advocated civilizationist racial uplift views—often cloaked in Christian rhetoric. Whereas black women radicals in the Communist Party endorsed anti-capitalism, black nationalist women promoted black capitalism, in the belief that the growth of black-owned businesses would bolster economic self-sufficiency and thus enrich and sustain black life.[16] On the other hand, black nationalist women embraced many ideas that challenged the status quo. Black nationalist women's endorsement of Afro-Asian solidarity, call for black separatism, support of African liberation struggles, and anti-imperialist critique of U.S. foreign policy—to name a few—were all ideas that were considered "radical" in relation to mainstream black political discourses of the twentieth century. More specifically, their ideas and activism reflected what political sociologist Craig Calhoun describes as tactical radicalism—an emphasis on "immediate change" and a willingness to use "extreme measures" to achieve their political goals.[17]

In their willingness to use such methods, black nationalist women leaders made a number of political missteps and errors in judgment and often pursued questionable alliances with individuals who did not share their vision. For instance, because black nationalist women generally embraced a biologically based understanding of race, they were willing to form political collaborations with well-known white supremacists in hopes of advancing their political goals. In the short term, these alliances proved somewhat advantageous—on several occasions, the white supremacists with whom these women collaborated used their political influence and material resources to support black emigration efforts. In the long term, however, these controversial alliances hindered black nationalist women's political goals. By forging these unusual alliances—however practical they appeared to them to be at the time—black nationalist women undermined their credibility in the eyes of many of their contemporaries. Yet understanding why they would take such measures—what, in their ideological makeup, gave them license to do so—is one of the fundamental goals of this book.

*   *   *

Perhaps the most important aspect of black nationalist women's political life was their interest in and commitment to black internationalism. Building upon a long and rich tradition and history dating back to the Age of Revolution, black nationalist women maintained a global racial consciousness and commitment to universal emancipation.[18] These women understood that the struggle for black rights in the United States as well as the fight for black political self-determination could not be divorced from the global struggles for freedom in Asia, Africa, Latin America and the Caribbean, and other parts of the globe. Using a variety of avenues, including journalism, print media, and overseas travel, black nationalist women articulated and disseminated global visions of freedom and sought to build transnational and transracial alliances with other people of color in order to secure civil and human rights.

While much of the scholarship on black internationalism centers on the ideas and political activities of towering individuals such as W. E. B. Du Bois, Paul Robeson, and C. L. R. James, this book emphasizes the significant yet largely underappreciated contributions of a diverse group of women activists and intellectuals. *Set the World on Fire* foregrounds the writings, speeches, and activism of black women leaders of all walks of life and explores how gender and gender relations shaped internationalist movements and discourses.[19] Moreover, this book highlights the interplay between national and geopolitical issues and makes visible the diverse and creative ways black nationalist women leaders built transnational networks with a diverse group of activists across the globe.

Whereas conventional historical narratives tend to privilege the political activities of the black middle class and elite, this book pays particular attention to the internationalist activities of working-poor women activists. It foregrounds the ideas and activism of impoverished black women activists and intellectuals with limited financial resources and, as a consequence, limited mobility. Amid the social and political upheavals of the twentieth century, impoverished black women activists and intellectuals devised a range of creative strategies to advance their internationalist agenda. These women often engaged in grassroots internationalism, articulating global visions of freedom and practicing black internationalist politics on the local level. Although many of the women in this book could not afford overseas travel, they sought to advance internationalism through their writings, community work, and local collaborations with men and women from various parts of the globe. By centering these women's grassroots internationalist politics, this book sheds new light on the crucial role working-poor women played in black internationalist movements of the twentieth century.

Similar to other black women internationalists of the period, the women in this book often articulated a proto-feminist consciousness—an opposition to gender inequality that predated the feminist movements of the 1960s and 1970s. Scholars often disagree on the precise terminology appropriate for describing black nationalist women's positions on women and gender issues. Yet, one thing is certain: black nationalist women during the early to mid-twentieth century often exhibited feminist beliefs and employed strategies that foreshadowed modern feminist movements of the 1960s and 1970s.[20] These women sought to empower other women in the African diaspora and rejected sexist perceptions of women as intellectually inferior to men.[21] They articulated a critique of male supremacy and attempted to change the patriarchal structures of the organizations in which they were active.[22]

Despite these overt expressions of feminism, black nationalist women's gender and sexual politics were far more complex. As black feminist theorist Joy James reminds us, black women activists and intellectuals were "not uniformly progressive." Indeed, black women's articulations of what James describes as "radical or revolutionary black feminism" stood side by side with "liberal and conservative feminisms and antiracism."[23] Not surprisingly, the women in this book critiqued male chauvinism and patriarchy, on one hand, and embraced traditionally conservative perspectives on gender and sexuality, on the other. In many ways, black nationalist women's ideological complexity mirrors the ideas and experiences of nationalist women in postcolonial Middle Eastern and South Asian societies.[24] While women in black nationalist movements during the early to mid-twentieth century found ways to challenge male patriarchy and even attempted to expand opportunities for women, their activities were still circumscribed by the masculinist traditions of nationalist discourses and movements in which black men were fighting to prove their manhood—often at the expense of women's rights and autonomy.[25]

*   *   *

At the heart of this book is an exploration of how black nationalist women "on the margins" struggled to make their way to the center—that is, the forefront of political movements for global black liberation.[26] These women, representing a subordinate group within the global racial and gender hierarchies, advocated immediate social changes and in so doing laid the political groundwork for a new generation of black activists and intellectuals engaged in struggles for freedom during the modern Civil Rights–Black Power era of the 1960s and 1970s. In their efforts to eradicate the global color line, the women profiled in this book adopted a practical and pragmatic approach to local, national, and global politics.[27] From the early twentieth century to the 1950s, these women devised a range of strategies and tactics, drew on an array of religious and political ideologies, and collaborated with activists and politicians of various political persuasions. Often with limited material resources and in the face of much opposition, these women attempted to transform American society and sought to improve conditions for people of color all across the globe.

Their stories capture the depth and complexities of the global black freedom struggle. Indeed, they illustrate the range of protest strategies and tactics individuals have employed in their efforts to resist domination, degradation, and exploitation. In addition, they enrich our understandings of how black nationalist women, particularly members of the working poor and individuals with limited formal education, have functioned as key leaders, theorists, and strategists at the grassroots, national, and international levels. What follows is an account of these women's stories in all their quirkiness, complexities, and paradoxes—filled with moments of tragedy and defeat but also filled with moments of triumph and hope.

CHAPTER 1

予

Women Pioneers in the Garvey Movement

ON APRIL 19, 1924, Eunice Lewis's editorial, "The Black Woman's Part in Race Leadership," appeared on the women's page of the *Negro World*— "Our Women and What They Think." A member of Marcus Garvey's Universal Negro Improvement Association (UNIA) residing in Chicago, Lewis crafted a succinct yet powerful article that embodied the spirit of the "New Negro Woman." "There are many people who think that a woman's place is only in the home—to raise children, cook, wash, and attend to the domestic affairs of the house," Lewis noted. "This idea, however, does not hold true to the New Negro Woman," she continued. The "New Negro Woman," Lewis insisted, was intelligent, worked equally with men, was business savvy, and, most significantly, was committed to "revolutionizing the old type of male leadership" in the UNIA and in the community at large.[1] Her comments, which coincided with the Harlem, or "New Negro," Renaissance of the period, signified a key shift that was taking place within the Garvey movement.[2]

Founded by Marcus Garvey, with the assistance of Amy Ashwood, in Kingston, Jamaica, in 1914, the UNIA (originally the Universal Negro Improvement Association and African Communities League) was the largest and most influential Pan-Africanist movement of the twentieth century. Emphasizing racial pride, black political self-determination, racial separatism, African heritage, economic self-sufficiency, and African redemption from European colonization, Garvey envisioned the UNIA as a vehicle for improving the social, political, and economic conditions of black people everywhere. From Kingston, Jamaica, Garvey oversaw UNIA affairs before relocating to Harlem, where he incorporated the organization in 1918. At its peak, from 1919 to 1924, the organization attracted millions of followers in more than forty countries around the world.

Like many black nationalists before and after him, Garvey maintained a masculinist vision of black liberation and thus believed that black men would ultimately lead the fight to improve conditions for black people in the diaspora.[3] Although he was not necessarily opposed to female leaders, Garvey sought to maintain a patriarchal model of leadership in the UNIA, which allowed women to serve as leaders only under the watchful eye of Garveyite men. Moreover, Garvey, as many other black men during the early twentieth century, endorsed Victorian ideals and exhibited the "spirit of manliness," a masculine sensibility that emphasized black men's respectability and ability to produce and provide.[4] Along these lines, Garvey not only upheld the belief that men were the vigilant protectors of black women and children but also embraced the view that women's natural place was in the home as wife and mother.[5]

Eunice Lewis's call for "revolutionizing the old type of male leadership" was therefore a direct challenge to the prevailing ethos of black patriarchy in the Garvey movement. Along with a cadre of women during this period, including Amy Jacques Garvey, Maymie De Mena, and Henrietta Vinton Davis, Lewis articulated a new and expansive vision of black women's leadership in the UNIA and in the community as a whole. These women, from a variety of socioeconomic backgrounds and social positions, adopted a proto-feminist stance in which they directly challenged male supremacy and attempted to change the UNIA's patriarchal leadership structure. In their efforts to "revolution[ize] the old type of male leadership," black nationalist women pioneers created opportunities for women to have greater visibility and autonomy than Garvey originally envisioned. Moreover, they devoted significant attention to women's issues and often defied prevailing gender conventions. In doing so, they articulated many of the same arguments and employed some of the strategies that were fundamental to feminist movements that emerged during the 1960s and 1970s.[6]

In addition to adopting a proto-feminist stance, women in the UNIA articulated several strands of black nationalism, drawing upon a rich and long tradition of black nationalist thought in the United States and across the diaspora. For example, they envisioned Africa as the homeland for black people and maintained the belief that black emigration would provide a means for black men and women to escape their second-class citizenship status and increase their political and economic power on a global scale. For many black nationalist women, Liberia represented the ideal location because of its ties to African Americans and its position as one of only two independent African nations during this period. Maintaining a cultural and racial bond with Africans on the continent and throughout the diaspora, women in the Garvey movement during the 1920s promoted Pan-Africanism and attempted to mobilize black men and women against racial discrimination, colonialism, and imperialism. They also advocated black economic self-sufficiency but did so within the framework of existing capitalist structures. To that end, they endorsed black capitalism, attempting to control the marketplace through the creation of black businesses and independent black institutions. By promoting all of these ideals, women in the Garvey movement played a pioneering role in twentieth-century black nationalism, laying the groundwork and theoretical foundations for the vanguard of nationalist women leaders who emerged in the three decades after Garvey's 1927 deportation.

Amy Ashwood and the Birth of the UNIA

Marcus Garvey's UNIA rose to prominence amid the social and political upheavals in the wake of World War I. A pivotal turning point in the history of the modern African diaspora, World War I, which began in 1914 and ended in 1918, mobilized thousands of black men to fight for the same democratic rights and privileges they were being denied at home.[7] The war also created a labor shortage in the United States, which provided a crucial opportunity for black men and women from various parts of the globe to gain employment in northern cities. Perhaps most significantly, the war dramatically altered the political consciousness of peoples of African descent in profound ways. In the war's aftermath, black men and women unequivocally rejected the racial discrimination that persisted in the United States and colonial territories in Africa, Latin America, and the Caribbean. When the war ended in 1918, Afro-Caribbean migrants, for example, who had served in the British West Indies Regiment, openly revolted against the British in a series of uprisings that swept the region.[8]

These political uprisings, combined with a number of historical developments of the era, including the Bolshevik Revolution in Russia (1917) and race riots in the United States referred to as the "Red Summer" (1919), created an atmosphere in which the UNIA emerged as the largest and most influential Pan-Africanist movement of the twentieth century.[9] Reflecting the rhetoric of self-determination, which gained increasing currency in mainstream political discourse after World War I, Garvey called on black men and women across the diaspora to help establish an autonomous black nation-state.[10] In Garvey's teachings, black men and women across the globe found the strategies and tactics to counter racial oppression and to advance universal black liberation.[11]

From the outset, black women were integral to the UNIA's growth and success. In 1914, when Garvey launched the organization, Amy Ashwood, who later became his first wife, served as its cofounder and first secretary.[12] Born in 1897 in Port Antonio, on the northeastern coast of Jamaica, Ashwood was one of three children and the only girl born of wealthy businessman Michael Delbert Ashwood and his wife, Maudriana (Maud) Ashwood (née Thompson). Shortly after Amy's birth, the Ashwood family relocated to Panama City, where Amy's father opened a bakery and restaurant during the construction of the Panama Canal. Concerned about the quality of education their children were receiving in Panama, Michael and Maud decided to bring the family back to Jamaica in 1904.

At age eleven, Amy began attending Westwood High School, a prestigious private school for girls that had been established by Reverend William Webb, a Baptist minister, in 1882. The first of its kind in Jamaica, Westwood provided an opportunity for all girls, regardless of class or race, to obtain quality educational training. There Ashwood was exposed to a diverse curriculum, which included courses in homemaking, biblical scripture, typing, and shorthand, as well as history, English, geography, mathematics, and science. Despite the first-rate education Westwood offered, the school's curriculum was, in many ways, a reflection of the British colonial system. When she began attending the school, Jamaica, the largest of the English-speaking Caribbean islands, had been under British colonial rule for more than two hundred years. Similar to other students who attended schools in British colonies during this period, Ashwood was primarily taught British history and, as result, had very little knowledge about black history and culture.[13]

Later in life, Amy credited her ninety-three-year-old great-grandmother, Boahimaa Dabas—"Grannie Dabas" as she was called—for making her aware of her African heritage and igniting her race consciousness and growing sense of Pan-Africanism. At age twelve, Ashwood began to ask Grannie

Dabas about her ancestors after an incident at school sometime in 1909. Recounting the event years later, Ashwood explained that teachers at West-wood had organized a mission fund that year to aid those in need. During a visit with Mrs. Webb, the wife of the school's founder, Ashwood disclosed the amount of money she managed to raise for the mission fund and was startled when Mrs. Webb expressed disappointment that the money would not be sent to Ashwood's "people" in Africa. "Being so young," Ashwood explained, "I was very puzzled by this bit of news and naturally asked the lady many more questions about Africa."[14]

Intrigued yet horrified by the information Mrs. Webb provided—about how black people had been captured by English slave traders on the shores of Africa and brought to Jamaica—Ashwood set out to find out more infor-mation about her ancestors. When her father became overwhelmed by the line of questioning, he took Ashwood to Grannie Dabas, who carefully recounted the difficult story of her capture on the Gold Coast at age sixteen and her life under slavery. According to Ashwood, her great-grandmother also described the "virility of her people and their prowess in war," inform-ing the girl that her great-great uncle was an accomplished military general of the Ashanti (Asante), one of the dominant ethnic groups in West Africa. This newfound knowledge of her family's history awakened Ashwood's racial consciousness and bolstered her confidence. "I was proud of myself [and] proud of my ancestry," she recounted years later. "I went back to school with a feeling of innate pride. I had a country, I had a name. I could hark back to my genealogy."[15]

By the time Ashwood met Marcus Garvey five years later, she had already developed a strong sense of race consciousness. However, her encounter with Garvey and subsequent relationship with him strengthened her interest in Pan-African politics. The two met in July 1914, when Garvey attended the weekly debate at the East Queen Street Baptist Church in Kingston. One of the featured speakers, Ashwood took the position that "morality does not increase with the march of civilization." Garvey, who Ashwood later described as a "stocky figure with slightly drooping shoul-ders," not only defended her point of view but also took the initiative to approach her afterward as she awaited her ride home. According to Ash-wood, Garvey immediately expressed his love, declaring, "At last, I have found my star of destiny! I have found my Josephine!"[16] By Garvey's account, the encounter was far less dramatic. He only recalled being intro-duced to Ashwood by a colleague. Although the specific details of their initial encounter remain a mystery, what is certain is that the encounter between Garvey and Ashwood marked the beginning of a vibrant political relationship.

Together, Garvey and Ashwood worked in tandem to launch what would become the largest and most influential Pan-Africanist movement of the twentieth century. Drawing inspiration from Booker T. Washington, founder of the Tuskegee Institute in Alabama, Garvey envisioned the UNIA as a benevolent organization committed to Washington's ideals of racial uplift, self-help, and social activism. Washington's *Up from Slavery* (1901), which emphasized the significance of black education, had a profound effect on Garvey, who upon reading it experienced an epiphany of his calling to become a "race leader."[17] Ashwood shared similar views to Garvey and credited their mutual interests in Pan-Africanism and racial uplift as the driving force behind the creation of the UNIA. Describing their collective political vision during these early years, Ashwood noted, "Our joint love for Africa and our concern for the welfare of our race urged us on to immediate action." "Together we talked over the possibilities of forming an organisation to serve the needs of the peoples of African origin," Ashwood explained, "[and] we spent many hours deliberating what exactly our aims should be and what means we should employ to achieve those aims."[18] Working closely together, Ashwood and Garvey began planning the first UNIA meeting.

Although historians have debated the extent of Ashwood's formal role in establishing the organization, none deny the fundamental importance of her organizational skills and social networks to the UNIA's success.[19] The organization's earliest meetings, for example, were held at the home of Ashwood's parents, and Garvey secured some of his earliest financial supporters through these contacts.[20] When the UNIA's headquarters relocated to Harlem in 1917, Ashwood remained actively engaged in the organization's affairs. In addition to serving as general secretary in the New York office, Ashwood played a fundamental role in popularizing the *Negro World*, the UNIA's official newspaper. "From midnight until four in the morning," she recalled, "Marcus and I would trudge around the streets of Harlem putting a slim copy of the *Negro World* under people's doors." By her own account, Ashwood also contributed to the financial growth of the UNIA, relying on her parents' money to meet some of the organization's growing expenses.[21] During the UNIA's early years, Ashwood helped to finance the Black Star Line Steamship Corporation (BSL), the UNIA's

FIGURE 1. Marcus Garvey on August 5, 1924. George Grantham
Bain Collection, LC-USZ61-1854, Library of Congress.

transatlantic steamship enterprise and the organization's largest and most significant business venture. In addition to helping raise the necessary funds for the BSL, she served as secretary and later as one of the directors.

In Harlem, Ashwood popularized black nationalist ideas on crowded street corners, using these public spaces as platforms to advance her political agenda.[22] Joining Marcus Garvey and a diverse group of other black stepladder speakers in Harlem, Ashwood began delivering public speeches on street corners in 1918. On several occasions, Ashwood publicly recited poetry, including Paul Laurence Dunbar's famous poem, "We Wear the Mask," which shed light on the strategies black people employed to survive segregation, oppression, and daily degradation. In one public speech, Ashwood reminded Harlemites that the struggles facing black people in the United States were intertwined with the challenges facing people of African descent throughout the globe. Underscoring her Pan-African vision, Ashwood passionately argued, "The Negro question is no longer a local one, but of the Negroes of the world, joining hands and fighting for one common cause." Reflecting her commitment to black political self-determination, Ashwood also reminded listeners that they "cannot attain Democracy unless they win it for themselves."[23] Ashwood's public speeches on Harlem street corners popularized the black nationalist objectives of the UNIA, brought greater visibility to the organization, and certainly helped to boost its membership. By 1919, the UNIA attracted an estimated 35,000 members in Harlem alone.[24]

Among her various contributions, Ashwood's early efforts to expand opportunities for women in the UNIA were perhaps the most significant. During its formative years, Ashwood maintained a vocal presence in the UNIA, encouraging the integration of women into the organization's leadership structure. Through her efforts, Ashwood ensured that women would be well integrated into the UNIA's constitution, and she also helped to create a system in which women would have opportunities to serve in both public and private roles. For example, each local UNIA division included a male and female president and vice president, and women actively participated in several auxiliaries that provided opportunities for them to develop leadership and organizing skills. Black women did not find equal opportunities to men in the UNIA, but the organization was, in some ways, one of the most progressive black political organizations of the period—when compared to other race organizations in which women were often confined to behind-the-scenes roles. Although Ashwood desired separate and equal roles for men and

women, the UNIA adopted a hierarchal structure in which women had separate but unequal roles. Still, Ashwood must be credited for advocating the
importance of women's leadership in the UNIA's early years, and her efforts
certainly provided invaluable opportunities for many black women to participate in the rapidly expanding Pan-Africanist organization.[25]

While the UNIA experienced significant growth during these years, the
personal relationship between Ashwood and Garvey became increasingly
contentious. On December 25, 1919, the two were married in an extrava-
gant ceremony at the UNIA's Liberty Hall, initiating what became a brief
and tumultuous union. Only three months later, the two were embroiled
in a bitter public divorce. Garvey accused Ashwood of being unfaithful and
drinking too much. Ashwood accused Garvey of abandoning the marriage
and prioritizing the UNIA over his new wife. Ashwood vehemently denied
Garvey's accusations and Garvey denied hers. In the end, the rumors alone
proved detrimental to Ashwood's reputation—far more than Garvey's.
During a period in which ideas of "respectable" black womanhood dominated public discourse, the accusations of adultery and alcoholism, whether
truthful or not, could easily taint a black woman's public image.[26] This was
certainly true for Ashwood, who encountered scorn and resentment from
some UNIA members in the aftermath of the divorce. Resilient in her
efforts to advance Pan-Africanist politics and now motivated by a desire
"to work in a more intimate fashion in order to help [black] women to
find themselves and rise in life," Ashwood set out to continue her political
work—far away from her ex-husband and the public spectacle surrounding
their divorce. In 1922, she left New York for London, where she joined a
vibrant community of black activists and intellectuals from Nigeria, Ghana,
Jamaica, and other British colonial territories.[27] In 1924, she helped to
establish the Nigerian Progress Union (NPU), an anticolonial organization,
with Nigerian activist Ladipo Solanke. Years later, in 1935, she opened the
International Afro Restaurant and then the Florence Mills Social Parlour,
which both provided significant spaces for black activists and intellectuals
in London to socialize and forge political alliances.[28]

Women, Gender, and Global Garveyism

Despite her departure from the UNIA, Amy Ashwood's efforts left a lasting
impact on the movement. In the United States, the organization witnessed
rapid growth in its female membership with women serving in various

capacities on national and international levels. Generally confined to the drudgery of domestic work, black women found a sense of empowerment in the UNIA, and the organization functioned as a political incubator in which many black women became politicized and trained for future leadership. Drawn to the UNIA by a series of factors, these women represent the widespread reach of Garveyism, which profoundly altered the lives of black men and women from a wide range of socioeconomic and educational backgrounds in various parts of the world. Indeed, the global reach of the organization cannot be overlooked. Whereas other race organizations of the period, including the National Association for the Advancement of Colored People (NAACP) and the National Urban League (NUL), maintained a membership base in the United States, UNIA chapters could be found in more than forty countries worldwide, including Costa Rica, South Africa, and Trinidad.[29] The global organization captured the imagination of a wide range of Afrodescended people across the globe, crossing cultural, ethnic, and class lines.

Throughout the United States, Canada, and other parts of the African diaspora, the UNIA played a critical part in fueling the racial consciousness of black women from all walks of life. Audley "Queen Mother" Moore, who became active in the Garvey movement in Louisiana, was drawn to Garvey's Pan-Africanist teachings during the early 1920s. Born in New Iberia, Louisiana, in 1898, Moore relocated to New Orleans with her younger sisters, Eloise and Lorita, where she worked as a hairdresser and later in domestic service.[30] Recounting a story many years later, Moore vividly describes the first time she heard Garvey speak in New Orleans, sometime around 1920: "We heard that Garvey was coming to New Orleans, but the police would not allow him to speak. Garvey came and they arrested him. The people raised so much sand until they had to let him out the next night." When local police officials tried to block Garvey from speaking during the second night, she and others pulled out guns in defense of Garvey's right to speak.[31] Moore's first encounter with Garvey that evening marked the beginning of her political journey into black nationalist and radical politics. In Moore's words, "Garvey brought something very beautiful to us—Africa for the Africans. He made us conscious of the fact that we belong to a big continent, with all of its gold and diamonds and riches. . . . That we were somebody . . . That we had a right to be restored to our proper selves."[32]

Similar to Moore, other black women credited Garvey for awakening their political consciousness during this period. Violet Blackman, a resident

of Toronto, Canada, praised Garvey for igniting her interest in race activism. Blackman, who had relocated to Toronto from the United States in
1920, joined the UNIA for the first time in Toronto, which provided one
of the few public platforms available for Canadian black men and women
during this period to challenge racism and discrimination. At the time she
joined the movement, Blackman recalls a period of intense antiblack racism
and racial segregation. "You couldn't get any position," Blackman said,
"regardless [of] who you were and how educated you were, other than
housework, because even if the employer would employ you, those that you
had to work with would not work with you." Like so many other black
men and women in Canada during this period, Blackman turned to the
Garvey movement as a step toward securing equal rights and opportunities.
"The UNIA was my heart and my soul and my life," Blackman admitted.[33]
As a member of the organization, Blackman found a vibrant community of
activists and intellectuals who were committed to improving the lives of
people of African descent. With the assistance of other Garveyite women in
Toronto, Blackman ran a children's program, hosted various community
events, and assisted younger black women seeking jobs in the area.[34]

Lucy Lastrappe, a native of Georgia who resided in Chicago during this
period, had similar memories of the UNIA. A gospel singer who went on
to sing the lead in a quartet called the Universal Four during the 1930s,
Lastrappe was drawn to the Pan-Africanist vision of Marcus Garvey. From
1922 to 1930, Lastrappe was an active member of the UNIA's Division No.
23 in Chicago. Recalling her activities years later, Lastrappe expressed a
sense of pride in her decision to become a Garveyite: "My work has not
been easy and I've had my bitters and sweets, but I love my work and love
the principles of the Universal Negro Improvement Association." "I have
had some good and bad times," she added, "but I'm still working in the
Cause of African Redemption, and . . . I want my work to be an inspiration
to some girl or boy to take up the work and carry on until Africa is
redeemed."[35] In black nationalist discourse of the period, African redemption meant the complete liberation of Africans and peoples of African
descent from racism, European colonization, and global imperialism. Lastrappe's comments underscore how this notion of African redemption was
a central component of Garveyite philosophy.

In an era of strict gender roles, involvement in the UNIA enabled black
women like Lastrappe to engage in political activities outside of the expected parameters of home and family.[36] The ratification of the Nineteenth

Amendment in 1920, which signaled an expansion of women's political power, ultimately failed to live up to its promises for black women and other women of color; it took more than four decades before they experienced the full benefits of suffrage.[37] Largely shut out of the formal political process, black women in the United States during the 1920s found opportunities to engage in political activity through predominantly black religious institutions and the black women's club movement.[38] In addition to these venues, women found some leadership opportunities in mainstream civil rights organizations such as the NAACP and the NUL. These opportunities, however, were limited in scope—often confined to behind-the-scenes roles.[39] With few visible leadership positions available to black women during this period, the UNIA provided a unique opportunity for women to maintain public roles. For example, when the organization relocated to Harlem, three of the six directors listed on the certificate of incorporation were women: Carrie B. Mero, an activist from Massachusetts, and Harlemites Harriet Rogers and Irene M. Blackstone.[40]

Of these three women, Blackstone was the most well known in Harlem circles. A clubwoman and suffragist who previously served as president of the Negro Women's Business League, Blackstone joined the UNIA in Harlem in 1917.[41] Initially believing that it was unlikely for black men and women in the United States to obtain full citizenship rights, Blackstone embraced Garvey's message and quickly became immersed in black nationalist politics. In addition to maintaining a position as one of the organization's directors, she became president of the New York UNIA Ladies' Division in 1917. During this period, Blackstone used her public platform in Harlem to advocate racial pride, boldly declaring in one speech, "I am American. I am black, and I am proud that I am black."[42] Reflecting her commitment to women's rights and leadership opportunities, Blackstone encouraged black women to leave white women's kitchens, urging them to build their own livelihoods by relying on their unique skills and creativity. In a passionate speech, delivered to a group of UNIA members in 1923, Blackstone advocated black economic empowerment and called on black men and women to boycott white-owned businesses.[43] "Why," she asked black Harlemites, "should all the white men come up here on your main streets—Fifth Avenue, Lenox Avenue, Seventh and Eighth Avenues [in Harlem] and have all of the business places?" "If you would boycott the white business man in Harlem," Blackstone continued, "you would find black businesses on the avenue."[44] Her comments underscore her endorsement of black capitalism as a vehicle for bolstering black economic power—an idea that was consistent with the UNIA's mission.

Several other black women in Harlem found similar visible leadership opportunities in the UNIA during the 1920s. This was certainly the case for Ethel Maud Collins. Born in Brown's Town, Jamaica, near Garvey's hometown of St. Ann's Bay, in 1892, Collins migrated to the United States during the Great Migration.[45] As thousands of black southerners abandoned life in the Jim Crow South, collectively resisting white supremacy and searching for better prospects in the urban North and West, Caribbean migrants also arrived in the United States in record numbers.[46] From 1899 to 1927, more than 140,000 Caribbean migrants entered the United States.[47] The period between 1922 and 1923 witnessed a sharp increase in Caribbean immigration before the restrictive Immigration Act of 1924 took effect.[48] The vast majority of these immigrants relocated to New York City. By the onset of the Great Depression, almost 20 percent of blacks in Harlem were of Caribbean origin.[49]

When Collins arrived in Harlem in 1920, she joined a vibrant community of Afro-Caribbean men and women. While the organization's base of support extended far beyond the city, the UNIA in Harlem became a significant political space for Afro-Caribbean men and women, as well as other peoples of African descent, to engage in the struggle to end global white supremacy. Though the specific circumstances surrounding her decision to join the UNIA are unclear, Collins became an active member of the Garvey movement within a year of arriving in the United States.[50] During the organization's heyday, Collins frequently attended UNIA meetings in Harlem, doing clerical work for the organization and investing in the Black Star Line.[51] A single woman who resided with her siblings, Collins operated a beauty shop from her Fifth Avenue apartment to maintain a livelihood and likely used it as a space to disseminate Garveyism.[52] By the late 1920s, she was appointed executive secretary of the Garvey Club in New York and acting secretary of the UNIA.[53]

Significantly, Collins's positions in the Garvey Club and in the UNIA brought her into contact with other black nationalist women in Harlem at the time, including Amy Jacques Garvey, who later became Garvey's second wife. Born to an educated middle-class family in Kingston, Jamaica, in 1895, Jacques Garvey relocated to the United States in 1917. As new black residents from the South joined a growing community of Afro-descended people in the city, Harlem witnessed a flowering of black intellectual and literary expression through various mediums, including poetry, literature, and music. The Harlem Renaissance, which began around 1918, also marked the emergence of the "New Negro," the antithesis of the submissive, passive, and accommodating "Old Negro."[54] Arriving in Harlem during this period, Jacques Garvey joined the community of "New Negro" migrants.[55] Although she would later deny it, Jacques Garvey was a close friend of Garvey's first wife, Amy Ashwood, who may have also played a significant role in Jacques Garvey's decision to join the UNIA. When Marcus Garvey and Amy Ashwood were married at Harlem's Liberty Hall in 1919, Jacques Garvey participated in the ceremony as Ashwood's maid of honor—a clear indication that the two women had formed a close bond of friendship and mutual affection.[56]

Like Collins, Jacques Garvey became increasingly active in UNIA affairs shortly after joining the organization. Unlike Ashwood, who maintained a very public presence, however, Jacques Garvey worked mostly behind the scenes. During her early years in the UNIA, Jacques Garvey served as the secretary in the UNIA's main office and helped Garvey plan his speaking tours. In 1922, months after Garvey's divorce from Amy Ashwood was finalized, Jacques Garvey became Garvey's new wife—a position she skillfully used to leverage her involvement and leadership in the organization. In only a matter of months, she became the most prominent woman in the organization, serving in a wide range of capacities, including spokesperson and archivist. In 1923, Jacques Garvey published the first edition of the *Philosophy and Opinions of Marcus Garvey*, a collection of Garvey's speeches and essays. "It is my sincere hope and desire," she explained in the book's introduction, "that this small volume will help to disseminate among the members of my race everywhere the true knowledge of their past history . . . and the glorious future of national independence in a free and redeemed Africa, achieved through organized purpose and organized action."[57] Embracing the core tenets of black nationalism, including black political self-determination, racial pride, and African redemption, Jacques Garvey played a crucial role in popularizing and preserving Garvey's ideas. When her husband was imprisoned in 1925 on charges of mail fraud, Jacques Garvey served as the de facto leader of the UNIA, overseeing much of the organization's day-to-day activities.[58] From 1924 to 1927, Jacques Garvey edited the women's page of the *Negro World*, "Our Women and What They Think," providing a significant platform for UNIA women to articulate their views without direct male censorship.[59]

While Jacques Garvey's leadership and influence was second to none, other women in the organization maintained critical positions in the UNIA, bringing a wide range of talents and skills "to the table." This was the case for Henrietta Vinton Davis, who became the organization's first female president and later maintained a number of prominent leadership positions in the organization. Born in 1860 in Baltimore, Maryland, Davis was the daughter of Mary Ann (Johnson) Davis and Mansfield Vinton Davis, a "distinguished musician."[60] During her early years, she attended the Boston School of Oratory, where she sharpened the oratorical skills that later proved beneficial to her involvement in the Garvey movement. In 1878, Davis became the first African American woman to be employed by the Office of the Recorder of the Deeds located in Washington, D.C.[61] A close associate of influential black leaders such as noted abolitionist Frederick Douglass, Davis was one of the most talented and prolific black actresses of the period and received widespread acclaim in several national newspapers.[62]

Unlike Jacques Garvey and Collins, who joined the Garvey movement in their twenties, Davis made the decision to join the UNIA much later in life. In 1916, at the age of fifty-six, the acclaimed elocutionist abandoned her acting career to become what one scholar describes as "a missionary in the cause of African redemption."[63] Although her involvement in the Garvey movement certainly enhanced her visibility and propelled her political career, Davis had already demonstrated engagement with political matters since the 1890s—in one instance, she wrote to Populist Party candidate Ignatius Donnelly to express an interest in supporting his 1892 campaign in order to better "serve [her] race and humanity." Especially drawn to Garvey's teachings on race pride and self-reliance, Davis became an active member of the UNIA in 1916, quickly moving up the ranks. Within three years, she became the UNIA's international organizer and concurrently maintained positions as vice president of the UNIA's shipping corporation and one of the directors of the Black Star Line. In the years that followed, Davis, who remained unmarried and without children, held a number of highly visible leadership positions in the UNIA, including secretary general and delegate to Liberia in 1924.[64]

Davis's unwavering commitment to mentoring others helped younger women advance in the Garvey movement. During the mid-1920s, Davis advised Maymie Leona Turpeau De Mena, who became another leading figure of the UNIA.[65] Born Leonie Turpeau in St. Martinville, Louisiana, on December 10, 1879, De Mena was one of eight children in a working-class household.[66] De Mena's father, Michel Turpeau, was a farmer who operated a lumberyard for a short period of time.[67] Isabella Turpeau, De Mena's mother, worked from home—raising her eight children with her husband's assistance until the two separated in 1881.[68] De Mena's brother, David Dewitt Turpeau Sr., later described the limited educational opportunities that were afforded to the Turpeau children: "To begin with we had no school to go to, if there were any disposition to give us any schooling. Not until my parents were separated and my mother moved to town was there any school opportunities given to us, and then it was most meager."[69] Though much of her early life is shrouded in mystery, census records reveal that De Mena relocated to Nicaragua during the early twentieth century but traveled frequently to the United States. In 1912, De Mena boarded the *Dictator* ship in Bluefields, Nicaragua, headed for New Orleans, Louisiana. By that time, she was a Nicaraguan citizen—a status she had acquired through her marriage to Francis H. Mena, a Creole planter and journalist from Bluefields.[70]

The circumstances surrounding De Mena's marriage to Francis H. Mena are unclear. What is certain, however, is that she became involved in the Garvey movement while residing in Nicaragua. By the early 1920s, approximately one-third of all UNIA chapters were located in Central America alone—including twenty-three in Costa Rica, eight in Honduras, and five in Nicaragua.[71] With these chapters in Central America, combined with the growing popularity of the *Negro World* newspaper, De Mena must have been exposed to Garvey's teachings long before meeting the charismatic black nationalist leader. When her marriage to Francis ended sometime around 1922, De Mena returned to the United States with her young daughter, Berniza, where she became increasingly active in the Garvey movement. Within a matter of years, she became one of the key women leaders, playing an instrumental role in promoting Garvey's teachings throughout the African diaspora and, on numerous occasions, serving as a translator and organizer during UNIA promotional tours with Henrietta Vinton Davis.[72] A gifted orator, De Mena traveled extensively with Amy Jacques Garvey in 1925, visiting UNIA divisions across the United States, galvanizing black men and women and garnering organizational support in the wake of Garvey's arrest and subsequent imprisonment.[73] In Virginia, for example, De Mena promoted Garveyism during the mid-1920s and oversaw the election of officers at the local UNIA division.[74]

In Sierra Leone, as in the United States, the UNIA similarly provided a vehicle through which black women could engage in black nationalist and

Pan-Africanist politics during the early twentieth century. The experiences of Adelaide Casely Hayford (née Smith) underscore the significant role the UNIA played in propelling Sierra Leonean women into political leadership during the 1920s. Born in 1868 into an elite Creole family in Freetown, Sierra Leone, Casely Hayford came of age during the period of British colonial rule. Originally founded by British abolitionists and philanthropists in 1787, Sierra Leone became a Crown colony of Britain during the nineteenth century, further expanding British colonial presence in West Africa. Like other Sierra Leonean women born into Creole elite society, Casely Hayford's upbringing was deeply influenced by traditional Victorian ideas of gender roles.

Casely Hayford's travels abroad planted the seeds that fueled her growing interest in feminist and Pan-Africanist politics—as it did for scores of other black women. In 1872, she migrated to London with her family where she studied at the Ladies College on the island of Jersey before going to study music in Germany. In 1903, she met and married Pan-Africanist Joseph E. Casely Hayford, a lawyer from Ghana, with whom she bore one child. In 1905, during one of her visits to Ghana, she emphasized the important role African women could play in the country's social and political development. Two years later, she relocated to Ghana to live with her husband but returned to Sierra Leone when the marriage ended in 1914. By several accounts, the relationship between Adelaide and Joseph Casely Hayford grew strained because of Adelaide's strong-willed and independent personality, which frequently clashed with her husband's own independence and strong will. Recognizing that the relationship could not be salvaged, the two mutually agreed to separate, although they were never legally divorced.[75]

In Freetown, where she took up residence, Casely Hayford articulated proto-feminism—using her speeches and writings to challenge male supremacy in African societies and endorse African women's political rights. Immediately after her arrival in Sierra Leone, Casely Hayford delivered a public lecture before congregants at the Wesleyan church on "The Rights of Women and Christian Marriage," no doubt drawing insights from her own personal experiences. In the subsequent months, Casely Hayford went on to deliver several lectures on women's rights, often speaking at women's forums and local churches.

Casely Hayford's entry into the Garvey movement sometime around October 1919 coincided with her growing interest in women's rights and education reform. With few opportunities for women to obtain a formal education in Sierra Leone during this period, Casely Hayford desired to open up a school for girls that would provide vocational training, teach African history and culture, and teach young girls how to be economically independent. Explaining her rationale years later, Casely Hayford noted that her "eyes were opened to the fact that the education meted out to [African people] had . . . taught us to despise ourselves." "Our immediate need," she continued, "was an education which would instill into us a love of country, a pride of race, an enthusiasm for the black man's capabilities, and a genuine admiration for Africa's wonderful art work."[76] These core tenets—race consciousness, black pride, African-centered education, and black self-sufficiency—were also central to the UNIA's platform. It is not surprising, therefore, that the UNIA provided a space in which Casely Hayford could advance her political work in Sierra Leone. In 1919, Casely Hayford became president of the ladies' division of the UNIA's Freetown branch, which provided a critical opportunity for her to work alongside likeminded African women in the organization.

Even though Casely Hayford parted ways with the UNIA in the summer of 1920 after tensions erupted over the use of money, her involvement in the Garvey movement crystallized her political views. Through her writings and speeches, Casely Hayford advocated black nationalism, Pan-Africanism, and feminism. In one article, published in the *West Africa* newspaper in 1922, Casely Hayford articulated African nationalist aspirations, noting that she was "looking forward . . . to a new day, in which Africa shall be allowed to expand and develop, along her own ideas and ideals."[77] Reflecting her commitment to racial pride and African-centered education, Casely Hayford stressed the importance of "educat[ing] and enlighten[ing] the African child without taking him too far away from his native environment."[78] She also called for more employment opportunities for people of African descent and emphasized the significance of black-owned businesses and institutions to better serve the needs of black communities. A "race woman through and through," as she described herself, Casely Hayford remained committed to racial uplift politics, public service, and leadership in black communities in Africa and in other parts of the globe.[79]

The Diverse Roles of Women in the UNIA

Although some women held formal leadership positions in the UNIA, this was not the case for most women, who comprised roughly half of the

FIGURE 2. The UNIA's Black Cross Nurses marching in Harlem
in 1922. George Rinhart/Corbis via Getty Images.

rank-and-file members.[80] Within the patriarchal structure of the UNIA, rank-and-file women often led from the margins, working to advance the goals of the organization primarily through their involvement in the UNIA's female auxiliaries—the Black Cross Nurses and the African Motor Corps.[81] Modeled after the American Red Cross, the Black Cross Nurses auxiliary was established by Henrietta Vinton Davis in 1921 in Philadelphia to provide a range of services in black communities.[82] Throughout the United States and around the world, these women not only offered medical services to black families but also provided health education.

The strategies Black Cross Nurses employed to administer their community work and the nature of their day-to-day activities varied from locale to locale. In Richmond, Virginia, the Black Cross Nurses auxiliary taught new mothers how to care for their babies, offered information about birth control, and organized community workshops on nutrition and sanitation.[83] In New Orleans, Louisiana, Black Cross Nurses often contributed to

relief efforts in the community and in nearby cities. After the Great Mississippi Flood of 1927, for example, members of the New Orleans division
provided assistance to flood victims in the Louisiana Delta.[84] In stunning
white uniforms, Black Cross Nurses in the United States often paraded
through city streets, deploying maternal images and symbols, singing the
UNIA's anthem, "Ethiopia, Land of Our Fathers," and carrying the organization's colorful flag.

Throughout Latin America and Caribbean, as in other parts of the
globe, Black Cross Nurses operated in their expected roles as mothers and
nurturers in black communities. They performed social welfare and organizational functions such as providing clothing for the needy, running soup
kitchens, and visiting the sick.[85] While men in the UNIA participated in
the African Legion, the organization's protective arm, female members of
the Black Cross Nurses were involved in the "motherly" duties of meeting
the physical and emotional needs of black communities—especially the
most marginalized groups. In Santiago de Cuba, for example, Black Cross
Nurses often cared for *braceros* who fell ill or were mistreated by local sugar-
cane companies. Facing a labor crisis during the early twentieth century,
sugar companies in Cuba obtained permission from the government to
import thousands of black workers, primarily from Haiti and Jamaica, to
work on sugar plantations. Despite the promise of better of wages, Caribbean
braceros in Cuba were ensnared into a system of exploitation that closely
mirrored slavery. With few public medical services available to *braceros*, the
UNIA's Black Cross Nurses in Cuba filled a significant void. In many
instances, these skilled nurses went into quarantined areas on sugar plantations to provide medical services for black *braceros* who were severely ill.[86]

Similarly, Black Cross Nurses in Belize initiated a series of community-
based initiatives to improve the quality of health services in black communities. Their strategies, however, were vastly different, reflecting class distinctions. In Belize, Black Cross Nurses were members of the Creole middle
class—descendants of African slaves and European slave owners. In the
complex social structure and racial schema of this British colony, these
middle-class women drew a sharp divide between themselves and working-
class, colonized, and immigrant women of color. Functioning as social
reformers, these women practiced "a maternalist politics of racial uplift,"
centering their social and political activism on improving conditions in
black communities yet seeking to increase rights for middle-class Creole
women at the expense of working-class and impoverished women. While

they attempted to assist impoverished mothers, Belizean Black Cross Nurses imposed their values on poor mothers, viewing them as morally inept. For the most part, Black Cross Nurses in Belize posed no threat to colonial authorities.[87]

In addition to serving as Black Cross Nurses, rank-and-file women in the UNIA, wherever they resided in the Black diaspora, often held positions as "lady presidents" of local divisions or participated in the Juvenile Divisions and the Universal African Motor Corps, the female version of the all-male paramilitary African Legion. Lady presidents of local divisions were charged with the task of overseeing the local female auxiliary.[88] In the African Motor Corps, Garveyite women learned military drills and a variety of automotive skills, including driving cars, taxis, and ambulances.[89] However, whether they maintained a position as a lady president of a local division, Black Cross Nurse, or member of the African Motor Corps, these women held restricted leadership positions and were always accountable to men in the organization.[90]

Rank-and-file women in the UNIA frequently challenged the organization's leadership structure, desiring more autonomous leadership positions without male oversight. During an afternoon session of the 1922 UNIA convention in Harlem, a group of Garveyite women publicly resisted their subordinate positions in the organization. Although they could serve as delegates to the organization's conventions, women encountered a number of difficulties being recognized by Garveyite men who presided over the sessions.[91] Insisting that they had not received "proper recognition" during previous sessions, these women addressed the convention with a list of grievances. "We, the women of the U.N.I.A. and A.C.L.," they stated, "know that no race can rise higher than its women." Reflecting their proto-feminist awareness, UNIA women went on to emphasize the value of women's autonomous leadership, which they argued was critical to "refine and mold public sentiment."[92]

Speaking on behalf of the women, Victoria W. Turner, a delegate from St. Louis, presented a list of five recommendations designed to improve the status of women in the organization. First, she asked that a woman be appointed the "head of the Black Cross Nurses and Motor Corps and have absolute control over those women." Second, Turner asked that women in the UNIA be given "more recognition by being placed on every committee" in order to be better informed about the inner workings of the organization. Third, she recommended having women leaders placed "in the important

FIGURE 3. The UNIA's African Motor Corps marching in Harlem
in 1924. George Rinhart/Corbis via Getty Images.

offices and field work of the association." Relatedly, the fourth recommenda-
tion called for women in the UNIA to be "given initiative positions, so that
they may formulate constructive plans to elevate our women." Finally, Turner
made a specific request that Henrietta Vinton Davis, founder of the Black
Cross Nurses, "be empowered to formulate plans . . . so that the Negro
women all over the world can function without restriction from the men."[93]

Several other UNIA women in the room chimed in, offering their support for Turner's recommendations. Clara Morgan, a Black Cross Nurse
from Chicago, chided male Garveyites in the room for ignoring women at
the convention. Women, she insisted, "were not willing to sit idly by and
let the men take all the glory while they gave the advice." Mrs. M. M. Scott,
an activist from Detroit, expressed similar sentiments, pointing out that
"whenever women began to function in the organization the men pre-
sumed to dictate to them."[94] Curiously, UNIA women made these demands
while Garvey was physically absent from the room, perhaps a strategic

move on their part.[95] When Garvey returned, he dismissed these women's concerns, suggesting that the resolutions were unnecessary since the UNIA's constitution already recognized women as leaders. Even though he insisted that he "didn't see any reasons for the resolutions," Garvey agreed to accept a modified version of resolutions four and five. To that effect, he suggested that rather than giving women "initiative positions . . . to formulate constructive plans to elevate [UNIA] women," as Turner had requested, they would instead be "encouraged to formulate [such] plans." Moreover, while he claimed to accept the premise that women should "function without restriction from the men," Garvey insisted on amending the fifth resolution to make it clear that there would be no "severance of the women from the men in the work of the organization."[96]

In the end, Garveyite women's actions at the 1922 convention did not precipitate any immediate or monumental changes in the UNIA. However, their actions did demonstrate the rhetoric and tactics they were cultivating as proto-feminists. Their resolutions also exposed the hierarchical structure of the organization, which failed to provide an equal place for women. Although Garvey claimed that the UNIA "was [an] organization that recognized women," he did not acknowledge that women held unequal positions to their male counterparts. In effect, the women's resolutions shed light on the core of the issue—opportunities for a handful of women to hold positions of prominence could not remedy the patriarchal leadership structure of the UNIA, in which women lacked full autonomy and equality. Espousing a proto-feminist politics, UNIA women openly expressed their growing sense of dissatisfaction in a male-dominated and masculinist organization and refused to sit quietly as Garvey and other men reinforced traditional gender constructions that limited leadership opportunities for women.

The Significance of the Women's Page

When Amy Jacques Garvey introduced "Our Women and What They Think," the women's page of the *Negro World*, in February 1924, she dramatically expanded rank-and-file women's influence, providing a public outlet from which to articulate proto-feminist views without direct male censorship.[97] From its first issue, the women's page of the *Negro World* openly challenged many of Garvey's views on women as well as the core principles of the UNIA. One of the featured articles, "The New Woman," written by Garveyite Saydee E. Parham, a law student residing in New York, challenged traditional notions of gender roles. A frequent writer for "Our Women," Parham discussed the process of evolution by which all species experience growth and maturation. Along these lines, she implied that women's roles and opportunities needed to expand in an ever-changing society: "From the brow-beaten, dominated cave woman, cowering in fear at the mercy of the brutal mate . . . from the safely cloistered woman reared like a clinging vine, destitute of all initiative and independence . . . we find her at last rising to the pinnacle of power and glory."[98] Blanche Hall reinforced these sentiments in her article, "Woman's Greatest Influence Is Socially," published in October 1924. "Show me a good, honest, noble man of character," Hall wrote, "and I will show you a good mother or wife behind him." Addressing the important responsibilities that women held in society and emphasizing men's dependence on women, Hall reminded readers that the UNIA could not advance without women's assistance. "There is much that the woman can do to make this organization a success," she carefully noted.[99]

Similarly, Carrie Mero Leadett, another frequent writer for "Our Women," demanded change within the UNIA along the lines of gender equality. A resident of New York, Leadett worked as a clerk at the UNIA headquarters in Harlem and for the organization's shipping company during the 1920s.[100] In her 1924 article, "The Negro Girl of Today Has Become a Follower—Future Success Rests with Her Parents and Home Environment," Leadett challenged young black women to build better futures for themselves through innovation rather than imitation. She went on to argue that although black women should aim for the same successes as women of other races, they needed to become leaders and not followers.[101] Florence Bruce reinforced this position in her 1924 article, "The Great Work of the Negro Woman Today." Bruce, an active member of the UNIA, was the wife of John E. Bruce, who served as a contributing editor of the *Negro World* from 1921 until his death in 1924. Citing women's impact in society since antiquity, Mrs. Bruce contended that women's influence would help the advancement of the UNIA and the black community. "No race has succeeded without a good and strong womanhood," she wrote, "and none ever will."[102]

Importantly, the debut of "Our Women" coincided with Garvey's legal troubles and increasing turbulence in the UNIA. A year prior to the introduction of "Our Women," Garvey had been convicted on charges of mail

FIGURE 4. Amy Jacques Garvey in 1940.
Afro-American, August 17, 1940, 2.

fraud, allegedly for using the U.S. mail to promote and sell stock for Black Star Line ships he had yet to purchase.[103] In February 1925, after his appeals were denied, he began serving a five-year term at the Atlanta Federal Penitentiary. During this period, Amy Jacques Garvey became increasingly involved in organizational affairs, serving as de facto leader in her husband's absence. With Garvey unable to wield full control from his Atlanta prison cell, Jacques Garvey used the pages of "Our Women" to articulate her proto-feminist views, openly denouncing what she described as the "antiquated beliefs" of men in the UNIA.[104]

With each successive issue of "Our Women," Jacques Garvey became increasingly more outspoken and critical of black men in the organization. Her article, "Black Women's Resolve for 1926," published during Garvey's incarceration, is a striking example. Without mincing any words, Jacques Garvey insisted that women in the UNIA were determined to have equal opportunities and were unwilling to allow male Garveyites to hinder their progress. "If the United States Congress can open their doors to white women," she wrote, "we serve notice on our men that Negro women will demand equal opportunity to fill any position in the Universal Negro Improvement Association or anywhere else without discrimination because of sex." "We are very sorry if this hurts your old-fashioned tyrannical feelings," she continued, "[but] we not only make the demand . . . we intend to enforce it."[105] Mirroring some of the women's earlier grievances at the 1922 convention, Jacques Garvey's statements underscore UNIA women's absolute frustration with male Garveyites who thwarted their efforts to obtain full gender equality within the organization.

Although women in the UNIA openly resisted male supremacy in the organization, this does not mean that all Garveyite women held this conviction or that these women did not at times accommodate these views. Indeed, UNIA women's views frequently reflected the dominant masculinist discourse of the period even as they fought to break free from traditional Victorian values. These inconsistencies were ever present in the articles of "Our Women."[106] For example, Amelia Sayers, an active member of the UNIA who worked as Jacques Garvey's personal assistant during the mid-1920s, wrote several articles for "Our Women" in which she accommodated Garvey's patriarchal stance. In her article, "Man Is the Brain, Woman Is the Heart," Sayers affirmed traditional gender roles and demonstrated her belief in the essentializing differences between men and women. Reducing women to emotional beings, Sayers asserted, "The man is the brain, but the woman is the heart of humanity; he its judgment, she its feelings; he its strength, she its grace, adornment and comfort." "Though the man may direct the intellect," she continued, "the woman cultivates the feelings." Sayers's statements diminished women's intelligence and wisdom, which she classified as exclusively male attributes.

Similarly, another Garveyite, identified only as Vera, reinforced sexist views on the pages of "Our Women." Vera's 1924 article, "The Ideal Wife," offered a succinct description of the *perfect* wife: "The woman who winds herself into the rugged recesses of her husband's nature, and supports and comforts him in adversity." Echoing Sayers's essentialist comments, Vera also employed the phrases "softer sex," and "ornament[s] of man" to describe black women.[107] Vera's statements, along with Sayers's views, reinforced Garvey's own metaphor of women as "nature's purest emblem" and certainly undermined UNIA women's earlier rejection of traditional gender norms.[108]

Significantly, these shifting views exhibit the contradictory and paradoxical nature of UNIA women's proto-feminist views and praxis. Women pioneers in the Garvey movement often wavered between feminist and nationalist ideals, articulating a critique of black patriarchy while endorsing traditionally conservative views on gender and sexuality. On one hand,

UNIA women embraced the "natural" roles of mother and wife and were often complicit in reinforcing masculinist discourses.[109] On the other hand, they attempted to subvert dominant views on gender and vigorously fought to expand women's leadership opportunities in the UNIA and in the community at large.

Within the confines of the UNIA's patriarchal structure, "Our Women" provided a unique space in which women, especially members of the rank-and-file, could publicly articulate their views on a range of issues.[110] On the women's page of the newspaper, Garveyite women endorsed anticolonial politics, calling for the "redemption of Africa" and advocating the unity of Africans on the continent and throughout the diaspora. Emphasizing the significance of race solidarity and political collaborations among people of African descent, Garveyite Eva Aldred-Brooks insisted that "race is stronger than politics" and praised the "darker races of the world [who] are determined to do their share in making the world safe for democracy."[111] She was not alone in her internationalist political vision. Writing in a 1924 editorial, Harlem-based Garveyite Saydee Parham assured readers that the liberation of Africa was imminent. Utilizing the rhetoric of Ethiopianism, race redemption ideas derived from biblical verses, Parham wrote, "The day is not far hence when Ethiopia shall stretch forth her hands unto God. The day is not far hence when Africa shall rise in all her glory and splendor and give out to the world a nation highly respected throughout its limits because of her governmental, industrial, commercial and cultural achievements." "When Africa shall take her seat in the great League of Nations of the world," Parham continued, "then we shall have everlasting peace, the brotherhood of man and the fatherhood of God."[112] Her comments underscored the anticolonial vision of Garveyite women writers and their belief in political self-determination as a right for peoples of African descent. Expressing similar sentiments, Mrs. Louise J. Edwards, a Garveyite activist residing in Coraopolis, Pennsylvania, called for the "rehabilitation of Africa and the restoration of the ancient glories of Ethiopia," describing it as the "ideal which the New Negro has fixed as his goal."[113]

Reflecting their commitment to racial pride, Garveyite women also wrote articles in "Our Women" featuring key black women historical figures, including famed poet Phillis Wheatley and women's rights activist Frances Ellen Watkins Harper.[114] "There is too much ignorance among us as to what our men and women . . . have accomplished," Jacques Garvey explained in one editorial.[115] "Our children, our young men and women become white hero worshippers; they see white; they imitate white," she continued.[116] To remedy the marginalization, exclusion, and distorted images of black men and women in popular culture and mainstream mass media, Jacques Garvey and other UNIA women used the women's page of the *Negro World* to highlight the work and accomplishments of people of African descent. Henrietta Vinton Davis, for example, wrote a series of articles in the newspaper on the historical contributions of black women abolitionists Harriet Tubman and Sojourner Truth. In another article, Garveyite Carrie Mero Leadett affirmed black beauty, encouraging black women to embrace their dark, natural hair. "Today if Mary Jones, a white girl, comes to school with her hair bobbed—tomorrow, many of our Negro girls [will] follow suit whether it is becoming to their features or not," Leadett explained. "Oh, if more of our girls would only 'be natural,'" Leadett added.[117] Ironically, although the women's page of the *Negro World* included articles that emphasized race pride and natural black beauty, it also included advertisements for skin lightening and hair-straightening products.

Despite its various contradictions, "Our Women and What They Think," which ran from 1924 to 1927, was especially significant. While Jacques Garvey offered no explanation for her decision to discontinue the page, it was likely related to her inability to secure consistent articles. In the months leading up to its demise, she frequently pleaded with UNIA women to send in articles for the page. The internal tensions in the organization, on account of Garvey's imprisonment, also contributed to the declining interest in the women's page and the newspaper in general. These organizational challenges, combined with Jacques Garvey's physical illness during this period, hastened the end of the women's page only three years after its debut.[118] Although it was short-lived, "Our Women" serves as one of the few surviving chronicles of rank-and-file women in the UNIA, unveiling their views, conflicts, and, above all, their efforts to foster change in the Garvey movement. In so doing, the women's page of the *Negro World*, perhaps more than the women's auxiliaries, propelled UNIA women into greater political visibility and influence.

Laura Adorker Kofey's Influence

Beyond the women's page of the *Negro World*, UNIA women found other public ways to challenge male patriarchy and articulate their commitment to black nationalist politics. The experiences of Laura Adorker Kofey, a UNIA organizer who rose to prominence during the mid-1920s, provide a striking example of how some women transgressed the bounds that were established within the patriarchal organization. Described by Amy Jacques Garvey as a "dynamic personality [and] quite the organizer," Kofey became a visible leader in the Garvey movement not long after Garvey's 1925 imprisonment, as more space opened for women in his absence.[119] During the mid-1920s, Kofey toured the United States and Central America, speaking at several UNIA divisions on Africa and African culture and displaying African art and artifacts. Through Kofey's charisma and zeal, thousands joined the UNIA during the short time that she served as an organizer, despite the suspicions surrounding Garvey's legal troubles. From 1926 to 1927, she traveled throughout the U.S. South, establishing new UNIA divisions in Louisiana, Alabama, and Florida. In Tampa alone, more than three hundred men and women joined the UNIA under Kofey's direction during the summer of 1927.[120]

Much of Kofey's experiences leading up to her involvement in the UNIA remains a mystery.[121] According to Kofey, she was an African princess, the daughter of "King Knesiphi," a paramount chief on the Gold Coast. "I am a representative from the Gold Coast of West Africa," Kofey explained in the *Mission Crusader*, "seeking the welcome of Africa's children everywhere."[122] In the absence of verifiable genealogy records, it remains uncertain whether Kofey was, as she claimed, from the Gold Coast or from the U.S. South, as several of her contemporaries suggested. However, Kofey certainly had strong ties to West Africa, including the Gold Coast and Sierra Leone. Several accounts confirm that she resided in West Africa, where she pastored a church in Asofa and served as a missionary in Kumasi during the early 1920s.[123]

Similar to UNIA leader Madame Maymie Leona Turpeau De Mena, who hid her southern roots and instead portrayed herself as an Afro-Nicaraguan immigrant, Kofey may have intentionally altered aspects of her early life to bolster her political work. If, in fact, Kofey's claims of Ghanaian birth lacked credibility, she can be credited for strategically crafting a public image that served to further her political goals. Portraying herself as an African princess certainly would have boosted her credibility in the eyes of many UNIA followers who embraced Garvey's Pan-Africanist message of global black unity and his emphasis on African heritage.

Kofey's position of prominence, however, was short-lived. By the end of 1927, her reputation became severely tarnished when a group of Garveyites grew suspicious of her immediate success. Sometime around August 1927, rumors began to circulate that Kofey was using her newfound success in UNIA circles to raise funds for her own purposes—to purchase, among other things, her own set of ships to relocate African Americans to West Africa.[124] As questions began to emerge about Kofey's intentions, several Garveyite leaders began to investigate Kofey's claims to African royal ancestry. In September 1927, Joseph A. Craigen, the executive secretary of the UNIA's Detroit division, openly denounced Kofey as a fraud, insisting that she was originally from Georgia. According to Craigen and several others, Kofey was born Laura Champion in Athens, Georgia; lived in Detroit from 1920 to 1924; and had traveled to London and West Africa as a Red Cross nurse. In a telegram sent to Garvey that month, Craigen made the UNIA leader aware of Kofey's alleged misrepresentations and warned, "If she is not advised to discontinue her activities in the association serious trouble will ensue which will entail serious complications."[125] Shortly thereafter, in February 1928, Garvey denounced Kofey in the *Negro World* newspaper, insisting, "This woman is a fake and has no authority from me to speak to the Universal Negro Improvement Association."[126]

Not long after her public dismissal from the UNIA, Kofey established the African Universal Church and Commercial League in Miami, Florida, teaching "a blend of Garveyism and religion."[127] Under her new organization, Kofey promoted West African emigration and economic self-sufficiency and encouraged black southerners to engage in a series of transatlantic business ventures.[128] Not surprisingly, Kofey continued to encounter resistance from male Garveyites in the movement who tried, on numerous occasions, to discredit the activist and hinder her religious and political work. On several occasions, members of the African Legion, the all-male paramilitary auxiliary of the UNIA, harassed Kofey during her sermons and attempted to disrupt her meetings by shooting out the lights. Despite moving her congregation to a new location in an effort to avoid confrontations with UNIA members, the threats and harassment remained constant. When their efforts failed to yield any results, a group of Garveyite men took matters into their own hands.

During an evening service on March 8, 1928, and in the presence of two hundred of her most avid followers, Kofey was assassinated. Pandemonium immediately broke out, during which time Kofey's followers seized Garveyite Maxwell Cook, a vocal critic of Kofey and close associate of Joseph Craigen, and began to beat him unmercifully. Within minutes, Cook lay dead on the floor as chaos continued to erupt in the sanctuary. When local police arrived on the scene, witnesses identified several suspects, providing conflicting accounts as to who actually pulled the trigger on Kofey. Claude Green and James Nimmo, two leaders of the UNIA's Miami branch, were eventually arrested and charged with first-degree murder. Inconsistent testimonies, however, resulted in their acquittal not long after. Although the two men were never convicted of Kofey's murder, they were present at the 1928 service and had, on several occasions, threatened Kofey prior to the shooting.[129]

In death, Kofey became a martyr, inspiring hundreds of black men and women who embraced her African-centered religious teachings. In the spring of 1928, they flocked to services in Miami, Palm Beach, and Jacksonville to pay their respects to Kofey. In the decades to follow, the African Universal Church, which Kofey had established in 1927, continued to advance her teachings throughout the United States and West Africa. In the early 1940s, church members in Jacksonville established a community called "Adorkaville" to continue to honor Kofey's memory.

Although Laura Adorker Kofey's experience represents an extreme case, it underscores the patriarchal ethos of the Garvey movement, which sought to limit the extent to which women could autonomously lead.[130] Women in the UNIA during the 1920s maintained some positions of leadership yet were expected to remain under direct male control and oversight. Even after leaving the UNIA, Kofey remained subject to the patriarchal control of male Garveyites. Kofey's bold decision to deviate from the socially acceptable gender roles and expectations in the Garvey movement ultimately cost the activist her life. However, if Kofey's assassination was meant to deter black nationalist women from stepping outside of the bounds of expected female leadership, then it failed to accomplish its intended purpose.

A New Phase of Black Nationalist Women's Activism

In December 1927, three months before Laura Adorker Kofey's assassination, Garvey was deported from the United States to his native Jamaica. The charismatic black nationalist leader had fought unsuccessfully to appeal his arrest and conviction on charges of mail fraud. From a New Orleans port, Garvey bid farewell to an estimated five thousand followers. While many of his opponents rejoiced in what they perceived as the complete demise of the UNIA, Garvey was determined to "devote every minute . . . to the great cause [of] universal freedom." "The fight [has] just started," he wrote optimistically to members of the Garvey Club in New York, "and I want you to look out for a greater and grander [UNIA]."[131]

Indeed, Garvey attempted to keep the organization afloat in the aftermath of his arrest, imprisonment, and subsequent deportation. In 1928, the black nationalist leader paid a visit to England, where he presented a petition to the League of Nations.[132] The following year, in the pages of the *Negro World*, he staunchly declared that "all roads shall lead [to] the 1st of August, 1929, where openeth the Sixth International Convention of the Negro Peoples of the World." Garvey urged "all [UNIA] branches and chapters . . . and all other organizations, societies and churches" to attend the 1929 convention to be held in August of that year. With plans to address a wide range of issues, including the launch of a new line of Black Star Line ships, Garvey predicted that the convention would be a "big time for the Negro race."[133] To some extent, he was right. By some accounts, the conference in Jamaica was just "as spectacular as the earlier ones in Harlem."[134]

Although the number of official UNIA delegates present—145—waned in comparison to previous conventions, women leaders were well represented at the conference. During the opening session, Maymie Leona Turpeau De Mena made a grand entrance during the street procession, "mounted on a grey charger with [a] drawn sword."[135] Her dramatic entry into the convention was certainly representative of the colorful pageantry associated with the UNIA. Even more, De Mena's entrance foreshadowed black women's ascendancy in black nationalist politics. Following De Mena's grand entrance, several other high-profile women leaders made their mark at the 1929 convention. During the opening ceremonies, which attracted an estimated twelve thousand attendees, Amy Jacques Garvey and Henrietta Vinton Davis joined Garvey on the platform.[136]

Despite the initial display of unity and cooperation, the 1929 UNIA convention was a hotbed of conflict. Still fuming with anger over the course of events that led him back to Jamaica, Garvey blamed his imprisonment and the UNIA's declining membership on "wicked, vicious and greedy men" in the organization. Without mincing words, he singled out Davis, accusing the influential woman leader of doing "nothing to give new life to the organization" during his time in prison. It is unclear exactly what

Garvey expected Davis to do for the UNIA during his imprisonment—beyond what she had done to actively support his mission during the organization's dark period. However, Garvey's public critique, in and of itself, served to undermine Davis's leadership and influence. Curiously, Davis made no public effort to respond to Garvey. She continued to participate in the convention but was careful and "conservative during most of the deliberations."[137]

Garvey's public critique of Davis during his opening ceremony offered only a glimpse into the growing fragmentation and internal dispute taking place within the organization. Calling for greater centralization and a change in UNIA headquarters, Garvey requested that all branches report directly to his new base in Jamaica instead of the former main office in Harlem. Rather than resulting in the unification of UNIA chapters, Garvey's suggestion further incited disagreements among his adherents. To be sure, these tensions had begun before August 1929, but the convention was the straw that broke the camel's back.

Fred Toote, a clergyman in the African Orthodox Church (AOC), an international religious order established in 1921 by Antiguan George Alexander McGuire, became the center of much of the conflict.[138] At the convention, Toote, who had served as acting president general during Garvey's imprisonment, found himself "with his back against the wall of the conversation . . . while he answered scores of questions leveled against him both by delegates on the floor and the speaker." Among the many issues on the table were questions over whether or not Toote, in his position as interim president general, fully complied with instructions from Garvey on how to conduct UNIA affairs during the black nationalist leader's imprisonment. Clearly frustrated by the public castigation, Toote promptly left the convention, returning to New York, where he and a group of loyal supporters established the rival UNIA, Inc.[139] Although Garvey envisioned the 1929 convention as an opportunity to revive the UNIA and bring greater cohesion to the organization, quite the opposite occurred. The Sixth International Convention resulted in even greater fragmentation and conflict.

Notwithstanding the UNIA leaders' skirmishes over power, funds, and resources, one of the other underlying tensions at the 1929 convention was the enduring gender politics in the organization. First, Garvey's public criticism of Davis during his opening ceremony underscores how easily women leaders could become scapegoats for the UNIA's failures. Certainly, regardless of her influence, Davis could not have been the sole or even primary reason for why the organization was in a state of disarray during Garvey's imprisonment. By insinuating as much, Garvey not only attempted to undermine Davis's leadership but also inadvertently over-looked the activist's long tenure of service, which had helped to catapult the organization's visibility and influence.[140]

Although many attendees at the 1929 convention witnessed Garvey's public scolding of Davis, few noticed another conflict brewing between a group of Garveyite men and Mittie Maude Lena Gordon, an activist from Chicago. Originally from Louisiana, Gordon grew up in Arkansas, which laid the foundation for her decision to embrace Garveyism later in life. In the aftermath of Reconstruction, the state became the site of one of the most fervent back-to-Africa movements of the nineteenth century.[141] Largely driven by the widespread racial oppression they encountered and deeply influenced by the teachings of Bishop Henry McNeal Turner of the African Methodist Episcopal Church, African American residents in Arkansas turned to the American Colonization Society (ACS) for financial aid to leave the country. Founded in 1816 by Reverend Robert Finley and a coalition of white slave owners and Quakers, the ACS opposed slavery in the United States.[142] While they supported abolition, members of the ACS maintained racial prejudices and established the organization on the belief that African Americans could not peacefully coexist with whites.[143] From 1817 to 1866, the ACS played a significant role in relocating an estimated thirteen thousand African Americans to Liberia and, in 1822, established the nation as a colony for free blacks.[144] While interest in emigration rapidly spread across the country, more than a third of the emigrants who relocated to Liberia originated from the state of Arkansas alone.[145] Although this "Liberia fever" significantly declined by the early twentieth century, it helped to lay the foundation for black southerners' interest in the teachings of Marcus Garvey and earlier black leaders, including Bishop Turner and African American educator Booker T. Washington.[146]

Having been exposed to the teachings of Bishop Turner, Gordon would have certainly found the principles and strategies of the UNIA to be familiar and appealing. Sometime around 1923, after settling in Chicago, Gordon became a member of the UNIA where she joined a vibrant community of black activists, including many who had also relocated from the South. In 1929, two years after Garvey was deported from the United States, Gordon decided to attend the convention in hopes that it would prove beneficial for improving conditions for black Americans. By her own account, she traveled with members of the New York–based Garvey Club to Jamaica in July of that year—in what appears to be the activist's only trip overseas. Though Gordon later claimed that she attended as a "private individual," as opposed to an "elected delegate or [UNIA] representative," her arrival in Jamaica two months prior to the convention—and her claim that she resided in Garvey's sister's home during this period—suggests that she was a leader or prospective leader of the organization.[147]

Gordon's experiences at the conference provide a glimpse into the enduring gender tensions in the UNIA. According to one account, when Gordon arrived in Jamaica that summer, Garvey "asked her to take charge of the divisions of the UNIA in Chicago." Apparently impressed with Gordon's speaking abilities, Garvey tapped her to be a new UNIA leader.[148] Though the full extent of Gordon's experiences remains a mystery, male Garveyites certainly resisted Garvey's efforts. Gordon claimed to have been "very disgusted with the manner in which certain officials were conducting themselves."[149] Referencing the course of events years later, Amy Jacques Garvey indicated, "The men at the Head of the Organization as usual, tried to hamper [Gordon]."[150] Jacques Garvey's comments, while brief, are indicative of the persistent gender politics in the UNIA, which remained an underlying issue at the 1929 convention in Jamaica.

*　*　*

Ultimately, while Garvey desired to use the convention as a launching pad for the organization's next phase of success, the convention brought more issues to the forefront and undercut Garvey's leadership and his organization. In other ways, however, the convention did serve as a launching pad—but not in the manner in which Garvey had originally intended. The widespread fragmentation that marked the internal collapse of the UNIA served as a blessing in disguise for women activists. In effect, the demise of the UNIA, as the most dominant mass organization of Afro-descended peoples, created an opportunity for women, in particular, to engage in black nationalist politics in new, idiosyncratic, and innovative ways. Certainly, women pioneers in the UNIA during the 1920s laid the foundation for women to have greater visibility and autonomy than Marcus Garvey originally envisioned. However, these efforts would only be fully realized during the post-Garvey era. In the absence of a strong and centralized UNIA and Garvey's looming presence, a number of women leaders—including some who had been snubbed at the 1929 gathering—emerged on the local, national, and international scenes, at once drawing on Garveyism and extending far beyond it.

Despite their contradictory experiences in the Garvey movement, women drew from the UNIA a wide range of skills, experiences, and networks from which they were able to build and expand in the decades to follow. Above all, they drew from the UNIA a sense of empowerment and foundational black nationalist ideals, including racial pride, political self-determination, and economic self-sufficiency. Building on yet also expanding beyond these core principles, women moved in various directions, utilizing black nationalism as an organizing tool around which to challenge global white supremacy during the twentieth century.

CHAPTER 2

৵

The Struggle for Black Emigration

STANDING BEFORE A CROWD of black Chicagoans in December 1932, Mittie Maude Lena Gordon made a bold statement. She insisted that she had a solution for black Americans who bore the brunt of the Great Depression. As she peered into the sea of faces in the audience at an old boxing ring in the city, Gordon passionately defended emigration to West Africa, arguing that "the Negro would escape from the economic, racial and political problems which confronted the race in the United States."[1] The forty-three-year-old activist stood five feet three inches tall and had a heavy build. She was light brown in complexion and had brown eyes with black straight hair that framed her round face. Described as a "very forceful and effective speaker," Gordon commanded attention when she spoke that evening, delivering one of the many passionate speeches that she would give across the city in years to come.[2]

Although some of Gordon's detractors dismissed her as a "rabble rouser" or as "uncouth," she attracted a following of thousands of black men and women in Chicago and across the nation.[3] Following her departure from Marcus Garvey's Universal Negro Improvement Association (UNIA) in 1929, Gordon went on to became one of Chicago's leading black nationalist "street scholars," speaking for the interests of the black working poor during a global economic crisis.[4] Similar to Amy Ashwood Garvey and civil rights leader Ella Baker who emerged as street scholars in Harlem during the 1920s, Gordon defied traditional middle-class expectations of black women in order to disseminate her nationalist philosophy during the years of the Great Depression.[5] Gordon was successful in popularizing these ideas and launched a vibrant emigration movement in Chicago in December 1932, which culminated in an unprecedented petition with signatures of an estimated 400,000 black Americans willing to leave the country. In August 1933, she sent this petition to President Franklin D. Roosevelt along with a request for federal aid to support emigration efforts. Inspired by FDR's promise of a New Deal to boost the economy, Gordon made an unconventional appeal to the state to allocate funds for black Americans desiring to leave the country. Her emigration campaign, which began in Chicago, would rapidly spread across the nation during the Great Depression.

Reflecting the rich yet complex intellectual milieu of the period, Gordon formulated her own religious and political philosophy, blending aspects of Garveyism with the teachings of Noble Drew Ali, founder of the Moorish Science Temple of America (MSTA)—the precursor to the Nation of Islam. To that end, she articulated a commitment to the core tenets of black nationalism—racial pride, African redemption (from European colonization), economic self-sufficiency, racial separatism, and political self-determination—and promoted an African American version of Islam. Significantly, she also maintained a black internationalist vision, linking the experiences of people of African descent with other nonwhite groups and calling for collaborations and alliances among people of color in their struggles against global white supremacy. Her internationalist vision resonated with Noble Drew Ali's Moorish American Islamic identity. With limited financial resources during a global economic crisis, Gordon skillfully organized black men and women in the city and established the Peace Movement of Ethiopia (PME)—the largest black nationalist organization established by a woman in the United States. Against the backdrop of the Great Depression, the PME functioned as a crucial space for working-poor black men and women to engage in black nationalist and internationalist politics—thereby providing a political alternative to the dwindling UNIA as well as the varied Communist-led groups and labor-oriented organizations of the period.

The widespread appeal of the PME and Gordon's emigration campaign underscores the continued salience and influence of black nationalist thought and praxis in the 1930s. During this era of global economic instability and political turmoil, a large segment of the black working class in the United States embraced black nationalism—especially the core tenets of black capitalism, political self-determination, and emigration—as viable solutions to achieve universal black liberation. Importantly, Gordon's founding of the PME and the remarkably popular emigration petition from working-class black Americans at the dawn of the New Deal exemplifies the important and wide-ranging political projects undertaken by black nationalist women in the aftermath of Garvey's deportation.

Mittie Maude Lena Gordon's Early Years

Gordon's childhood was critical in shaping her interest in black nationalist politics as an adult. Born Mittie Maude Lena Nelson on August 2, 1889, in rural Webster Parish of Louisiana, Gordon spent her early childhood in Louisiana, but it was not long before her family moved to Hope, Arkansas, in an effort to find better job and educational opportunities.[6] The school system in Webster Parish thwarted her parents' plans to provide a decent education for Gordon and her nine siblings. According to Gordon, "School facilities for colored children were so bad in Webster Parish, that the third-grade was as high as one could go, because pressure was so strong against educating [N]egroes."[7] Local resistance against black education coupled with vast disparities in quality between white and black schools confirmed her parents' decision to move out of Webster Parish in 1900. The family moved to Hope after Gordon's father, Edward Nelson, became a minister in the Colored Methodist Episcopal Church (CME) that year and asked to be transferred to Arkansas.[8] To his dismay, however, the educational opportunities for African Americans in Arkansas were no different from what he had left behind.

Nelson, the son of a former slave who had been denied access to formal education, was determined to secure the best educational opportunities for his children. When the local school districts in Arkansas failed to provide viable options, Nelson began to homeschool his children with the limited education that he had received. This choice had a significant impact on the formation of Gordon's nationalist ideology. According to Gordon, her father devoted much time to the teachings of Bishop Henry McNeal Turner, laying the foundation for her decision to embrace Garveyism later in life.[9] Born near Abbeville, South Carolina, in 1834, Turner became a minister in the Methodist Episcopal Church in 1851 and went on to join the African Methodist Episcopal Church seven years later. During the late nineteenth century, Turner began advocating for emigration after his political prospects abruptly ended after Reconstruction. Convinced that extinction was the only likely outcome for African Americans who opposed emigration, Turner appealed to African Americans to leave the country, and between 1891 and 1898, he made several trips to the African continent. Similar to other black nationalists of the period, Turner maintained a civilizationist perspective, believing that emigration to West Africa would blaze a path toward modernity in Africa.[10] His writings underscore his nationalist vision and strong affinity for Africa—ideas that Gordon began to embrace at an early age.

During these formative years, Gordon was also exposed to the harsh realities of Jim Crow and the scope of the black condition in America. As she traveled with her father to church events across the South, Gordon encountered the same racial disparities that she witnessed in her own community. She wrote, "In travelling, I found thousands of people suffering under the same conditions as we." It was during this period that she began to develop a deep sense of race consciousness, which only intensified after witnessing a lynching in 1898, two years after the landmark *Plessy v. Ferguson* decision upheld the constitutionality of racial segregation. As Gordon later explained, "I saw a lynch mob of 1600 men pass my home when I was nine years old. They lynched this man, Will Streake, near Dorlean, Louisiana. Since that day I have been the most unhappy person that ever lived."[11] Her statements reveal the traumatic social impact of lynching in black communities and capture the lingering pain of those who witnessed racial violence.[12]

In 1900, at the age of fourteen, Gordon married Robert Holt, a bricklayer who was more than thirty years her senior, in Hampstead, Arkansas.[13] Although the full circumstances remain a mystery, it is likely that her marriage was arranged by her parents—perhaps driven by economic necessity. Her marriage to Holt resulted in the birth of two children—Lucille and John. When Holt passed away in 1906, Gordon became a dressmaker in an effort to take care of her two young children.[14] Her relocation to the urban North during the World War I era marked a key turning point in her life. Like many other black southerners who collectively resisted Jim Crow and white supremacy, Gordon headed North during the early years of the Great Migration.[15] Sometime around 1913, she arrived in East St. Louis, Illinois, as a widowed mother in hopes of building a new life in the aftermath of her husband's death.[16] Her life was forever shattered in the summer of 1917 when the East St. Louis race riot erupted over labor-related conflicts and growing white resentment toward the rapid influx of black southerners.[17]

Although the specific details are unclear, Gordon's ten-year-old son, John, sustained significant injuries during the riot, resulting in his untimely death shortly thereafter.[18] Gordon offered no details on the matter in any of her personal writings—a likely indication that she did not want to recall the painful incident—but one can easily imagine that the riot sparked many intense emotions in the grieving mother. When Marcus Garvey delivered an impassioned speech in New York denouncing the riot, Gordon might have heard about it or read its transcript in a local newspaper.[19] Describing the riot as "one of the bloodiest outrages of mankind" and a "crime against the laws of humanity," Garvey called on black Americans to "lift [their] voice[s] against the savagery of a people who claim to be the dispensers of democracy." "White people are taking advantage of blackmen," Garvey added, "because blackmen all over the world are disunited."[20] Garvey's powerful comments might have resonated with Gordon.

In the immediate aftermath of the riot, Gordon relocated to Chicago, joining thousands of other black residents pouring into the city. Since the late nineteenth century, Chicago—known as the "City of the Big Shoulders" —was a major commercial and manufacturing hub, providing an array of job opportunities in factories, stockyards, and railroad yards.[21] As opportunities expanded in mass production during the early twentieth century, Chicago became "a city of migrants."[22] During the first wave of the Great Migration, which began in 1915, the black population in Chicago rapidly grew. In 1910, 44,000 black men and women resided in city. From 1915 to 1920, an estimated 50,000 black southerners migrated to Chicago in search of better job opportunities, primarily in industrial and domestic service and in an effort to escape the racial violence of the South.[23] While Gordon and other new migrants in Chicago inevitably faced a host of social challenges, including many of the same ones they encountered in the South, urban migration still offered some glimmer of hope.

Abandoning the Jim Crow South, Gordon and other working-class "New Negro" migrants joined a thriving black consumer culture and intellectual community in Chicago.[24] Shortly after relocating, Gordon married William, a fellow southerner.[25] Born in Thomasville, Georgia, in 1873, William Gordon had worked as a farmhand in Florida until the age of eighteen, when a local railroad company employed him. He relocated to Chicago in 1918 and within two years was employed as a laborer at a local iron mill.[26]

Although it is unclear exactly how the Gordons met, the two married in 1920 and, three years later, began attending UNIA meetings located not too far from their home.[27] Gordon noted that she had joined "every movement . . . that claimed to better [the] race's condition," but "I had a greater hope in the U.N.I.A., than any other movement." Moreover, Gordon found Garvey's message of African pride and black self-sufficiency appealing: "[Garvey] gave us light on Africa and taught us nationhood."[28]

Wholeheartedly embracing Garvey's teachings, Gordon became an active member of the UNIA, quickly moving up the ranks. After only a few years, she was appointed "lady president" of a local UNIA division in Chicago. This position gave her the responsibility of overseeing the women's division, but her authority was limited because women who served as lady presidents did not lead autonomously. In each UNIA division, the lady president was expected to answer to the male president, who had the final say and often amended women's reports to the division at large.[29] Notwithstanding its limitations, Gordon's tenure as lady president provided a meaningful opportunity for her to hone her leadership and organizing skills and brought her into contact with hundreds of Garveyites.[30] Moreover, the position provided an opportunity for Gordon to work alongside notable Garveyite women, including Amy Jacques Garvey and Maymie De Mena, who became Assistant International Organizer for the UNIA in 1926.[31]

Gordon's leadership in the UNIA would be short-lived, however. In 1929, two years after Garvey's deportation, Gordon attended the UNIA's Sixth International Convention in Kingston, Jamaica, where she encountered male resistance to her leadership. Determined to advance black nationalist politics, Gordon set out to find other political alternatives in Chicago. Her restaurant proved especially crucial for her engagement in nationalist politics. In 1927, two years before she left the UNIA, she and her husband had opened up a small restaurant, conveniently located in the back of their apartment on State Street. What began as a delicatessen—selling a few carryout items—became a full-fledged restaurant in 1932 until it ran out of business in 1934.[32] Though short-lived, the opening of the restaurant underscored Gordon and her husband's belief in the value of economic self-sufficiency and black capitalism—central tenets of black nationalist philosophy. In addition to helping her build a livelihood, business ownership also bolstered Gordon's engagement in politics.[33] Similar to Amy Ashwood Garvey, who owned a London restaurant that became a central meeting space for Pan-African leaders during the mid-1930s,

Gordon used her restaurant as a physical space to strategize and develop relationships with potential allies.[34]

Ashima Takis and the Pacific Movement of the Eastern World

During the early 1930s, Gordon used her restaurant as a central location for intellectual exchanges with a wide range of individuals, including a man who called himself Ashima Takis. Born in the Philippines in 1900, Takis, whose birth name was Policarpio Manansala, arrived in Chicago sometime during the late 1920s. Posing as Japanese, Takis spoke to local black residents at UNIA meetings in the city and across the U.S. Midwest.[35] In 1931, UNIA leader Maymie De Mena invited Takis along with a few other Asian speakers to appear at various UNIA public events.[36] It is unclear whether De Mena was knowledgeable about Takis's actual ethnic identity. Takis later insisted that De Mena asked him to pose as Japanese, but given his tendency to misrepresent information, this claim was probably fabricated.[37] Although the specific details are murky, extant records reveal that De Mena was largely responsible for Takis's involvement in multiple UNIA divisions. Intent on convincing black audiences that the UNIA "was sponsored and encouraged by the Japanese government"—perhaps hoping to bolster the UNIA's global political standing and to improve morale in the movement at a moment of uncertainty—De Mena enlisted Takis's speaking services in Chicago, Cincinnati, and Columbus.[38]

Takis's speaking tour coincided with a period in which the U.S. government had adopted several policies that excluded Asians from American citizenship and limited the number of Asian immigrants entering the country. The racist "yellow peril" ideology of the late nineteenth century, which stemmed from white fears and anxieties over Asian immigration, had persisted well into the twentieth century. Reflecting a pattern of anti-Asian policies—including the 1882 Chinese Exclusion Act and 1907 regulation that barred the entrance of Japanese and Koreans from Hawaii—the U.S. government passed the 1924 Immigration Act that declared all Asians "racially ineligible for citizenship."[39] The global economic crisis during the early 1930s, which resulted in more competition over jobs and resources, served as a catalyst for rising anti-Asian sentiment in mainstream American discourse.

The negative images and stereotypical depictions of Asian cultures that dominated Western mass media mirrored the pervasive global racist attitudes toward African Americans. These similarities underscore how the historical experiences of peoples of Asian and African descent have been intertwined for centuries. Indeed, both groups have experienced racial oppression and as a result have collaborated to resist racism and discrimination.[40] Following the abolition of slavery during the mid-nineteenth century, thousands of Chinese and Indian laborers were sent to work on sugar plantations in the Caribbean, including Trinidad, Cuba, and British Guiana (now Guyana). The manner in which Asians were brought to the Caribbean mirrored the kinds of experiences that Africans endured during the transatlantic slave trade. Under the trans-Pacific "coolie trade," as it became known, Asian laborers were often transported to the Caribbean in the same ships that had once carried Africans and, in many cases, were captured and coerced into a life of plantation labor.[41]

Although Asian indentured servants were generally given contracts ranging from five to eight years, they had no guarantees that they would be able to return to their native lands. With no means of enforcing these contracts, many Asian indentured servants found themselves in a perpetual state of servitude with minimal financial compensation—if at all. The lack of economic and political power under a system of white domination and control mirrored the experiences of Africans under chattel slavery. These overlapping histories provided impetus for Afro-Asian solidarity as a revolutionary collective effort to challenge racial oppression throughout the diaspora. In nineteenth-century Cuba, for example, people of African descent joined forces with people of Asian descent to challenge the Spanish empire.[42]

In a similar vein, several black leaders in the United States during the twentieth century pursued collaborations with Asian activists in a unified effort to contest the global color line. Recognizing the shared historical experiences of peoples of Asian and African descent, civil rights leader W. E. B. Du Bois, UNIA leader Marcus Garvey, and others emphasized the significance of Afro-Asian solidarity as a viable strategy for combatting racial oppression. A number of earlier historical developments strengthened this point of view, including the Russo-Japanese War (1904–5), in which the Japanese military defeated Russian warships. For Du Bois, Garvey, and many others, Japan's military victories served as a symbolic triumph against global white supremacy. Years later, the 1931 Japanese invasion of Manchuria reinforced some of these sentiments among certain members of the African American community. In September 1931, the

Japanese military invaded Manchuria, initiating what would result in a brutal fourteen-year occupation of the country. While many disparaged Japan's
imperialist impulse, some praised the nation's success in expanding its territory and influence.[43] This was certainly the case for Takis, who began
speaking in black communities during this period, strategically masking his
Filipino identity and claiming to be Japanese.

It was during one of Takis's speaking services in Chicago that Gordon
first encountered the Filipino activist and, shortly thereafter, arranged for
them to meet at her restaurant on State Street. During the meeting, Takis
shared with Gordon his plans to establish the Pacific Movement of the
Eastern World (PMEW), a pro-Japanese organization that supported the
unification of people of color globally.[44] Gordon found the proposition
appealing but admitted that she was most intrigued by Takis's support for
black political self-determination and emigration. "I had already decided to
go ahead with the [PMEW]," she later remarked, "after I found there was
no hope of our going to Africa through the U.N.I.A."[45] Gordon and Takis
collaborated in the months that followed, circulating an emigration petition
in Chicago and later in Indiana, until their relationship began to unravel
sometime in the fall of 1932. While FBI records indicate that the source
of the conflict was financial, Gordon attributed the conflict to ideological
differences.[46] Recounting the course of events years later, Gordon insisted
that she parted ways with Takis because he proposed emigration to Manchuria, then occupied by Japan, instead of West Africa.[47]

Gordon's statements reveal the contradictory nature of her political
ideas. On one hand, her collaboration with Takis offers a glimpse into Gordon's global vision and growing interest in black internationalism. In fact,
Gordon would later amplify her efforts to forge transnational solidarities
with Asian activists and other activists of color from across the globe. However, her resistance toward Takis's proposal also underscores Gordon's early
struggles to reconcile her Pan-Africanist vision with her desire to forge
alliances with other people of color. Because of her affinity for Africa as the
homeland of black people and her belief that emigration was a crucial step
toward its "redemption," Gordon maintained the view that Africa provided
the only logical destination for people of African descent. While Gordon
viewed Japan as a model and potential military ally, she was unwilling to
support black emigration to Japan's newly conquered territory.[48] Finding
little success in Chicago, Takis headed to St. Louis, Missouri, where he
forged ahead with plans to launch the PMEW.

Ideological Foundations of the Peace Movement of Ethiopia

In the aftermath of her falling out with Takis, Gordon decided to establish her own organization, building on her prior experiences and drawing inspiration from several black political and religious movements of the period. In December 1932, Gordon held another meeting at her restaurant as she had done only months before. This time, however, she met with her husband, William, and a group of twelve other black Chicagoans and laid out plans for what would become the PME.[49] This was a response to new developments nationally—including a presidential campaign that had just elected Franklin D. Roosevelt, promising a new era of government activism in the face of economic crisis. However, it was also an outgrowth of the experiences of Gordon and others in the new black-led political, religious, and social organizations that surged across the Midwest as elsewhere over the course of the 1920s.

According to Gordon, the process of arranging the PME's first meeting was a rather difficult task: "[The] people had lost confidence in men after the defeat of the U.N.I.A., and refused to follow another man."[50] This was certainly an overstatement, but it exemplifies Gordon's frustration with Garveyite men for what she viewed as their inability to effectively lead the UNIA. Gordon insisted that she only accepted the position after failing to locate a "strong man" to do the job, yet she had already secured her position as founder and president by planning, initiating, and facilitating the first meeting. Moreover, ten men were present at the PME's founding meeting, including Gordon's husband, William, who had also been active in the Garvey movement during the 1920s. Gordon's suggestion that there were no "strong men" available, along with her apparent apprehension and attempt to underplay her own leadership role, was especially significant, however. It captured the struggle that many proto-feminists endured as they advocated for an expansion of women's leadership roles while reinforcing traditional roles and expectations.

Despite these apprehensions, Gordon went through with plans to establish the PME, drawing inspiration from Garvey's UNIA. The PME's motto—"One God, One Country, One People"—was a rephrasing of the UNIA's motto—"One God, One Aim, One Destiny."[51] Likewise, the PME's official constitution reflected the same tone and language from Garvey's 1920 Declaration of the Rights of the Negro Peoples of the World.[52] For example, it underscored Garvey's "race first" philosophy and strong commitment to emigration: "Our aim is to return to our motherland, to our

FIGURE 5. Mittie Maude Lena Gordon. Earnest Sevier Cox Papers, Box 39, 1821–1973, Rare Book, Manuscript, and Special Collections Library, Duke University, Durham, N.C.

true name, to our own language and to our true religion. Therefore, let Africa be free for Africans, those at home and those abroad. We believe in the National-Hood of all Races, and the right of all national movements." To further reinforce the influence of Garvey's ideas, Gordon included a short but significant clause in the PME's constitution: "We freely coincide with [the] Nationalistic principles laid down by the Hon. Marcus Garvey."[53] With these words, Gordon revealed much about how she envisioned the organization; rather than pledging full allegiance to Garveyism, she chose instead to "freely coincide," indicating an effort to draw some distance from Garvey.

Further illustrating the black nationalist leader's efforts to depart from Garvey's UNIA, Gordon drew on the idiosyncratic Islamic teachings of Noble Drew Ali and integrated symbols of Ali's MSTA into the PME's official documents.[54] Although Garvey's UNIA was not directly affiliated with any church or religious organization, it did appeal to black churchgoers, and Garvey's own Christian faith certainly influenced his beliefs. Garvey used religion and religious rhetoric to advance his "race first" philosophy. Moreover, he received considerable support from members of the African Orthodox Church (AOC), an international religious order that taught a blend of Pan-Africanism, Ethiopianism, and Garveyism.[55] Established in 1921 by George Alexander McGuire of Antigua, the AOC generally attracted West Indians who were sympathetic to Anglicanism and others who embraced Roman Catholicism and the teachings of the Episcopal Church.[56] While not a religious organization per se, the UNIA was closely affiliated with the AOC, and many of its members embraced a black reinterpretation of Christianity.[57]

Unlike the UNIA, the PME promoted a non-Sunni presentation of Islam. Emphasizing Noble Drew Ali's teachings and the principles of the MSTA, Gordon encouraged her followers to "[trust] in Allah, [follow their] leader, and [look] East to Africa."[58] While there is no extant evidence to suggest that Gordon converted to Moorish Science, founding documents of the PME reveal that she certainly drew inspiration from many of Ali's teachings. Founded by Ali, who according to tradition was born Timothy Drew in North Carolina in 1886, the MSTA held its first meeting in Newark, New Jersey, in 1913 but gained a significant following in Chicago during the late 1920s.[59] Sometime around 1927, Ali established Temple No. 1, the headquarters of the MSTA, on Indiana Avenue on the Southside of Chicago.[60] Given the close proximity of the MSTA's headquarters to Gordon's apartment, Gordon likely crossed paths with Ali. Advocating Islam as the true religion of black people and emphasizing an alternative identity, Ali taught his followers that they were "Asiatics" and "descendants of Moroccans" rather than "Negroes," "blacks," or "colored people."[61] Blending together elements of Islam, Freemasonry, Christianity, Theosophy, and Pan-Africanism, Ali published the *Holy Koran* (or *Circle Seven Koran*) in 1927, which maintained that African Americans—along with a host of other groups, including the Japanese, the Indians, and the Chinese—were "the descendants of Canaan and Ham and therefore the original Asiatic nations."[62]

These teachings held sway with many black men and women during the post–World War I era—a period that witnessed a number of historical developments, including the relocation of millions of African Americans from the South to the Northern region, growing unrest in urban cities, and a global depression. Many black men and women, especially those residing in the urban North, envisioned membership in the MSTA as a way to distinguish themselves from their enslaved ancestors. According to MSTA doctrine, black people would not have been enslaved if they had rejected Christianity and honored the Islamic religious practices of their ancestors. Ali maintained the belief that he could alter the destiny of black people by erasing all ties to slavery and offering an alternative racial history and identity. Amid the political and economic upheavals of the period, these ideas served to bolster racial pride and certainly fueled hope. Within the black nationalist political milieu of the post–World War I era—no doubt influenced by the popular Garvey moment—Ali's religious ideas gained currency.[63] Not surprisingly, the two movements were closely aligned. Ali's *Holy Koran* acknowledged Garvey's UNIA as a forerunner to the MSTA.[64] The two men maintained a cordial relationship during the 1920s, and in the aftermath of Garvey's deportation, Ali envisioned the MSTA as a successor to the UNIA.[65] During the early 1930s, the MSTA attracted many former UNIA members who certainly embraced this point of view.[66]

For Gordon, Ali's teachings had particular appeal because they offered an alternative to mainstream Christianity, which she viewed as the religion of white oppressors. Though she did not require or even advocate for membership in the MSTA, Gordon used her weekly meetings as a forum to endorse Ali's new Islamic ideas—a move that underscores the diverse religious and political thinkers from which Gordon drew. Along these lines, Gordon actively propagated the symbols and rhetoric of the MSTA. The PME's letterhead, for example, bore the same Islamic symbols—the star and crescent—that appeared on Ali's "Nationality and Identification Cards," which he issued to his followers.[67] Furthermore, at the weekly meetings in Chicago, Gordon and other PME leaders openly denounced Christianity and described Islam as the true faith of black people.[68] As her husband, William, later explained, "We don't have a connection with the Moslems but just believe in the Moslem faith." "At our meetings . . . we talk about worshipping Allah," William continued, "[and] we also believe that Mohammed is the prophet of Allah, just like Jesus Christ was the prophet of God."[69] His comments underscore how

FIGURE 6. "Members of the Moors [Moorish Science Temple], a Negro religious group of Chicago, Illinois." Schomburg Center for Research in Black Culture, Photographs and Prints Division, The New York Public Library.

Gordon and her followers formulated an ideology based on the Islamic teachings of Noble Drew Ali.

Even as she drew inspiration from Ali's Islamic teachings, Gordon's ideas were also informed by her own Christian upbringing, and she recognized the utility of Christianity in attempting to expand the reach of her political message and increase her following. Similar to Ali, Gordon appropriated the worship practices and "biblical tropes and characters" of black churches while claiming full allegiance to Islam.[70] While indicating that the PME was "built . . . from a Biblical standpoint," for example, the PME's constitution included a clause that suggested its members believed in one God—"Allah, the God of the universe." Throughout its pages, the PME's constitution also included a number of well-known biblical verses such as Psalm 19:14—"Let the words of my mouth, and the meditation of my heart be always acceptable in thy sight, O' Lord my strength and my Redeemer."[71] Notwithstanding their support of many of Ali's teachings and efforts to appropriate the religious leader's rhetoric and symbols, Gordon and her followers did not adhere to the distinct rituals and practices of the MSTA. Members of the PME, for example, did not adopt the surname "Bey" or

"El"—a common practice for Ali's followers—or wear the Turkish fez, the MSTA's official religious dress for men. For Gordon, the rejection of mainstream Christianity and promotion of Islam was both a religious and political move. By telling her followers to embrace an idiosyncratic ideology that fused Christianity and Islam, Gordon, like Ali, constructed a unique religious identity that defied mainstream religious expressions.[72] Gordon's propagation of Ali's Islamic teachings functioned as a counterhegemonic response to white domination, and her organization provided a platform for blacks in Chicago and across the urban North to assert their political and religious agency.[73]

Rank-and-File Members of the Peace Movement of Ethiopia

The PME provided a crucial space for working-poor black men and women in Chicago to engage in black nationalist and internationalist politics during the economic crisis of the 1930s. With the onset of the Great Depression in 1929, many of these men and women were unemployed and struggling to make ends meet. As the nation sunk deeper into the Depression, Chicago faced a number of challenges. The city, which bore the full force of the Great Migration—with an estimated black population of 492,000 by 1950—economically collapsed.[74] Only months after the 1929 stock market crash, Jesse Binga's State Bank, the preeminent black-owned bank in the city, had been forced to close. By 1934, most of the residents in Chicago's "Black Belt"—the predominantly African American community on Chicago's Southside—were on government relief.[75] Worsening conditions for black residents in Chicago and other Northern urban cities coincided with the declining influence of mainstream race organizations. During the early years of the Depression, Chicago's National Association for the Advancement of Colored People (NAACP) and National Urban League (NUL) lost a significant amount of their funding from African Americans and white philanthropists. The lack of financial resources, coupled with changes to the local NAACP's and NUL's leadership, underscored these organizations' instability and their inability to confront the growing problems of poverty in the city's black communities.[76]

Around the same time that Gordon established the PME, the United States Communist Party (CPUSA) was beginning to gain traction in black communities across the country.[77] The 1931 Scottsboro case, in which nine young black boys were sentenced to death after being falsely accused of raping two white women in Alabama, became a significant recruiting tool for the party. Signifying the party's commitment to eradicating racial injustice at home and abroad, Communists initiated a national and international justice campaign for the Scottsboro boys.[78] The CPUSA's growing popularity in various parts of the country, including Chicago, offered black Americans political opportunities in which to merge racial and economic concerns.[79] Black women, in particular, found in the party a space in which to advance black leftist and feminist politics.[80]

Although the CPUSA provided a space for black women to engage in the struggle for racial advancement, the organization maintained a male-centered version of radicalism.[81] Women's roles were still limited in the predominantly white and male organization. Black women in the CPUSA functioned as "outsiders within," never fully participating on an equal level with their white male counterparts.[82] Gender politics, however, were not the only deterrents for some black women. Individuals like Gordon rejected Marxism, choosing instead to embrace black capitalism as a more viable political strategy. Similar to Garvey, Gordon and her followers maintained the belief that black economic development was possible within a capitalist system.[83]

Whereas some black activists during this period forged an idiosyncratic politics that drew on both Garveyism and Communism, Gordon and those who joined the PME viewed these two positions as ideologically incompatible.[84] Writing in 1937, Gordon insisted that the sole purpose of the CPUSA was to "destroy any race-conscious movement" and prevent the establishment of an autonomous black nation-state. Within the context of the Great Depression era, which ushered in a period of intense repression of Communist organizing in the United States, Gordon's words reflect a sense of distrust that some activists had for the Communist Left during this era—specifically, a fear that any Communist affiliation might bring unwanted attention and thereby hinder their political agenda.[85] However, her rejection of Marxism and decision to remain distant from the Communist Left also capture the range of black radical politics during the Depression. Gordon's PME provided a different avenue for black radical activists who were unwilling to affiliate with the Communist Left.

From the outset, the PME promoted a vision of Pan-African unity, appealing specifically to "black men and women whose hearts beat in unison with the race."[86] This is why Gordon chose to emphasize "Ethiopia" in the organization's name. A common trend of blacks in the African diaspora, Gordon used the term "Ethiopia" to refer to all peoples of African descent. Rooted in the ideological underpinnings of Ethiopianism—race redemption ideas derived from biblical Ethiopia—Gordon's use of the term in 1932 was symbolic. Significantly, the establishment of the PME coincided with the reign of Ethiopia's Emperor Haile Selassie, who had been crowned two years prior.[87] By her own statement, the reference to Ethiopia derived from the biblical verse Psalm 68:31, which reads, in part, "Princes shall come out of Egypt, and Ethiopia shall soon stretch forth her hands unto God."[88] Like many black nationalists before her, Gordon drew inspiration from the biblical verse, which served as a prophetic reminder of inevitable black redemption.[89] This is exemplified by the PME's installation ceremony script, which reads, in part, "I shall . . . to the best of my ability spiritually, mentally, and physically defend the cause of the Peace Movement of Ethiopia . . . and protect the morale of our members to the end that God's divine purpose be accomplished in the ultimate redemption of Africa."[90] Gordon's decision to include these words in the script signifies her belief in the message of Ethiopianism, her commitment to worldwide black liberation, and her steadfast belief that emigration would hasten the redemption of Africa.[91]

The height of Gordon's PME coincided with the women's peace movement of the period—a transnational effort to advance peace and nonviolent activism in the aftermath of World War I. Led primarily by middle-class white women reformers, the women's peace movement provided a crucial public platform for women in various locales to agitate for pacifism and social reform during the twentieth century. Under the auspices of organizations like the Women's International League for Peace and Freedom (WILPF), the Women's Peace Society, and the Women's Peace Union, women in the United States, Britain, and other parts of the globe employed a myriad of strategies and tactics intent on preserving peace and stability. Despite internal racial tensions in the movement that reflected the Jim Crow era in which it emerged, middle-class black women, including well-known black clubwomen Addie Hunton and Alice Dunbar-Nelson, found a space in the movement in which to advance their race work. As members of WILPF, Hunton, Dunbar-Nelson, and others forged interracial transnational alliances in their efforts to challenge racism and discrimination.[92]

Gordon may have drawn inspiration from the women's peace movement of the period—even though she did not explicitly address the movement in her writings. Similar to women activists in WILPF and other groups, she and other leaders in the PME endorsed pacifism, calling on their members not to serve in the U.S. military.[93] While their reasons for promoting this stance were far more complex, Gordon and other PME leaders emphasized the need for "peace and harmony" in the organization's constitution. In later years, Gordon would also discourage her supporters from fighting in World War II. This was also consistent with various groups of the era, including Father Divine's Peace Mission—an interracial religious organization that attracted a large following in the urban North in the 1920s and 1930s.[94] Whereas Father Divine's Peace Mission advocated pacifism in all contexts, Gordon's PME endorsed pacifism insofar as it opposed the use of military force by the U.S. government and other white imperialist nations during this period. Gordon and her supporters recognized the significance of violence and military force in opposition to global white supremacy and racial oppression.

During the early 1930s, Gordon began holding public meetings all across the city in an effort to persuade black men and women to join the PME. Sam Hawthorne, a native Mississippian from Center in Attala County, who had relocated to Chicago in 1927, first crossed paths with Gordon sometime during the early 1930s. He recalled hearing Gordon speak "in public, on the streets," and remembered other black Chicagoans enthusiastically talking about her.[95] Deeply moved by the activist's teachings, Hawthorne became a PME member and later established a chapter in his hometown. Another black resident in Chicago recalled hearing Gordon speak at a local park, drawing crowds of former UNIA members. Describing her as a "rebel," the individual assumed that Gordon had been speaking on behalf of the Communist Party though he or she angrily concluded that Gordon had "no damn program." Criticizing Gordon for integrating "lots of biblical crap" in her speeches, the individual suggested that Gordon's appeal was only due to her ability to stir her listeners' emotions.[96]

Evidently, this individual was no fan of Gordon's, but his or her comments, along with Hawthorne's recollections, offer glimpses into how Gordon used city parks and street corners as platforms to disseminate her nationalist ideas and build momentum for the movement. Like Garvey had done in Harlem years prior, Gordon used speeches in public spaces as opportunities to attract new members. Her efforts were fruitful. Surviving organizational records reveal that the PME drew a significant following of black men and women in Chicago and across the country during the 1930s.

In the Midwest—specifically the states of Illinois, Indiana, Michigan, Kansas, Minnesota, Missouri, Wisconsin, and Ohio—the PME boasted an estimated 2,027 members, which included an estimated 868 women.[97]

The weekly meetings of the PME's main division, held at the Boulevard Hall on East 47th Street in Chicago, often drew from 200 to 350 people.[98] Usually held on Sundays, the meetings began with prayer and then proceeded to the readings of minutes from the previous meeting, reports from local officers, updates from the varied divisions, and, occasionally, elections of officers to any vacant positions. The meetings were facilitated in a strict fashion, reflecting the organization's hierarchical structure of leadership. During one meeting, for example, Gordon admonished attendees for not following the correct protocol to address the executive board. She carefully reminded them that "no speaker would be permitted to talk before . . . giving the president of that local [division] their subject" for review.[99]

These meetings provided an intellectual space for working-poor black men and women to engage in black nationalist discourses and address important issues of the day. Each PME meeting centered on key themes for discussion, and Gordon, along with various other male and female leaders in the organization, presented speeches that addressed these matters and then provided opportunities for members of the audience to raise questions. In one meeting, for example, the subjects of discussion were as follows: "Can the black man be completely independent in the U.S. Government? What steps could be taken to bring about a permanent solution to the race problem in the U.S.? Should the matter be delayed or should the black man act now?" In another instance, PME leaders and members discussed the key question, "Why should the black man choose Africa as his destination?"[100]

Reflecting on the history of race relations in the United States, PME leaders offered poignant examples to help reinforce their positions. During one meeting, they reminded those in attendance that President Abraham Lincoln had once proposed deporting former slaves to Haiti and Liberia upon the abolition of slavery. Moreover, they read excerpts from Chief Justice Taney's racist ruling in *Dred Scott v. Sandford* (1857), which had declared African Americans to be *noncitizens* of the United States. By evoking these earlier historical developments in their weekly meetings—and thereby deemphasizing other developments such as the Fourteenth Amendment, which effectively overturned the *Dred Scott* decision—PME leaders made it quite clear that in their view, race relations had not improved much since the nineteenth century and blacks were "not citizens of America, but citizens of Africa."[101] Hundreds of working-class black men and women in Chicago embraced this message.

Although the PME received considerable support from black working-class Chicagoans, many middle-class and elite race leaders opposed the organization and its goals. According to one 1936 *Chicago Defender* article, some race leaders in Chicago were greatly "disturbed by this bombshell which threatens to wreak havoc on all the progress the race has made in this country since emancipation." One anonymous race leader insisted that the PME's agenda was motivated by cowardice: "Action by this group of mis-led Negroes shows a cowardly attitude of running away from a problem instead of standing and fighting it out."[102] He went on to criticize the organization's makeup, noting that no scientists, engineers, or doctors were members of the PME, alluding to the fact that Gordon's organization lacked the backing of the "better class of Negroes."[103] Expressing similar sentiments, Claude Barnett, founder of the Associated Negro Press, described Gordon and PME members as "a crude, ignorant lot."[104] These comments offer a glimpse into the class divisions within black communities over the question of emigration. The black masses often embraced emigration plans in their quest for economic and social autonomy, whereas members of the black middle class and elite generally resisted these efforts.[105] No doubt social status informed these perspectives as members of the black elite often saw their prospects for further economic and political advancement in the United States in a more favorable light. Those who struggled to meet their day-to-day needs, however, generally expressed a greater willingness to leave the United States—regardless of their views on black nationalism.

Despite the resistance that Gordon and her supporters faced from some race leaders, the organization continued to gain momentum. In addition to the weekly meetings on the Southside of Chicago, the PME began to hold meetings in various parts of the city, and its influence began to spread across the nation. This expansion can be credited to Gordon's commitment to "street strolling" along with her followers' active recruiting efforts. With the help of Harry Collins, a PME organizer, the organization opened a new branch in East Chicago, Indiana, during the early 1930s with an estimated 400 members. Another organizer, Tommie Thomas, managed to maintain a PME branch in Grady, Arkansas, for a short period of time until the group dissolved in 1940. Likewise, Leonard Robert Jordan oversaw a PME branch in Jersey City, New Jersey, while fellow PME member William Ashley Fergerson formed a local chapter in Palatka, Florida, after reading about the PME in the *Pittsburgh Courier*.[106] The median age of the organization's membership was between forty and fifty, representing the age group that would have been most impacted by the Garvey movement.[107] The only surviving membership roll, obtained by FBI officials in 1942, indicates that the organization had an estimated 4,100 official members in chapters all over the country, including the states of Illinois, Washington, Indiana, Maryland, Arizona, Mississippi, Missouri, Arkansas, Pennsylvania, and Florida.[108] The majority of the PME's membership—about 65 percent—was male.[109]

Gender Roles and Women's Leadership in the PME

Despite the strong representation of men in the PME, women held a variety of visible leadership roles and decision-making positions in the organization. In addition to Gordon as president, women served as national organizers while others were members of the organization's board of directors and supervisors of PME chapters. Alberta Spain, who Gordon carefully mentored during the 1930s, served as secretary and a member on the organization's executive council.[110] Likewise, Mrs. W. L. Stubbs served as one of the executive officers. Details about these women's personal lives are scarce, but organizational records reveal that they both became actively involved in the PME shortly after its debut in Chicago. As executive officers, both women were granted a number of leadership duties that distinguished them from the lay members of the organization. As members of the executive council, they were responsible for "decid[ing] all questions arising between [l]ocals, subordinated Society appeals, International questions and all matters affecting the good and welfare of the organization and the members at large." As members of the PME's executive council, they also had the power to approve and reject the appointments of officers in the organization.[111]

While women like Spain and Stubbs maintained positions on the PME's executive board, other women supervised local divisions of the organization. For instance, Lydia Jernigan, a homemaker, served as supervisor for the PME chapter in Galesburg, Illinois, during the 1930s and early 1940s.[112] Born in Mayfield, Kentucky, in 1888, Jernigan had relocated to Illinois with her stepparents and eight siblings during the Great Migration. Her spouse, Hampton Jernigan, a native Mississippian, worked in a local metal factory

in 1920 and, later, as a watchman for a railroad company before losing his
position sometime during the late 1930s.[113] While Lydia Jernigan oversaw
the local PME chapter in Galesburg, other women in the PME served as
secretaries and others as "lady presidents." In the PME, women leaders
had much more flexibility than in the Garvey movement. Under Gordon's
leadership, the title "lady president" was used as a way to distinguish
between male and female leaders; there is no evidence to suggest that "lady
presidents" in the PME were solely confined to a woman's division.

Moreover, women leaders in the PME were not expected to answer to
male leaders in the organization. All members and leaders of the PME were
answerable to Gordon, who set the parameters for each division and position. While she worked in conjunction with members of her executive committee, often seeking their advice and making decisions based on a majority
vote, Gordon exerted control by chairing weekly meetings, limiting who
could serve in leadership positions, and carefully overseeing the activities
of each division.[114] As "lady presidents" of a local division, women leaders
in the PME under Gordon's leadership regardless of who actually
presided over the specific chapter. Second, although many men in the PME
served as presidents of local divisions, the position was not gender specific.
Female presidents (and vice presidents) could be found in a number of
local PME divisions. Mary Bailey, for example, was appointed president of
the PME chapter in Pittsburgh.[115]

Even though Gordon's PME provided a platform for black nationalist
women to serve in multiple leadership capacities, the organization still upheld certain traditional gender roles. The organization's constitution explicitly stated that while lay members, regardless of sex, could hold leadership
positions, women could only hold the office of president when "there is
not sufficiency among the male[s]."[116] Given the predominance of men
in the organization, this clause is peculiar but not entirely surprising. It
demonstrates how Gordon, like other black nationalist women during this
period, attempted to uphold the patriarchal and masculinist ideals generally
endorsed by black nationalist organizations.

The PME's Protective Corps division further illustrates this point. Modeled after the UNIA's African Legion—a military division comprising male
Garveyites—the Protective Corps represented the paramilitary division of
the PME.[117] Similar to the UNIA's African Legion, the purpose of the PME's
all-male Protective Corps was to provide the protective arm of the future
black nation-state. Foreshadowing the Deacons for Defense and Justice, an

armed self-defense civil rights organization that emerged during the Black Power era, members of the PME's Protective Corps were trained in military discipline.[118] The inclusion of the Protective Corps in the PME underscores the longstanding significance of the principle of armed self-defense in the black nationalist tradition.[119] Although the PME did not publicly endorse armed self-defense—as did later black nationalist groups—the organization's leaders understood its utility as a viable method for securing civil and human rights. Not surprisingly, members of the PME's Protective Corps carefully guarded weekly PME meetings in Chicago and other parts of the country in order to ensure that activists would be ready to respond to white supremacist violence.

Black Emigration and FDR's Promise of a New Deal

One of the primary goals of Gordon's PME was to advance the cause of black emigration to West Africa—a political strategy long employed by black nationalists who saw no contradiction in making financial demands of the state or of individual white citizens while endorsing economic self-sufficiency and black political self-determination. One of the earliest efforts to advance emigration to Africa had been led by Paul Cuffe (or Paul Cuffee), a wealthy African American businessman and an avid sailor who traveled extensively to and from West Africa during the 1800s. In 1811, he visited Sierra Leone, where he began to forge ties with the nation's leaders and arrange plans for relocation. Convinced that people of African descent could not live without discrimination in the United States, Cuffe worked tirelessly to recruit individuals who were willing to leave the country. In 1815, he successfully led a group of thirty-eight individuals to Sierra Leone, using his own funds to cover travel expenses. In the years following Cuffe's death in 1817, the American Colonization Society (ACS) actively supported black emigration to West Africa.

During the American Civil War (1861–65) and Reconstruction (1865–77), black emigration from the United States to Liberia gradually declined as leaders such as Frederick Douglass openly criticized the ACS and African Americans' efforts to relocate. African American leaders such as Bishop Henry McNeal Turner, however, helped to revive the movement during the late nineteenth century. Convinced that the United States had accumulated an estimated $40 billion for centuries of exploitation, Turner demanded that the U.S. federal government compensate black Americans by covering relocation expenses.[120] Years later, in 1922, Garvey followed suit, supporting Mississippi Senator T. C. McCallum's proposal to seek federal assistance to purchase or negotiate "a piece of land where the Afro-American could move towards independence under the tutelage of the United States government."[121]

Gordon's petition, therefore, was hardly unique. Similar to individuals like Garvey and Bishop Turner, Gordon believed that the U.S. government should provide financial aid in support of black emigrationist efforts. And similar to Turner, Gordon envisioned federal aid for black emigration as reparations for years of slavery and racial oppression. These convictions certainly guided her decision to launch an emigration campaign during the early 1930s. But, even more, Gordon's emigration campaign became a crucial recruiting tool for the PME, designed to mobilize mostly working-class black Americans during the Depression—first targeting black men and women in Chicago and the U.S. Midwest and gradually including those located in various parts of the nation.

Although Gordon and other PME leaders were already committed to the idea of black emigration when she launched the organization, the election of Franklin D. Roosevelt in 1932 served to bolster their cause. FDR's promise of a "new deal for the American people"—long before the idea became a reality—strengthened PME leaders' resolve to advocate emigration to West Africa.[122] These men and women envisioned the New Deal as the source from which they would be able to secure federal funds to leave the country. In August 1933, several months after FDR's inauguration, Gordon and founding members of the PME completed the final draft of a pro-emigration petition addressed to FDR. At the time they began drafting the petition, several New Deal programs were already in place, including the Federal Emergency Relief Act—passed by Congress in May 1933 to provide hundreds of millions of dollars in aid for unemployed Americans. From the start, African American activists were concerned that the new programs would not provide economic security for dispossessed, unemployed black men and women across the country, and by 1933, evidence of exclusionary practices was clear.[123] Still, this did not deter Gordon and other PME leaders from demanding federal aid for black emigration. To the contrary, they skillfully invoked FDR's language in an effort to bolster and legitimize their demands.

From its opening lines, the PME's drafted petition called on FDR to provide federal aid for black emigration, citing the promises of the New

Deal. "Whereas the Congress has empowered the President to exercise his judgment in the present crisis in a manner suited to the exalted office and provided means to execute his plans for the amelioration of distress and the restoring of normalcy," they argued, "we, the subjoined signatories, American citizens of African extraction, individually and collectively join in respectfully petitioning the President to consider our proposal, confident that his conclusions will be for the best interests of our families and of the community at large." The petition went on to emphasize the stringent economic conditions that black Americans faced, arguing that emigration would hasten the end of the Great Depression: "The distress of the unemployed is most severely felt by such of the uneducated American Negroes who abhor alms, both public and private, in any guise; [thus] the removal of a half million of the poorest from a competitive labor market, at the time, would tend to relieve to that extent the condition and opportunities of the remainder."[124] Moreover, they advocated emigration as a logical response to the nation's economic crisis and as a viable solution to African Americans' harsh conditions within the context of the Depression. "Hungry, cold and miserable," they argued, "the pursuit of life, liberty and happiness in America appears futile." "Given an opportunity in our ancestral Africa," they continued, "the knowledge of farming and of simple farm machinery and implements, which we have acquired here, would enable us to carve a frugal but decent livelihood out of the virgin soil and favorable climate of Liberia."[125]

While Gordon and her supporters were endorsing black emigration to Liberia—to escape the economic and political upheavals in the United States—the country was undergoing an economic and political crisis of its own. In addition to insurmountable debt and growing accusations of political corruption, Liberia was also embroiled in an international scandal concerning charges of labor exploitation.[126] Despite these realities, Gordon and her supporters remained steadfast in their belief that Liberia was a haven for black men and women and a viable space in which to rebuild their lives and advance the black nationalist project of nation building.

What is also striking about the petition is the way Gordon and her supporters creatively evoked the language of American citizenship while making an unconventional request to renounce U.S. citizenship. Although many Americans turned to the growing welfare state for aid to maintain a livelihood in the United States, Gordon and her supporters were seeking aid to establish a home elsewhere. Importantly, Gordon and her supporters called themselves "Americans of African extraction" in their emigration petition to FDR and as "Ethiopians" or "Liberians" in other documents.[127] This emphasis on an African identity underscores how PME activists imagined themselves as part of a diasporic polity even as they evoked the language of U.S. citizenship to frame their demands to the state.

With this completed petition in hand in August 1933, Gordon and fellow PME leaders moved quickly to solicit signatures from PME members and other black residents who supported emigration to West Africa. Convinced that an impressive number of signatures would improve their chances of obtaining federal support, these activists initiated a vibrant grassroots nationalist movement, which would eventually evolve into a nationwide—and later, international—emigration campaign. Using the networks she had already developed as a former UNIA member in the city and through the process of grassroots organizing, Gordon popularized her ideas widely and circulated the emigration petition, which called for relocation to "Liberia or some other place or places in Africa where [blacks] could work out [their] own destiny independently of white people."[128]

The interest generated by Gordon's ideas was so great that she arranged several mass meetings in Chicago to collect signatures from African Americans willing to leave the country—and to recruit new PME members. In one mass meeting, held in late August 1933, seventy volunteer secretaries—mostly women—were stationed at thirty-five tables at an old boxing ring to record the names and addresses of interested black Chicagoans. In the weeks that followed, Gordon and PME members continued to collect the names of emigration supporters across the U.S. Midwest and throughout various parts of the country. By October 1933, PME volunteers had collected the names and addresses of black men and women interested in emigration in neighboring states, including Indiana and Missouri. To expedite the process, PME volunteers asked each signatory to provide the names of family members and friends who might be interested and urged loved ones to sign the petition.[129] This method of obtaining signatures proved to be successful. In only a matter of months, Gordon and her followers managed to collect an estimated 400,000 signatures from black men and women expressing a desire to emigrate from the United States to West Africa. On November 15, 1933, Gordon mailed a copy of the petition to FDR.[130]

Gordon's popular emigration petition, along with the PME-sponsored organizing efforts that made it possible, underscores the continued salience of black nationalist thought and praxis during the 1930s. Moreover, it reveals the crucial role women played in popularizing these ideas during the post-Garvey era. Against the backdrop of the Great Depression, Gordon's PME offered an alternate space for black activists, mostly members of the working poor, to endorse the principles of black nationalism and agitate for black political rights. For these men and women, emigration to West Africa was a viable response to the continued subjugation, disenfranchisement, and economic disparity facing people of African descent in the United States. Similar to earlier black nationalists, Gordon and her supporters in the PME maintained the belief that federal support provided the most feasible means for making their dreams a reality. To be sure, these activists lacked the financial means to advance emigration on their own. But, even more, they reasoned that the U.S. government owed them some amount of financial support—as a form of reparations for centuries of forced labor by their ancestors. "We were torn from our original homes and kindred people against our will," they carefully explained in the petition.[131]

*　*　*

Not long after sending the petition to FDR in November 1933, Gordon received a two-sentence response from Jay Pierrepont Moffat, a U.S. diplomat and State Department official. He began, "The receipt is acknowledged, by reference from the White House . . . regarding the desire of a number of [N]egro citizens of the United States to emigrate to Liberia, and requesting the assistance of the United States Government to this end." Without providing any additional explanation, Moffat went on to reject Gordon's request in no uncertain terms: "It is regretted that at present this Government has no funds available for such a purpose."[132] Gordon was not surprised, but she was disappointed. Later, she argued that the U.S. government did have the means to help blacks relocate to West Africa. In a letter to one political ally, she argued, "Harry Hopkins, Federal Relief Director, [unveiled] a federal plan to spend an initial $25,000,000 in buying land to segregate the poor (presumably Negroes) in the arid West and in the sandy wastes of the cut-over lands of the North." As such, she reasoned that the "the government disproves its own claim that it has no money for the purchase of land."[133] From her vantage point, New Deal funds could provide a viable financial source for aiding black men and women willing to leave the country.

   Although she likely viewed the State Department response as an obsta-
cle, Gordon remained undeterred in her efforts to advance universal black
liberation through emigration. Within weeks of receiving the letter, the
black nationalist leader launched yet another pro-emigration petition,
building on the growing momentum among her followers. Moreover, she
began to make steps toward expanding her base of support. While most of
Gordon's activities during the early 1930s had been confined to Chicago
and other areas of the U.S. North, the black nationalist "street scholar"
decided to target the Jim Crow South—where she and most of her followers
had resided before the Great Migration. In 1936, she appointed a national
organizer to lead the charge. Her name was Celia Jane Allen.

CHAPTER 3

卆

Organizing in the Jim Crow South

IN 1937, CELIA JANE ALLEN arrived at the home of George Green, a black preacher and farmer, in Long, Mississippi—a small community located between Greenville and Leland on the Washington County and Sunflower County line.[1] The sixty-two-year-old preacher might have been caught off-guard by this new visitor, but Allen's arrival was certainly intentional. She wanted a place to stay, but even more, she wanted to secure Green's support for her political activities. Allen, a native Mississippian who had been residing in Chicago, traveled back to Mississippi on behalf of the Peace Movement of Ethiopia (PME) to promote emigration to West Africa. Her arrival in Mississippi coincided with a tumultuous period in the state's history. Like other states in the former Confederacy, the lives of black men and women in Mississippi were dominated by Jim Crow segregation, exclusion, racial violence, and terror. By the early twentieth century, white mob violence was part of the fabric of black life in Mississippi. Described by one historian as the "most race-haunted of all American states," Mississippi was the site of 476 recorded lynchings—representing 13 percent of the nation's recorded lynchings—from 1889 to 1945.[2] In this tense racial climate, Allen arrived at Green's home in Long, Mississippi, intent on organizing rural black residents around the issue of emigration. Although Green was initially skeptical of Allen, he eventually conceded and allowed the activist to stay in his home.[3]

In the ensuing months, Allen went on the mission to establish local branches of the PME in Long and later in Matherville—a remote plantation community in southeastern Mississippi a few miles away from the Alabama border on the Clarke County and Wayne County lines.[4] Later recounting her activities, Allen noted that she was "successful in getting many thousands to heed the call and sign their names." "Many places I was in danger, and was advised not to mention to the people about going to Africa," she continued, "but I never ceased to plead with them and was successful to leave the South without any trouble."[5] By her own account, she managed to secure more than four thousand signatures from black residents in Mississippi, Alabama, Tennessee, Kentucky, and Missouri during the 1930s.[6] In 1942, in a letter to one political ally, she claimed to have collected over a million signatures of black residents who were willing and ready to abandon life in the United States for the prospect of a better one in West Africa.[7]

Allen's organizing activities in the Deep South were part of the PME's strategy after their failed petition to the Roosevelt administration in 1933. In the years after the FDR petition, PME founder Mittie Maude Lena Gordon and her supporters began to extend their political activities to the South, specifically targeting rural black sharecroppers. In 1936, Gordon appointed Allen as one of the PME's national organizers sent to organize southern blacks in rural areas. From 1937 to 1942, Allen led a grassroots black nationalist movement in Mississippi and in neighboring states—advocating for Pan-African unity, economic self-sufficiency, and political self-determination during a period of economic instability. Drawing upon the southern black nationalist tradition—popularized by Bishop Henry McNeal Turner of the African Methodist Episcopal (AME) Church, Tuskegee Institute founder Booker T. Washington, and others—Allen called on impoverished black men and women in the region to set their sights on Liberia, where PME leaders had received some assurances that relocation would be welcomed.

Deploying black nationalist theory and rhetoric, including the tenets of black political self-determination, racial pride, and economic self-sufficiency, Allen worked within the organizing tradition as she attempted to garner support for her cause. Centered on transforming the political consciousness of individuals in order to build greater participation in civic and political life, the organizing tradition, as opposed to the emphasis on large-scale and short-term public events known as the mobilizing tradition, represented the bottom-up, community-based political activism that was vital to the development of local leaders. Reflecting the grassroots and community-based tradition of struggle, the organizing tradition rested upon a "developmental style of politics," which allowed for identifying and

FIGURE 7. State of Mississippi. Map created by Alice Thiede.

nurturing local leaders.[8] This philosophy undergirded Allen's activities in Mississippi during the 1930s and 1940s as she worked to galvanize rural black men and women and advance black nationalist politics.

With the focus on building relationships and developing local leaders, Allen led a pro-emigration campaign in the U.S. South, which she envisioned as a viable solution to the social, economic, and political challenges facing black men and women in the United States and across the African diaspora. Her political ideas, however, were far more complex. Embracing a biological conception of race, Allen pursued an unlikely political alliance with Mississippi Senator Theodore G. Bilbo, a well-known white supremacist who actively supported racial separatism—and, by extension, black emigration. Recognizing his influence in the state during this period, Allen sought out Bilbo's support for her political activities and imagined that she might be able to use her ties to the senator to advance the movement. To that end, Allen tried, though unsuccessfully, to obtain Senator Bilbo's aid to curb white mob violence—for the purpose of rallying support among black sharecroppers interested in emigration.

Allen's story sheds new light on the range and complexity of black women's activism in the Jim Crow South, shifting the focus from local struggles for voting and citizenship rights. While many southern black women of various economic backgrounds were actively involved in mainstream civil rights organizations and women's clubs, others found a space in black nationalist organizations like the PME in which to agitate for black political and economic rights.[9] Allen's efforts to organize rural black men and women in Mississippi and in other nearby states underscore the continued salience and influence of black nationalism in the Jim Crow South during the 1930s and 1940s. Significantly, Allen's activities highlights the crucial role women played in sustaining black nationalist politics and reveals how these women strategically adapted their actions and ideological messages to fit the local settings in which they worked.

Celia Jane Allen's Early Years

Similar to many working-class black women living during the early twentieth century, Celia Jane Allen left no personal archives and few writings. She was born in Mississippi—the specific location is unknown—and, during the first wave of the Great Migration, relocated to Chicago, where she resided at 442 Bowen Avenue.[10] Mittie Maude Lena Gordon and other PME

FIGURE 8. Executive Council of the Peace Movement of Ethiopia, including Mittie
Maude Lena Gordon (front row, center) and Celia Jane Allen (front row, center-
right). Earnest Sevier Cox Papers, Box 39, 1821–1973, Rare Book, Manuscript,
and Special Collections Library, Duke University, Durham, N.C.

leaders who worked alongside Allen referred to her as "Mrs. Allen," but
since there is no record of a previous unmarried name—or, for that matter,
a Mr. Allen—they may have referred to her as "Mrs. Allen" out of respect
and because of her age. The only surviving photo of Allen suggests that
she might have been around forty years old during the late 1930s (see
Figure 8).[11] Very little else about Allen's personal life is known.

Although Allen disclosed few details about her personal life in her correspondence and interactions with others, census records offer some clues.
Curiously, no one by the surname "Allen" appears in census records for
Chicago during this period—who also fits all of the details Allen provided
in her writings. Though multiple individuals with the same name resided
in Chicago, they neither resided on Bowen Avenue nor had a birthplace
listed as Mississippi. In 1940, when census takers arrived at 442 Bowen

Avenue in Cook County, Chicago, they encountered a thirty-five-year-old African American woman by the name of Ruth Dorsey. Born in Mississippi in 1905, Dorsey had relocated to Chicago sometime during the mid to late 1920s. She arrived in the city during the Great Migration when thousands of other African Americans abandoned life in the Jim Crow South.[12] While residing in Chicago with her mother and her husband, Frank, Ruth Dorsey, like countless other black women in urban areas, worked in domestic service.[13]

During the early 1930s, Dorsey lost her job as a domestic worker and remained unemployed until 1940.[14] Her experience mirrored those of other black women residing in Chicago and other cities. By January 1931, more than a quarter of all employed black women residing in urban areas lost their jobs. Though Dorsey admitted receiving some type of income—most likely federal relief—in 1940, her financial situation was probably still dire. Federal funds provided minimal relief for African Americans, who received less than their fair share. The Federal Emergency Relief Administration (FERA), which spent $4 billion primarily in direct financial aid for the needy, extended more funds to white Americans than black Americans. New Deal policies, which promised to improve socioeconomic conditions for all Americans, ultimately offered to African Americans a "raw deal."[15] For black women, the extremely limited job opportunities during the economic crisis and rampant racial inequalities in federal relief programs created a dismal atmosphere. Some black women in the urban North participated in "slave markets," accepting extremely low pay for domestic work.

Although Celia Jane Allen's living arrangements are unclear, her ability to use Dorsey's address for the purpose of receiving mail during the 1930s and 1940s suggests that the two women may have been related, intimately involved, or otherwise well acquainted. It is also likely that Allen was a boarder (or lodger) in Dorsey's apartment even though Allen was not present when census takers arrived at the home in 1940. While the full circumstances surrounding Allen's early life in Chicago remain a mystery, surviving records reveal that she became a member of the PME sometime in 1933. During the economic and political upheavals of the Depression, Gordon's PME provided a significant platform for working-class blacks in the city and other parts of the country to engage in nationalist politics.[16] With local chapters of the Universal Negro Improvement Association (UNIA) in a state of decline, the PME emerged as the largest black nationalist organization in Chicago.

Like many of the black men and women who joined the PME, Allen was especially drawn to the organization because of its emigrationist platform and commitment to economic self-sufficiency and racial separatism. Allen insisted, "I want to do all that I can do in the fight in the helping to provide ways and means for the [N]egroes to be immigrated to Africa from whence we came." "We can only plead to the gods of this country to send us to Africa," she continued, "where we can work and make a living and be a pure black race."[17] Allen's comments capture her commitment to racial separatism, her Pan-African vision, and her sustained belief that emigration was a vehicle for realizing black unity and bolstering black political and economic self-determination. For Allen and the thousands of men and women who joined the PME, emigration to West Africa appeared to be a logical response to the racial hatred that permeated much of the nation and a first step toward building better livelihoods during a global economic crisis.

By 1937, Allen became one of the PME's key recruiters in the U.S. South. Gordon and other members of the PME's executive council identified Allen as the ideal candidate to facilitate this process—perhaps because Allen was familiar with the area or had volunteered to go. The transient nature of Allen's life suggests that the activist enjoyed a mobility that made it possible for her to be an effective organizer. As a national organizer, Allen was expected to be away from home for extended periods of time, and she was also expected to travel frequently throughout the Jim Crow South. If Allen was married or, at the very least, had familial ties to Chicago, the decision would have been a difficult one to make. Moreover, as an organizer, she received little financial support from the PME. By one account, the organization provided $5 to cover traveling expenses, but Allen ultimately bore the brunt of the financial costs.[18] The personal sacrifices and financial commitment associated with Allen's political organizing activities might have been deterrents. Even more, the decision to return to Mississippi must have caused Allen some anxiety. Allen's few surviving letters capture her sense of fear as she traveled throughout the South to recruit new members and promote the message of black emigration. Naturally, she worried that her life would be in danger, and with limited financial resources, she had no clear sense of how her basic necessities would be met.[19] Her unexpected arrival at Reverend Green's home in Mississippi underscores the uncertainty associated with her political activities during this period. Notwithstanding her fears and anxieties, Allen remained committed to the task of promoting black emigration in rural black communities in the Jim Crow South.

Building a Movement in Mississippi

During the late 1930s, when Celia Jane Allen ventured out into the state to begin organizing rural blacks, white mob violence had become commonplace in Mississippi. Though there appears to be fewer lynchings in Washington County—where Reverend Green resided—than in other parts of the state, white vigilantes were active in every region of the state, and black residents could not escape this sobering fact.[20] An estimated 12.7 percent of those who were lynched in the state—from 1889 to 1935—were accused of rape.[21] However, records of the period only confirmed what journalist Ida B. Wells had long acknowledged: whites used the threat of rape as a means of terrorizing black Americans in order to keep them "in their place."[22] Though white vigilantes generally targeted black men, women were also victims of white mob violence.[23] Between 1880 and 1930, at least 130 black women were lynched in the Southern region.[24] In the state of Mississippi, roughly eighteen black women were victims of mob violence during this period.[25]

Significantly, one of the most infamous lynchings of the period took place in Duck Hill (Montgomery County) in 1937. In April of that year, a mob of white men seized Roosevelt Townes and Robert McDaniels, two African Americans who had been accused of murdering a local white merchant. After mob leaders hung Townes and McDaniels to a tree, hundreds of local whites watched on as they used gasoline blowtorches to burn the men alive. The Duck Hill lynching might have gone unnoticed, as many other acts of racial violence in Mississippi during this period, were it not for the fact that someone in the crowd chose to take photographs. Images of the gruesome scene later circulated across the nation as Congress debated the passage of a federal anti-lynching bill.[26] Despite the public outcry, no one was ever arrested for the murders. These incidents, combined with a string of highly publicized black lynchings, helped the state gain its reputation as "the land of the tree and the home of the grave."[27]

Despite the clear danger associated with organizing in rural Mississippi during this period, black activists of various political persuasions attempted to galvanize black men and women in the state. Civil rights organizations and women's clubs—including the National Association for the Advancement of Colored People (NAACP) and the National Association of Colored Women (NACW)—maintained an active presence in the state, providing a platform for black residents to challenge white supremacy and agitate for social and political rights.[28] These groups, which generally appealed to black middle-class and elite activists, promoted racial uplift politics, publicly decried the extreme educational disparity in the state, and lobbied for improved educational opportunities for black Mississippians.[29] During the Depression, many black sharecroppers in the state turned to the Southern Tenant Farmers Union (STFU), an interracial organization that challenged the discriminatory politics of New Deal programs.[30]

During this same period, members of the Communist Party began to mobilize black Mississippians, articulating a radical black internationalist and anticapitalist political vision. The party, however, was unable to attract a significant following in the state as a result of limited resources.[31] By 1936, the combined party membership for Mississippi and two other states—Alabama and Georgia—was 425, representing a significant decrease from two years prior when the party boasted 1,000 members in the city of Birmingham alone.[32] The exact figures are murky, but the Communist Party yielded far less success in organizing blacks in Mississippi during the 1930s than it did in other Southern states.[33] Additionally, the party's influence began to wane considerably in the South during the late 1930s—at the very same moment that PME organizers began to target the region. As a result, the Communist Party posed little competition to the PME, which also targeted the working class, despite different ideological commitments, methods, and goals.

Against this backdrop, Allen showed up at Reverend Green's home unexpectedly, asking for a place to stay. Born in Mississippi in 1875, Green was a widower who resided on a farm he rented with his aunt and several other relatives.[34] A sharecropper by day, Green was also a preacher at a local church and may have had ties to various other churches in the region. As a preacher, Green would likely have many local connections, and his endorsement of the organization and its platform would certainly make Allen's work a bit easier. While it is plausible that someone—perhaps a black churchgoer who read about the PME's popular emigration campaign in Chicago—suggested that Allen stay with Green, the preacher had never heard of Allen or the PME prior to the activist's arrival.[35] Pointing out the limited opportunities available for Southern blacks and insisting that emigration to Liberia offered the most viable solution, Allen convinced Green to become a PME member and also help her establish a series of local chapters. Although Green later shrewdly told FBI officials that Allen never made him aware of the organization's stance on black emigration, his writings confirm his full knowledge of the PME's aims and his conscious decision to join the movement.[36]

Green's endorsement of the PME marked a turning point in Allen's political activities in the area. His involvement certainly strengthened Allen's ability to garner support for her cause. As a minister who had been residing in the area for quite some time, Green occupied a place of privilege in the black community. Unlike Allen, who was fairly new to the community, Green was likely already well connected, and as a spiritual leader, he wielded some amount of influence and respect.[37] Green's support provided Allen with access to a public meeting space where she could address local residents. Largely shut out of the formal political process during this period, black churches, like black-owned businesses and other institutions, provided a significant space for black southerners to meet, plan, and disseminate ideas.[38] These churches provided crucial spaces for African Americans during the Jim Crow era to challenge discrimination and white supremacy.[39]

While Green provided Allen with access to a physical meeting space, the preacher's support also provided a buffer of protection from those who might have questioned a woman's ability to autonomously lead. Concerns over the proper roles and responsibilities for women often dominated discussions among black churchmen and black nationalists who, more often than not, advocated for a strict gendered hierarchy of leadership. While men recognized women as the "backbone," they were generally less willing to accept women in positions of visible leadership with authority over both men and women.[40]

Significantly, the PME did not maintain a strict gendered hierarchy, thereby providing a space for women to articulate proto-feminist views. Unlike women in the UNIA during the 1920s, women in the PME could be found serving in a variety of visible leadership roles from national organizers to members of the executive board.[41] This is not to suggest that the organization maintained gender egalitarianism or that Gordon herself promoted gender equality. To the contrary, Gordon maintained a masculinist vision of black liberation, and while she remained at the forefront of black nationalist politics, she still desired to establish a black nation-state led by strong black men. Along these lines, her views were strikingly similar to UNIA women during the 1920s who sought to expand opportunities for women's leadership yet also reinforced traditional roles and expectations.[42]

However, women in the PME articulated proto-feminism in ways that were noticeably different from the first generation of women activists in the UNIA. While women in the UNIA during the 1920s used the pages of the *Negro World*, the official Garveyite newspaper, to publicly challenge male chauvinism and patriarchy in print, women in the PME were often silent on these issues in their writings. Surviving primary sources suggest that PME women were less interested in advocating for a black proto-feminist agenda in writing compared to vocal nationalist women like Amy Jacques Garvey. Their actions, however, spoke louder than their words or lack thereof. Despite the absence of overt feminist writings, the women in the PME maintained positions of leadership and authority over both men and women and engaged in activities that sometimes challenged the gender and sexual conventions of their time. Allen's decision to travel alone and live away from home for extended periods of time, particularly as a woman who may have been married, offers a case in point. Similar to black women in the Communist Party during this period, Allen defied traditional expectations about "respectable" black womanhood.[43]

Moreover, Allen carefully walked a fine line between leading as a woman and adhering to the black nationalist (masculinist) belief in the primacy of black male leadership. When Allen began to organize in Mississippi, she skillfully asserted her leadership in a way that would not appear threatening to male members of the community. Her decision to collaborate with Reverend Green was strategic in this regard. With Green's endorsement and through his connections, Allen quickly tapped into a widespread network of churchgoers, friends, and relatives located in various parts of the state.[44]

During her stay in Mississippi, Allen contacted thirty-nine-year-old black resident Thomas H. Bernard, an associate of Reverend Green. Born in Matherville, Mississippi, in 1898, Bernard worked as a sharecropper during his teens until 1918, when he was drafted for the U.S. Army at the age of twenty.[45] By the time Allen arrived in Mississippi in 1937, Bernard was still residing in Matherville with his wife, Alee, and his mother, Delia. By his own statement, Bernard's interest in the PME was directly linked to his encounter with Allen during her visits.[46] A few years later, he recalled his motivations for joining the PME, indicating that he found the organization appealing because of its commitment to "get[ting] its members back to Africa, their fatherland" and its emphasis on "peace at all times." As a World War I veteran, Bernard was especially intrigued by the organization's instructions that members should "file conscientious objector forms . . . in order that [they] would not have to fight for the United States" in the event of another war.[47]

Bernard's interest in relocating to "the fatherland" suggests that he imagined himself as part of a diasporic community of black men and women who would ultimately be (re)united in Africa.[48] One of Allen's surviving poems, "Freedom's Wind Is Blowing," captures these same sentiments: "We are a nation / Must go free and stay free forevermore / We are thirty million strong / We bid you all adieu." After recounting "four hundred years" of the transatlantic slave trade, black enslavement, and racial oppression in the U.S. South, Allen called on blacks in the diaspora to take a definitive stance toward racial progress. Exemplifying the masculinist undertones associated with black nationalist discourses, Allen's poem appealed directly to black men to lead the way:

> The black man now must stand alone
> And let the nations see
> That he now has a worthy cause
> And surely must go free
>
> His Fatherland is calling him
> And homeward he must go
> He has no envy in his heart
> But [b]id you all adieu[49]

Like many other black nationalists, Allen desired to be (re)united with other blacks in the diaspora and envisioned the PME, in particular, as a vehicle for advancing black emigration and thereby establishing an autonomous black nation-state.

Importantly, Allen's poem, "Freedom's Wind Is Blowing," highlights the central tenets of black nationalist thought—black liberation, racial unity, black self-determination, and self-sufficiency. These ideas, which were popularized by Marcus Garvey during the 1920s, had already been firmly rooted in black culture since the early nineteenth century. While Allen's poem addresses many of the core themes reflected in Garvey's own poetry, it also underscores the ways in which Allen and other PME activists drew on the ideas of earlier black nationalists. Her reference to Africa as the "fatherland," as opposed to the "motherland," is more consistent with nineteenth-century black nationalist writers, including Bishop Henry McNeal Turner and Alexander Crummell, the Episcopalian priest and educator who established the American Negro Academy in 1897.[50]

Given the widespread influence of Turner, Washington, and other early black leaders in the South, it is not surprising that Garvey had found a significant following in the Southern region. By the mid-1920s, his organization, the UNIA, claimed five hundred divisions and branches across the U.S. South.[51] The UNIA, which eventually witnessed a sharp decline in membership following Garvey's arrest and imprisonment on charges of mail fraud, played an integral role in the politicization of many Southern black activists.[52] In Mississippi, Garveyism held sway among black tenant farmers and sharecroppers—many of whom read the widely circulated Garveyite newspaper, the *Negro World*, which encouraged local residents to set up their own divisions. By 1921, thirty-four UNIA chapters were established in the state largely as a result of the efforts of individuals like local black farmer and preacher Adam D. Newson.[53] As in other locales, UNIA women in Mississippi were largely involved in the movement as Black Cross Nurses, providing a range of social services for members of the black community.[54] By the late 1920s, however, the UNIA branches in the Southern region began to wane.

When Allen went to Mississippi to organize for the PME, local UNIA organizers were struggling to keep their chapters afloat.[55] It is likely that Allen was already tapped into this network of Garveyite activists on account of Mittie Maude Lena Gordon's ties to the UNIA. Certainly, Allen's emphasis on racial pride, black emigration, political self-determination, and economic self-sufficiency resonated with many black southerners during this period. As the UNIA began to lose its stronghold in the Southern region, the PME emerged as a viable alternative for local black residents interested in black nationalist politics.[56] Organizing on their own terms without Garvey's direct influence or authority, PME activists attempted to build a wide coalition of black supporters in the region, advocating for emigration as a vehicle for black social, political, and economic progress. While there is no doubt that these activists tapped into many of the nationalist ideas that were firmly rooted in black politics and culture during this period, they also employed new tactics that helped to propel the movement. For example, PME organizers were able to convince local black residents to join the movement by insisting that they had already secured land in West Africa. While Liberians had welcomed their interest, the PME had yet to secure land there.

Black nationalists' views on Liberia during this period reflected a long-standing interest in emigration firmly rooted in black political thought since the eighteenth century.[57] While earlier black intellectuals and activists looked to various other nations, including Sierra Leone, Haiti, and Canada, as potential sites for black relocation, Liberia became the focal point of black emigrationist movements during the nineteenth century. The surge of interest in Liberia during this period can be attributed in part to the American Colonization Society (ACS), which financially backed emigrationist efforts during the early to mid-nineteenth century while endorsing white supremacist views. Although emigrationist movements declined during the mid-1860s, African American leaders such as Bishop Henry McNeal Turner of the AME Church helped to revive it. Turner became one of the most vocal proponents for emigration to West Africa, utilizing a variety of outlets, including his newspapers, *The Voice of Mission* and the *Voice of the People*, to spread his ideas. Bishop Turner advocated emigration to Liberia as the best means of improving the social and economic conditions of black men and women. His efforts resulted in the emigration of an estimated five hundred African Americans to Liberia during the 1890s. Following the Supreme Court ruling in *Plessy v. Ferguson* (1896)—which formally established Jim Crow segregation laws—many black southerners abandoned life in the United States in pursuit of new opportunities in Liberia. In Arkansas, an estimated one hundred African American men and women relocated to Liberia with the aid of the ACS during the late 1890s. The Garvey movement of the early twentieth century would help to further ignite interest in Liberia despite Garvey's unsuccessful efforts to create a UNIA colony in Liberia in the 1920s.

Ultimately, then, Allen's activities in Mississippi during the 1930s and her interactions with Senator Theodore Bilbo represent a continuum of black mobilization around the issue of emigration to Liberia and black nationalists' willingness to ally with white supremacists to facilitate emigration. By the time she arrived in Mississippi in 1937, PME leaders had made some strides in their efforts to advance black emigration and emphasized (and sometimes exaggerated) this point to pique the interests of prospective followers. In April 1936, T. Elwood Davis, then aide to Liberian President Edwin Barclay, extended what appeared to be a favorable response to black emigration to the country. Citing President Barclay's commitment to making Liberia a "respectable and attractive place in which Negroes the world over may find it the true asylum from those handicaps and oppressions peculiar to other places where they are domiciled," Davis assured Gordon and her supporters that they would receive a warm welcome.[58]

Circumstances were far more complicated, however, and President Barclay had a number of stipulations for prospective emigrants. In a subsequent article, published in the *Chicago Tribune*, President Barclay addressed the issue of emigration yet emphasized the need for a certain class of black emigrant: skilled laborers. The newspaper article further elaborated on this issue, indicating that Barclay preferred "skilled artisans, trained agriculturalists, business men with capital, and young physicians willing to go into the interior and develop the aborigines."[59] This description hardly described Gordon and her supporters, but Gordon remained convinced that the invitation to Liberia, regardless of Barclay's stipulations, was an invitation nonetheless. Significantly, Gordon's acceptance of Barclay's request for volunteers to "develop the aborigines" in Liberia also reveals her civilizationist views toward indigenous African people—ideas that were characteristic of earlier black nationalists.[60]

By not disclosing all the stipulations outlined by Barclay, Gordon managed to convince her supporters that with the promise of land in Liberia, black residents would soon be able to begin the process of leaving the United States. In addition, when Allen arrived in Mississippi in 1937, the PME was in the process of sending a small delegation to Liberia to assess conditions in the country and begin negotiations with Liberian officials.[61] Therefore, when Allen began organizing in Mississippi, she emphasized these developments to convince Thomas Bernard and other black Mississippians that the PME and its leaders were making tangible steps toward realizing their goals. Over the course of her time in Mississippi, however, the PME's plans for relocating to Liberia began to fall apart. In October 1938, two PME representatives—black Chicagoans Joseph Rockmore and David J. Logan—traveled to Liberia to meet with officials to sort out logistics for relocating.[62] They returned to the United States, however, with more stipulations from President Barclay. In addition to agricultural skills, President Barclay now requested that each emigrant bring at least one thousand dollars to establish himself or herself in Liberia.[63] Much like Barclay's earlier requests, these new stipulations were unreasonable for PME activists—most of whom were unemployed and on government relief during this period.

FIGURE 9. Liberian President Edwin Barclay. George Grantham
Bain Collection, LC-B2-6416-4, Library of Congress.

Yet, they remained optimistic even in the face of these obstacles, maintaining the belief that emigration to West Africa would soon be realized.

Maintaining a deep sense of urgency, Allen pled with local residents in Mississippi to join the PME, which she described as the "only safe way to Africa." "I tried very hard," she later noted, "to make my people see that our time is winding up in this western world."[64] Her efforts were fruitful. Bernard was convinced, and like Reverend Green, he agreed to become a member of the organization. Shortly thereafter, he and Allen established new PME chapters in Mississippi, which attracted an estimated three hundred members. Much like her experiences with Green, Allen played an instrumental role in Bernard's quick transition from member to leader. By 1942, Bernard was not only a member of the organization but also a local organizer in Matherville who in turn went on to help establish more chapters of the PME in the neighboring state of Alabama.[65]

Local residents' descriptions of Bernard during this period reveal much about how he utilized the organizing tradition among everyday black people in the rural South. One anonymous local resident complained to federal authorities that Bernard's involvement in the PME incited some tensions in Matherville. According to the informant, "T.H. Bernard was constantly agitating the colored folks in that vicinity against white people." "He possessed a typewriter in his home, carried a little black satchel, and carried on considerable correspondence with some peace organization in Chicago, Illinois," the individual added. Interestingly, the only surviving photo of Allen shows the activist also holding a black satchel, symbolically forging a connection between the two organizers who worked in tandem during the Depression era. Described as a "whiteman hater" by one of his neighbors, Bernard engaged in door-to-door canvassing, attempting to solicit help "in obtaining freedom of the [N]egroes from the slavery of the whites."[66] Another anonymous black resident later recounted that during the process of canvassing, Bernard called for a militant response to racial oppression, attempting to enlist help to "actively revolt against white people" in the area. The individual also claimed that Bernard carried a gun.[67]

These descriptions about Bernard's activities provide a glimpse into the diverse protest strategies that PME activists employed during their political work. Whereas Allen centered her political activism on convincing local black residents to join the PME, advocating for black political self-determination, and insisting that black emigration was imminent, Bernard may have desired an immediate overthrow of the white power structure.

If, in fact, the FBI informant looked askance at Bernard's alleged militant approach, others seemed to embrace it. During the late 1930s, Bernard's door-to-door canvassing garnered considerable support in the local community, and within months of joining the movement, he had established two PME branches, consisting of "about 300 members" in Wayne County, Mississippi.[68] One local white resident later observed, "[Bernard] wielded considerable influence with his fellow [N]egroes."[69]

Together, Bernard's chapters in Matherville and Green's PME chapter in Long provided crucial spaces for black men and women to become involved in nationalist politics, drawing widely on the networks of church-goers and using the church as the central meeting place. The extent of the utilization of the church and the overtly Christian ethos mark striking differences between PME chapters in the South and the organization's main chapter in Chicago. While Gordon and PME leaders in Chicago promoted a syncretic version of Islam based on the teachings of Noble Drew Ali, PME activists in the South toned down their Islamic rhetoric—evidence of the activists' flexible organizing strategy. In addition, the PME's weekly meetings in the South mirrored a typical church service. These weekly meetings, generally held immediately after church services, began with a prayer and the reading of biblical scriptures. For example, in Florida, William Butler, a deacon of the Mount Carmel Freewill Baptist Church in Toddsville, later recalled that PME organizer William Ferguson shared information about the organization shortly after the pastor had delivered his sermon.[70] Another local resident, Rosa Boyd, recalled the same organizer showing up at Allen Chapel, a Methodist church in Hicksville, Florida, asking the pastor for permission to address the congregation at the conclusion of the service.[71]

These examples offer glimpses into how PME activists in the South skillfully used black churches as platforms from which to spread their nationalist ideas and recruit new members while downplaying their Muslim connections. Notwithstanding the tensions that often existed between black churches and black activists, these examples also illustrate the inextricable relationship between black religion and politics and reveals that black churches had a profound impact on the development of the PME's nationalist movement in the South.[72]

With access to this crucial meeting space as well as an introduction and tacit endorsement from the local minister, Allen and other PME organizers shared their nationalist ideas hidden from white interference and control.

Local leaders used the meetings to not only bring members of the community together—through prayer, bible study, and quiet reflection—but also discuss key issues and keep local residents abreast of current developments. Reflecting the legacy of oral traditions in African and African American cultures, PME leaders used these meetings to read aloud from newspaper articles and letters from Gordon.[73] Many of Gordon's letters contained references to international developments—an indication that Gordon wanted to make sure that her followers did not lose sight of global freedom struggles of the era. For example, in a 1942 letter to Bernard, Gordon reflected on the challenges that Indians endured under European colonialism and staunchly declared, "When India is free all colonial people and subjects throughout the world will be free." "It will cost much bloodshed," she predicted, "but it WILL COME."[74] In a subsequent letter to Tommie Thomas, a PME organizer in Arkansas, Gordon emphasized the link between the challenges facing African descended people and the plight of Indians. "The India situation is somewhat connected," she argued, "and the complete freedom of India will bring complete freedom to the American black people, because the same men are holding them in slavery."[75]

While the caste system in British India was not entirely the same as the racial hierarchy in the United States, and the racial demographics in both countries were vastly different, Gordon recognized that the struggle against white supremacy in the United States was intertwined with the larger struggle against white imperialism worldwide.[76] Her comments allude to the overlapping histories, shared struggles, and political solidarity between Indians and African Americans.[77] Linking local and national concerns to global ones, Gordon used her letters as a way to disseminate her black internationalist ideas to Southern followers. In this way, the PME's weekly meetings provided an intellectual space for local blacks, many sharecroppers and tenant farmers, to engage black internationalist discourse at the grassroots level.

FBI Surveillance and Black Radical Politics

The PME's success in the Jim Crow South during the late 1930s can be attributed, in part, to its leaders' ability to evade federal authorities. Many of Allen's activities went undetected by federal officials, who were far more preoccupied with suppressing communism than monitoring the activities of a black nationalist woman.[78] Ironically, despite one local resident's complaints about Bernard, FBI officials did not begin to investigate the PME in the South until the outbreak of World War II—when they became aware of Gordon's efforts to dissuade her followers from fighting in the war and her growing interest in Afro-Asian solidarity. Although Gordon remained committed to black nationalism, she also endorsed an internationalist vision that called for political collaborations with other people of color across the globe. Much like Madame C. J. Walker—the first African American female millionaire who had established the International League of Darker Peoples (ILDP) in 1919 with Marcus Garvey and other notable black leaders—Gordon espoused a commitment to the "confraternity among all dark races," believing that the plight of blacks in the United States was linked to that of all nonwhites globally.[79]

In May 1934, Gordon sent a letter to Kenji Nakauchi, then Japanese Consul General in Chicago, introducing her organization and requesting his support. "We are seeking the assistance and cooperation of your people in this our darkest hour," she wrote. "We have suffered untold misery in America over three hundred years and now our condition is far worse than ever," she continued. Gordon requested a "private interview" and assured Nakauchi that she would be willing to "meet on [his] own terms."[80] In another letter to Sadao Araki, a Japanese military general, Gordon requested a truce between the PME and "the dark skin people of the East[ern] world."[81] Making it clear to Araki that she and her supporters were "not [enemies] to the Japanese," Gordon called for peace and unity between the two groups. "This war is between the white man and the Japanese and we are not included," she added.[82] This letter, sent to Nakauchi right after the Japanese attack on Pearl Harbor in December 1941, drew the attention—and certainly the ire—of federal authorities, who were determined to squash pro-Japanese movements in black communities.[83]

In the months to follow, FBI officials sent informants to PME meetings in Chicago where they began to build a case against Gordon. Their investigations led them to the Jim Crow South, where FBI officials set out to interview several PME leaders and activists who frequently corresponded with Gordon—as well their neighbors and friends. Though interested in determining if Gordon or other PME leaders were popularizing pro-Japanese sentiments in the South, FBI officials also desired to learn more about the PME's connections to Africa. When they arrived in Mississippi,

FBI agents uncovered a world of grassroots black nationalist activists organizing in rural areas. By 1941, the PME boasted 733 official members in Mississippi—individuals who had purchased a PME membership card for ten cents each and likely attended meetings on a frequent basis. An estimated 351 of these individuals were women and approximately 346 were men (the sex of thirty-six individuals is unknown).[84] Members could be found in various parts of the state—from Bolivar County in the Delta to the central Mississippi counties of Attala and Madison. Most PME members—an estimated 179 individuals—resided in Bolivar County, 105 in Attala County, and 135 in Madison County. These figures capture the widespread geographical reach and effectiveness of PME organizers, who used a range of tactics and strategies to recruit new members and sell their nationalist vision(s) during the 1930s.

PME women organizers' emphasis on building relationships and developing local leaders played a vital role in propelling the movement to state and regional prominence. Celia Jane Allen's relationship with Joella Johnson provides a striking example of this correlation. Sometime in 1938, Johnson, a forty-eight-year-old wife and mother of two, made the decision to join the PME.[85] Born in Mississippi in 1890, Johnson was residing in Long, Mississippi, during the Depression when she crossed paths with Allen during one of Allen's public talks on emigration. In Mississippi and across the Southern region, Allen had been taking her message to "churches, schools, on the streets and in hundreds of homes" in an effort to convince local black residents that emigration to West Africa was a logical response to the challenges facing black Americans and a necessary step toward universal black liberation.[86] Later recounting her activities, Allen expressed deep despair over the conditions of black southerners: "Hundreds of the poor people were being driven from their farms. . . . Conditions are such that many children are not able to go to school for the lack of shoes, clothing and food." "I have met so many of them," she continued, "and have had the opportunity to get them to sign the [emigration] petition or [recite] our one prayer." [87] Moreover, she added, "I tried very hard to make my people see that . . . the PEACE MOVEMENT OF ETHIOPIA, which was founded and led by Mme. M.M.L. Gordon, is the only safe way to Africa, which means freedom and justice."[88]

Perhaps Joella Johnson was one of the individuals that Allen described —one of the many black southerners "being driven from their farms." For much of the nineteenth and twentieth centuries, Mississippi was, like other

states in the Southern region, largely agricultural. In the aftermath of slavery, sharecropping became the primary means by which Southern farmers
earned a living. However, for freedmen and women, tenant farming only
created a cycle of unending dependency and debt with little prospect for
land ownership.[89] During the 1930s, conditions became even more dismal,
despite, and ironically because of, the federal government's attempts to
boost the economy with the implementation of the New Deal.[90] Policies
such as the 1933 Agricultural Adjustment Act (AAA), intended to increase
failing crop prices, made payments to landowners to reduce their crop production. The act required landowners to share the payment with their tenants and sharecroppers, but few did, resulting in the displacement of
thousands of land tenants, sharecroppers, and small landowners—most of
them being African Americans.[91] As landowners began to eliminate their
small plots and as farms became more mechanized, the systems of land
tenancy and sharecropping began to decline in the region. Allen's encounter with Johnson in 1938, then, coincided with the beginning of a major
shift in the Southern economy, and Johnson must have been affected by
these developments.[92]

Johnson's interview with FBI officials in 1942, though rife with contradictions, offers some important clues on why she joined the movement.
Importantly, Johnson admitted to FBI officials that she was already familiar
with the PME before she met Allen. She credited a woman activist by the
name of "Mrs. Brooms" from Chicago who first told her about the organization and its goals. Yet, a careful reading of the FBI records reveals that it
was Celia Jane Allen who left a lasting impression on Johnson.[93] From the
outset, Johnson denied membership in the PME and tried, to little avail, to
maintain a level of secrecy about her involvement in the political movement. In one instance, she informed FBI officials that she was unable to
read and write even though she had numerous letters in her possession.[94]
Though Johnson blatantly denied any knowledge of Allen's nationalist
agenda, she did admit to hearing Allen publicly "say something about
Africa." In addition, while she suggested to FBI agents that she hardly knew
anything about the organization or Allen for that matter, she admitted wel-
coming Allen into her home for two nights.[95]

Understandably, Johnson was not forthcoming with FBI officials.
Nonetheless, her actions are quite revealing. Her carefully crafted re-
sponses, which attempted to downplay her intelligence, interest in the
organization, and knowledge of its leaders, affirm her close affiliation

with the organization. Certainly, Johnson wanted to protect the organization and its leaders—so much so that was she was willing to withhold crucial information. Her refusal to admit her full involvement in the PME was a survival strategy. She was not oblivious to the consequences of her political actions or the reprisals that might have followed if she disclosed too much information.[96]

Cognizant of the racial hierarchy that circumscribed the lives of black men and women, as well as the looming presence of the state, Johnson strategically withheld valuable information from white FBI officials and played into their preconceptions.[97] In so doing, she covertly challenged the social order, and by claiming to be oblivious of Allen's activities, Johnson attempted to ensure the future success of the PME's emigration campaign. Not only was Johnson knowledgeable about Allen's activities, but other sources reveal that she was drawn into the movement on account of Allen's recruiting efforts.[98] The two days that Allen spent in Johnson's home could not have been coincidental. Similar to her earlier experiences with Reverend Green, Allen may have identified Johnson as a potential leader of the movement. Therefore, Allen's request for a place to stay was, in all likelihood, also an attempt to build a relationship with Johnson and her family, as well as an opportunity for Allen to help groom Johnson for future leadership roles in the organization.

In the immediate aftermath of Allen's short stay in her home, Johnson helped to establish a new local PME chapter and served as the chapter's "lady president."[99] This provides yet another example of how the organization provided a space for women to serve in visible leadership roles. A survey of the list of officers in PME chapters across the state of Mississippi reveals that all chapters had both male and female officers. One of the local PME chapters in Matherville ("local # 10"), for example, boasted nine officers—three of whom were women serving in varied leadership capacities as president, vice president, and secretary.[100] Johnson's title also underscores how women activists in the PME had to carefully navigate black nationalist spaces. While Johnson was responsible for overseeing both men and women in the local chapter, the very use of the title "lady president" captures the gender politics at play.[101] In the PME, the title was used as a way to distinguish between male and female leaders; "lady presidents" in the PME were not confined solely to a woman's division (as was the case with Garvey's UNIA). In Johnson's case, she worked alongside Reverend Green, who served as the chapter's male president in Long, Mississippi.[102]

Significantly, Gordon administered organizational instructions to both Johnson and Reverend Green—an indication that their leadership roles were complementary or equal.

Maintaining frequent communication with these local organizers, Gordon offered advice when needed, made suggestions for how the organizers should conduct their affairs, and provided words of encouragement in moments of despair. Writing to Johnson in 1942, Gordon urged her not to become "discouraged because of those who differ with you." Echoing Garvey, who popularized the slogan during the 1920s, Gordon advised Johnson to "preach 'AFRICA FOR THE AFRICANS' everywhere you can."[103] In another letter, after Reverend Green reported acts of white supremacist violence directed against PME members, Gordon followed up with a detailed letter, offering words of encouragement. "We hope you will soon find out the truth about the brutality to some of our members," she noted. "Tell your people to be of good cheer for those that are suffering now will not have to suffer much longer." Vaguely referencing recent developments in East Africa and India, Gordon advised the Reverend Green that in only a matter of time, black people would "win our fight without opposition."[104] She expressed similar sentiments in a letter to Sam Hawthorne, a Mississippian who joined the PME in Chicago and later returned to the Southern region to help establish a new chapter. Gordon urged Hawthorne "not to be discouraged because the people are slow to see the light." "It takes time to wake sleeping people," she added.[105] Reinforcing these views in a letter to Bernard, Gordon optimistically declared, "Everything is working in our favor all over the world. In the very near future . . . the black man will be free."[106] Gordon's words provided much-needed hope and encouragement when circumstances appeared bleak for black southerners.

The Struggles Within the Struggle

In addition to unwanted attention from the FBI, PME organizers' political activities in the Jim Crow South were hampered by growing tensions among its leaders. Reflecting on her tenure in the PME, Allen described a strained relationship with Gordon during the early 1940s. According to Allen, Gordon "became [jealous] and envious" of her success in organizing blacks in the Southern region and, in response, started to "press and ignore" her.[107] The activist also bitterly complained that she had a "very hard fight with so many preachers and [professors]" while organizing in Mississippi, Alabama,

Kentucky, Missouri, and Tennessee. Convinced that many of these black "preachers and professors" only opposed emigration because of their desire to "exploit [their] own race," Allen openly criticized their attempts to block her efforts. "If the poor masses could see why they are trying to block this [emigration] measure," she argued, "they would ignore that kind and would be too glad to go [to Africa]."[108] To a large extent, Allen's critiques were unsubstantiated, especially considering the assistance she received from local preachers like Revered Green. At the same time, her statements offer a glimpse into the conflicts and class divisions that often existed in black communities regarding the question of emigration.

Political opposition and internal conflicts, however, paled in comparison to the white supremacist violence Allen encountered during this period. In one instance in 1938, while moving from plantation to plantation in an attempt to convince black sharecroppers to sign the PME's "back-to-Africa" petition, Allen encountered a group of hostile white landowners near Bamboo Road in Leland, Mississippi. Black sharecroppers in the area had expressed a genuine interest in the organization, but when she showed up with plans to organize these men and women, a group of white landowners drove the activist out of town with threats of violence and intimidation.[109] Black residents who openly supported the organization and its goals also faced a number of reprisals, in some cases "being beat almost to death."[110] Indeed, political organizing in the Jim Crow South was no easy task, and PME activists during the Depression era had to devise a range of creative strategies and tactics to deal with some of the challenges that they encountered.

In light of such violence, their alliance with a well-known white supremacist was perhaps the most questionable and seemingly paradoxical strategy these activists employed. In the immediate aftermath of the Bamboo incident, Allen wrote a letter to Mississippi Senator Theodore G. Bilbo—unbeknownst to Gordon—asking the senator for a letter "authorizing us to organize in your state, a letter to be shown to any authority questioning our right to organize for this purpose."[111] Her odd request arrived on Bilbo's desk in June 1938—only months after Gordon had begun corresponding with the senator to secure his support for the passage of an emigration bill. An ardent separatist, Bilbo had committed much of his political career to upholding white supremacy.[112] By 1936, he had already developed a reputation as one of the most virulent racist politicians in the country.

While other white separatists certainly maintained the same views, Bilbo stood out. He unabashedly expressed overt racist remarks in public, often using derogatory language to describe African Americans and other non-whites.[113] His politics certainly reflected his racist views. While he supported New Deal policies, he eschewed what he saw as FDR's attempt to advance "racial egalitarianism."[114] In the late 1930s, he became a major opponent of the federal anti-lynching bill, vowing to fight it until "hell freezes over."[115] Although the senator condemned lynching, he resisted federal intervention, viewing it as the ultimate threat to white superiority.[116]

On the surface, the collaboration between white supremacists and black nationalists may seem surprising. Whereas white supremacists promoted racial terror and violence, black nationalists openly condemned racial oppression. Moreover, black nationalists rejected the white supremacist belief that members of the white race were biologically superior to blacks. Black nationalists embraced the idea that people of African descent were morally superior to whites—on the basis of their history of suffering.[117] This, however, did not prevent some black nationalists from collaborating with white supremacists for a myriad of political reasons. During the nineteenth century, for example, a number of black nationalist figures, including Martin Delany and Bishop Henry McNeal Turner, procured assistance from the ACS.[118] Years later, in 1922, Garvey held a controversial meeting with Edward Young Clarke, acting imperial wizard of the Ku Klux Klan, in Atlanta.[119] In the years to follow, Garvey maintained close contact and collaborations with several white supremacists—including Senator Bilbo.

Accepting biological notions of race, which have since been repudiated, many black nationalists found common cause with white separatists on the matter of "racial purity." These men and women could not realize their goals "without the actual biological perpetuation of the race." Therefore, black nationalists attempted to closely monitor and control black sexuality.[120] One of Allen's surviving letters to Bilbo underscores this fact. "I am tired of looking [at] white ladies and [N]egro men locked arms walking up and down the street [and] white women pushing half [N]egro babies," the activist bitterly complained.[121] In all likelihood, these occurrences were far less common than Allen suggested. However, by expressing these views to Bilbo, Allen was certainly appealing to the senator's own hatred for race mixing.

Because black nationalists and white separatists both rejected race mixing and desired racial separatism, they often stood on the same side of the emigration issue. To be sure, black nationalists advocated for voluntary emigration as opposed to compulsory emigration. Nevertheless, some black nationalist leaders attempted to use collaborations with influential white separatists as a means of bolstering their political leverage and thus securing their ultimate goal of racial separatism.[122] The questionable collaborations with white supremacists incited much tension and disagreement in black nationalist circles and, not surprisingly, drew sharp criticism from other black activists.

In Celia Jane Allen's case, her collaboration with Senator Bilbo reflected her understanding of the consonance of their respective racial ideologies, shared interests in emigration, and the value of Bilbo's enormous power and influence in Mississippi and as a U.S. senator.[123] Bilbo was, as his biographer has argued, "the state's dominant political personality of the era of segregation."[124] His popularity in the state was second to none, and black nationalist organizers were not oblivious to this fact. During the late 1930s, as she began to organize black men and women in the Jim Crow South, Allen used her connection to Bilbo as a recruiting tool. Allen also appeared to be deeply moved by her correspondence with the senator. "It is very encouraging to have the privilege to write a United States Senator," she later admitted to Bilbo. Alluding to the significance of receiving letters from someone with an official title and position of authority, Allen added, "I am filled with enthusiasm when I read a letter from the U.S.A."[125]

By telling local residents in Mississippi that the PME had not only secured land in Liberia but also had the support of the most influential white politician in the state, Allen hoped to win the support of those who might have been skeptical or too fearful to join the movement. Somehow, the very notion that Bilbo supported the PME organizers' efforts seemed to place some black Mississippians at ease. This certainly was true for Reverend Green. In March 1938, months after joining the PME and helping Allen establish a local chapter, Green wrote to Senator Bilbo to express his enthusiasm for the emigration campaign. "I thank you for the good you are doing for this Black race [of] mine," Green wrote. After noting that Allen was residing in his home in Long, Mississippi, at the time of his writing, Green went on to ask Bilbo to corroborate the story that Allen had been circulating. "I understand from Mrs. Celia J. Allen [of] Chicago that you give her authority to organize the Black people in the State [of] Mississippi," Green wrote, "so I would love to read a letter [of] permit from you to be read to my people."[126]

Green's comments to Bilbo in 1938 are quite revealing. While he offered no clear indication as to why he seemed to maintain some skepticism about

Allen's claims, it is evident that he or others in the community maintained some misgivings at the time the letter was written. It is also evident that Allen shrewdly used the PME's affiliation with Senator Bilbo as a way to somehow authenticate her political activities in the face of local resistance. On one hand, Allen reasoned that some skeptical black residents might be more willing to get on board if they believed that the organization had the backing of a well-known U.S. senator. On the other hand, Allen hoped that the senator's sponsorship could secure black nationalists some protection from white violence. She reasoned that local whites might refrain from challenging her work if they viewed her as operating within the bounds of white supremacy—rather than in defiance to it.

She must have been disappointed, then, when Bilbo failed to provide the letter of support that she (and Reverend Green) requested.[127] Although Bilbo responded to both Allen and Green, he did not mention the letter. Not surprisingly, he used the opportunity to demean the activists, emphasizing what he saw as the benefits of slavery—giving black people access to "the Christian religion and the white man's civilization"—and reinforcing the need for black men and women to leave the United States. "In this wonderful country of Africa," Bilbo wrote in his response to Green, "the black man will have a country all his own where he can work out his own salvation without any hardships and discriminations that he has to undergo in this country."[128] In his response to Green and Allen, Bilbo thanked the PME activists for their efforts to advance black emigration and encouraged them to ask other senators to support the idea—all the while evading their questions and requests.

*   *   *

In 1941, Celia Jane Allen wrote a short report of her organizing activities in the South to be included in a PME pamphlet. In the most detailed surviving firsthand account of her activities during this period, Allen constructed a narrative that would circulate across the nation and ultimately end up in the hands of federal officials. After recounting her many speeches to black residents in Mississippi and across the South, the activist expressed a deep sense of satisfaction that she never gave up and, in the end, was "successful in getting many thousands to heed the call and sign their names."[129] In all, Allen worked tirelessly to organize rural blacks in the South for a period of six years.[130] While it is impossible to verify the actual numbers, Allen had a meaningful impact in the South. Of the estimated four hundred thousand signatures from black residents in support of the PME's emigration plans, a significant number came from black residents in Mississippi and neighboring states.[131] Far beyond the petitions, however, Allen contributed to keeping black nationalist ideas alive in the U.S. South during a period of economic and racial turmoil. With few options during a global economic crisis, black southerners found hope in Allen's teachings—hope that their lives would improve by joining forces with the PME.

Despite or perhaps because of her invisibility, Allen managed to sell her Pan-Africanist vision to countless black men and women—as evidenced by the number of individuals she successfully recruited as new PME members and the numerous new chapters she helped to establish in the region.[132] Her reliance on the organizing tradition—the slow and long-term grassroots political work that received little attention or fanfare—was especially crucial in this regard. Drawing on the social networks of black churchgoers and using the church as the primary physical space to disseminate her ideas, Allen advocated for racial pride, black political self-determination, and economic self-sufficiency across the U.S. South; built lasting relationships with countless men and women; and played a key role in developing local leaders. Even after she ceased political organizing in the region, she remained in frequent contact with local activists—in one instance, writing Thomas Bernard during World War II to inquire about the well-being of his family.[133]

Allen's commitment to relationship building and the development of local leaders helped to propel the PME's emigrationist movement to regional and national prominence. While Allen's activities did not dismantle white supremacy, they did leave an indelible mark on the lives of many black men and women in the U.S. South. So significant was Allen's influence that FBI officials tried, though unsuccessfully, to interview her during the 1940s. She managed to evade them, perhaps with the assistance of the same local residents who withheld information from authorities. Even after Allen went into obscurity around 1942, local activists continued to launch new PME chapters in Mississippi and nearby Alabama.[134] Through Allen's efforts, black men and women like Reverend George Green, Joella Johnson, and Thomas Bernard came to embrace black nationalism as a viable political strategy in response to racial discrimination and exclusion, Jim Crow segregation, and white mob violence. These individuals, in turn, helped to spread black nationalist ideas throughout the South during the 1930s and beyond.

CHAPTER 4

⤳

Dreaming of Liberia

WHILE ACTIVISTS IN the Peace Movement of Ethiopia (PME) were working to expand the organization's influence in the United States, they were also attempting to extend their global reach and strengthen their diasporic networks and collaborations. Central to the organization's mission was a commitment to black emigration to West Africa as a step toward improving social conditions for African Americans and uniting black men and women throughout the diaspora. From the late 1930s onward, PME activists across the country amplified their transnational activism and deepened their internationalist focus. In a 1938 letter to Mississippi Senator Theodore G. Bilbo—the outspoken white supremacist and ardent separatist who had found common cause with the PME—Florence Kenna, a PME member in Chicago, praised the senator for his efforts to advance black emigration to Liberia. "I have read an article in the newspaper," she wrote, "pertaining to your request to this government to raise money, to send all people of African [descent] back to their home in Africa; to inhabit our motherland." "I congratulate you," she continued, "and I do hope that your determination for this program will never cease [until] the millions [of] sons and daughters of Africa be sent back home to serve our God and our maker under our own vine and fig tree."[1] Kenna's letter of support was one of many that arrived on Senator Bilbo's desk from black nationalists across the country during the late 1930s.[2] These men and women lauded the senator's efforts to pass the Greater Liberia Bill, dubbed the "Back to Africa bill," which called for millions of dollars in federal aid to relocate African Americans to

Liberia and surrounding territories.[3] Arguing that racial separatism would improve the lives of both blacks and whites, Bilbo called on his colleagues in the Senate to back the bill. Civil rights leaders across the country vehemently opposed the bill, arguing that as citizens of the United States, black people had no business relocating elsewhere.

While many race leaders openly denounced the bill and its controversial author, black nationalist men and women found it to be a glimmer of hope. Amid the social and political upheavals of the period, Bilbo's controversial Greater Liberia Bill stirred long-held nationalist aspirations of establishing an autonomous black nation-state on the African continent. For black nationalists like Florence Kenna, the Greater Liberia Bill represented a viable step toward improving the social conditions of black men and women in a world deeply divided by the color line.[4] In Kenna's political vision, black emigration would serve a twofold purpose: to provide a means for black men and women to escape their second-class citizenship status in the United States and to increase their political power on a global scale. The Greater Liberia Bill, then, was a welcome proposition for black nationalists who maintained this point of view.

During this period, a cadre of black nationalist women leaders, including Mittie Maude Lena Gordon and Ethel Waddell, emerged as key proponents of the Greater Liberia Bill, publicly lobbying for its passage at the local and national levels. Similar to Marcus Garvey, these women leaders were willing to work in tandem with white supremacists on the basis of their mutual interest in racial separatism.[5] Unlike Garvey, however, black nationalist women during the 1930s relied heavily on the support of white supremacists and played a far more proactive role in fostering these relationships in hopes of attaining their political goals.

Though controversial and paradoxical, this decision to collaborate with white supremacists was neither irrational nor haphazard. To the contrary, through these collaborations with seemingly unlikely political allies, black nationalist women sought to influence the direction of national and global public policy. At the same time, their collaborations were acts of performance that were shaped by historical convention.[6] During a period of Jim Crow segregation and black disenfranchisement, these women activists were cognizant of their positions as outsiders in a white-dominated and patriarchal society. As such, they envisioned alliances with influential white male supremacists as a means to bolster their cause and secure federal legislation to improve conditions for blacks in the United States and across the African diaspora. An exploration of black nationalist women's political collaborations with individuals like Senator Bilbo reveals the pragmatic and strategic steps, negotiations, and compromises that activists were willing to make in order to advance black nationalist and internationalist politics during a global economic crisis.

Liberia in the Black Nationalist Imagination

During the 1930s, many black nationalist men and women maintained a utopian vision of Liberia as a haven for black men and women throughout the diaspora. Viewing the United States as irredeemably racist, these men and women championed black emigration to Liberia in their writings and speeches. "Our condition is growing worse each day," Mittie Maude Lena Gordon wrote in a 1934 letter to a political ally, "and our only hope is to go back to our own country, AFRICA." "We want to go to this part of Africa[:] LIBERIA," she quickly added.[7] On the pages of Madame Maymie De Mena's newspaper, the *Ethiopian World*, black nationalist men and women engaged in lively discourse on Liberia, grappling with its significance for the future of the black race and encouraging readers to rally in support of the nation. A gifted journalist and experienced political activist, De Mena had established the *Ethiopian World* in 1934 after a short stint in Father Divine's Peace Mission.[8] Appealing to black nationalists in the United States and other parts of the globe, De Mena pledged to provide "clean, constructive, fearless and progressive journalism that will help the race to find its true and noble place among the other great races of our common human family."[9] In order to help advance the race, De Mena envisioned emigration as a viable solution. She believed that relocation to Liberia would simultaneously help black Americans and improve conditions in Liberia.

In a 1934 speech to Universal Negro Improvement Association (UNIA) supporters in Harlem, De Mena also encouraged the resettlement of black Americans to Liberia in light of that nation's political turmoil.[10] In 1930, Liberian President Charles D. B. King and members of his administration became embroiled in an international scandal surrounding charges of slavery and political corruption. The conflict, which had reached a boiling point during the late 1920s, began many years earlier in 1914 when Liberian officials made an agreement to provide contract labor in Fernando Po, a small island in the Gulf of Guinea. By the start of World War I, the Spanish colony had a shrinking labor force with an increasing demand for labor on the island's cocoa plantations. Based on the terms of the agreement, laborers from Liberia were expected to work in Fernando Po for one to two years and receive compensation at the end of their term. From the beginning of the agreement in 1914 to 1927, thousands of Liberian laborers were sent to the colony. However, after a series of developments, including questionable recruitment practices and financial constraints, Liberian officials proposed to end the flow of workers to the Spanish colony in late 1927.[11]

In the subsequent months, Liberian officials faced increasing international scrutiny over their labor practices, resulting in an investigation by the League of Nations. Critics accused the Liberian government of condoning modern-day slavery as others questioned the ability of the nation's leadership to rule effectively. Though members of the international community focused primarily on Liberia's involvement in the scandals, deplorable conditions on the Spanish colony also played a key role.[12] The charges of slavery and political corruption that were leveled against Liberia negatively impacted many black Americans' view of the nation. In the aftermath of the scandals, many black Americans lost faith in Liberia as a potential haven for black people.[13]

However, for black nationalists, the problems in Liberia only bolstered their interest in the nation by confirming the need for black emigration. In a poem entitled, "Liberia," written after the Liberian scandals, PME member Albert McCall emphasized the need to establish an independent black nation in Liberia to alleviate some of the nation's social problems: "Liberia, Liberia, here we come / Sound the bugles and sound the drums / We are coming to build up a government . . . / We will build up a government like they have here; / Because [there is] nothing but trouble makers on every hand."[14] Deploying civilizationist rhetoric, McCall appealed to black men and women in the United States, noting, "You are the men and women that Liberia needs / And we'll make an army of men like you / I am sure all of you have agreed, / To go back to Liberia to live / Where you won't have to be lynched and killed."[15] McCall's comments simultaneously capture his Pan-Africanist vision and his assumption that Americanization would fundamentally improve conditions for Liberians. Writing in the *Ethiopian World*, De Mena expressed similar sentiments: "In spite of whatever assurance the League [of Nations] may give in their final decision on Liberia, the inspiration of National service and self sacrifice must continue to be numbered by our people everywhere. The call is to ask the youth all over the world to make it a duty . . . to utilize the opportunity which now presents itself for greater and more useful service to your race."[16]

Other black nationalist leaders appealed to black youth across the African diaspora to take up the cause of aiding Liberia in its time of need. Charles Mitchell, who served as U.S. ambassador to Liberia, challenged younger UNIA members at a meeting in Harlem to take advantage of emigration opportunities: "Liberia . . . is the land of opportunity [especially] for young people with adequate financial backing."[17] Similarly, members of the Harlem-based African Reconstruction Association (ARA)—a relatively small nationalist organization established during the early 1930s to "promote and encourage immigration and colonization into undeveloped areas . . . of Negro nations"—called on young black Americans to support nation-building efforts in Liberia.[18] The organization's leaders, Harlemites Bernard Mason and W. A. Ramsey, emphasized the economic opportunities for black men and women in Liberia and requested help to "colonize 50,000 or more Negroes there."[19] Laced with paternalist undertones, Mason's and Ramsey's statements further demonstrate nationalists' view of Liberia as a country in complete disarray and desperately in need of black Americans to come to its aid.

Significantly, Mason, Ramsey, and other ARA leaders continued to envision emigration to Liberia as the primary means of uplifting the black race generally. These activists emphasized emigration to West Africa as the most viable means of racial progress on a global scale.[20] Members of the ARA, for example, laid out their case for emigration in the pages of the *Ethiopian World*, pointing out the need for a physical home for peoples of African descent: "The program of finding a home by immigrating and assisting in developing the Republic of Liberia is [our] only aspiration." "Losing possession of the land and control of natural resources," they continued, "we have become a poverty-stricken, unprotected people, merely engaged in a struggle with empty hands against tremendous odds for recognition."[21] Establishing a black nation-state in Liberia, they reasoned, was the ultimate solution.

In a weekly meeting of the ARA, black nationalists in Harlem gathered to listen to Liberian doctor S. S. Sesvir, who argued that African Americans could earn a substantial living by engaging in agricultural work in Liberia.[22] Writing in a 1934 newspaper article, Lloyd Graves, a member of the ARA, insisted, "Liberia is the land of opportunity. . . . Some day we will be glad to go there, knowing there will be no more jim-crowism, no more segregation, no more lynching and brutality cast upon our people, knowing that we will be respected by men as men."[23] Garveyites Peter M. Easley, Leroy

Edwards, and S. Campbell expressed similar sentiments in a pro-emigration petition, which emphasized the prospect of relocating to a country that seemed to offer financial stability for black Americans during the Depression.[24] With limited job opportunities and minimal federal relief, Cora Lee Frazier, a member of the PME, lamented, "I have 5 children [and] I don't see any future for them here . . . I have always wanted to be free. If we stay here we will all go to [nothing]."[25] Another black resident from Washington, D.C. added, "We are tired [of] beg[g]ing for jobs and home relief . . . we want to go to Africa."[26]

What is especially striking is that black nationalists imagined Liberia as a place of wealth—not the country steeped in millions of dollars in debt as it were. Perhaps this point of view resulted from a lack of knowledge regarding Liberia's economic conditions, wishful thinking, or a little of both. Still, the vision of Liberia as a place of wealth offered some hope for black nationalists during an economic crisis in the United States. Expressing this highly romanticized view of Liberia, black nationalist Albert McCall declared in one poem, "There is fruit in Africa worth while eating / We don't have to stay here and take a white man's beating." He went on to emphasize Liberia's alleged thriving job market, insisting that "Liberia has many towns, where work can easily be found."[27] W. E. Johnson, a graduate of Howard University's Dental School, lent his support to black emigration, arguing that "Africa offers great opportunities for us." Reflecting the civilizationist rhetoric in black nationalist discourse, Johnson added, "We could bring about trade relations with America etc. . . . . If we remain here we must apply for relief, charity [but] if we go to Africa we can solve our problem."[28]

McCall's and Johnson's descriptions were exaggerated, and conditions in Liberia were far different from what they imagined.[29] In reality, the Great Depression of the 1930s had devastating economic consequences for Liberia, as it did for other nations across the Black diaspora. During the Depression, Liberia's financial debt grew rapidly as international demand for Liberian rubber and other exports declined.[30] However, by envisioning Liberia as a haven with unlimited possibilities, black nationalists found an escape, if only imagined, from both the reality of life for black men and women in the United States and the real socioeconomic challenges in Liberia. This utopian vision, along with a desire to improve the lives of African descended people, strengthened black nationalists' resolve to advance black emigration during the social upheavals of the 1930s.

Allies on the Outside and Rivals Within

The rise of Jim Crow in the United States coincided with the rise of a racial caste system that swept across the globe. The United States was very much a part of constructing this racial caste system as much as it was a product of it. The U.S. occupation of Haiti from 1915 to 1934 exemplified the process by which the United States exercised territorial, economic, and political control over people of color.[31] The American policies in Haiti were certainly not unique. To the contrary, these policies exemplified a larger pattern of U.S. foreign relations during the twentieth century and, indeed, much earlier.[32] They also reflected a larger system of global white supremacy that was not particular to the United States.

The global color line, which W. E. B. Du Bois first described in a 1900 speech at the Pan-African conference in London, appeared to be fixed in place despite the persistent struggles and protest movements that emerged in the United States and abroad.[33] At its core, the global color line—which described both European colonialism in Africa and Asia and U.S. expansionism in Haiti, the Dominican Republic, and other countries—was deeply rooted in the eugenicist thinking of the day.[34] These beliefs influenced many Europeans and Americans of the twentieth century to conceptualize race as both biological and overly deterministic and provided these individuals with a justification for discrimination, racism, and global imperialism.[35] Many black men and women also accepted this form of racial thinking, albeit in different ways. Black elites such as Du Bois eschewed racial determinism, while black nationalist leaders like Garvey maintained essentialist views, glorified blackness, and emphasized the importance of racial separatism, racial purity, and self-determination.[36] In the same vein, Mittie Maude Lena Gordon, Maymie De Mena, and other black nationalist women during the Depression era embraced a biological conception of race and advocated for racial separatism and black political autonomy.[37]

During the mid-1930s, Gordon initiated a massive letter-writing campaign aimed at attracting support from powerful whites who also embraced biological conceptions of race and championed racial separatism. In 1934, one of her letters arrived on the desk of Earnest Sevier Cox, a white supremacist from Richmond, Virginia. An author and explorer who had traveled extensively throughout the African continent, Cox was an avid proponent of black emigration, maintaining the belief that it was necessary for "racial purity."[38] His first book, *White America*, published in 1923, championed white supremacy, calling on white Americans to "preserve ethnic purity, for upon his shoulders was the burden of civilization and progress." In 1924, Cox's popularity began to expand as his book drew the attention of white supremacists and, unbeknown to him at the time, black nationalists in Richmond and across the country.[39] In September of that year, after hearing Garvey speak at a local event, Cox became a UNIA supporter, embracing Garvey's pro-emigration message. In the ensuing months leading up to Garvey's 1927 deportation, Cox maintained consistent correspondence with Garvey and worked closely with numerous Garveyite leaders across the country.

When she launched her letter-writing campaign in 1934, Gordon strategically targeted Cox. In four detailed pages, Gordon laid out for Cox her case for emigration to West Africa. First, she described her efforts to obtain 400,000 signatures for an emigration petition, which she mailed to FDR in 1933. She went on to assure Cox that although the U.S. federal government had denied her request for financial support, she had obtained "assurance that the governments of [Liberia and Ethiopia] would welcome mass immigration of American Negroes." Convinced that she might be able to persuade the U.S. government to release New Deal funds for black emigration, Gordon appealed to Cox to lend his support to her organization and her cause: "We ask you, therefore, to take up our appeal."[40] Impressed by Gordon's "dignified and moving petition to the President of the United States," Cox eagerly accepted the invitation.[41]

Interestingly, once Cox expressed a willingness to support Gordon's plans, the tone of Gordon's letters shifted drastically. Moving from a rather neutral tone in her initial letter, Gordon's subsequent letters took on a more submissive tone, which underscores her attempts to coax her new white ally. Now addressing her new ally as "my dear Mr. Cox," Gordon skillfully asserted, "Let me give expression to my heartfelt gratitude for your continued interest in the welfare of our people. Please be assured that your benevolent attitude will spur us on to greater effort and greater hope in its ultimate success."[42] In a subsequent letter, Gordon continued to praise Cox, noting, "Words are inadequate to express our appreciation . . . accept my personal thanks together with the great appreciation from all our good and humble members, for the kind interest you are showing on our behalf."[43] Gordon's statements to Cox, as well as the tone in which they were expressed, capture the activist's concerted efforts to secure a new political ally through a series of performances.[44] Gordon's change in tone and

FIGURE 10. Earnest Sevier Cox. Earnest Sevier Cox Papers, Box 39, 1821–1973, Rare Book, Manuscript, and Special Collections Library, Duke University, Durham, N.C.

description of her supporters as "good" and "humble" reveal, among other things, a conscious attempt to perform an act of submission and deference to white male control.

Gordon's strategy worked. In return, Cox appeared especially eager to offer advice and direction, clearly moved by Gordon's apparent admiration. "No one could receive a higher compliment than you have paid me," Cox noted. Responding to Gordon's initial letter, Cox went on to outline a list of steps for Gordon to take to secure federal support for emigration plans. In addition to contacting the American Colonization Society (ACS), Cox advised Gordon to make arrangements to see FDR, seek endorsement from the Liberian government, and work toward an emigration petition through the Virginia General Assembly.[45] However, Gordon was two steps ahead of Cox—she had already attempted to obtain support from FDR and had initiated a letter-writing campaign directed toward Liberian officials months prior. In her response to Cox in September 1934, Gordon offered him thanks for his suggestions but carefully explained her own attempts to secure Liberian support through a series of letters sent to politicians in Cape Palmas. After acknowledging her failed efforts to obtain support from Edwin Barclay—who assumed the Liberian presidency in 1930—Gordon made one request to Cox: "It would be a great move if you succeed in getting President Barclay of Liberia to send his approval of our petition to the President of the United States."[46]

Cox failed to secure President Barclay's direct support for emigration plans; however, he was able to use his connections to advance Gordon's plans in other ways. By Cox's own statement, he turned to "capable white people who are in sympathy with our cause" to assist Gordon and her supporters. By 1936, Cox was able to persuade members of the Virginia General Assembly to pass a resolution recommending that the U.S. Congress provide federal assistance for black emigration.[47] This signified an important development in Gordon's pro-emigration campaign. While the Virginia resolution was a far cry from the federal legislation Gordon and her supporters desired, it represented a step closer to their goal. Writing to Cox days later, Gordon expressed her gratitude on behalf of the PME but skillfully downplayed her own involvement in the matter: "We were profoundly awed, utterly surprised and received with great enthusiasm your special message of good news to-day. . . . Words are far from inadequate to even attempt to tell you of the esteem and respect this organization holds for you and your mastery in winning this colossal victory."[48]

Although Cox's support helped to propel Gordon's political career—by increasing media coverage of her activities and thus extending the reach of her message—it also drew some unwelcome attention and public criticism. Mainstream white news outlets mocked Gordon and the PME, while others simply ignored their existence. Writers of one article for *Time* magazine chose to emphasize Gordon's outward appearance rather than her political message, describing her as a "portly mulatto." Others portrayed her as a fanatic who maintained an obsession for Garvey and described her organization disparagingly as a "repatriationist cult."[49]

Though Gordon seemed to weather the storm of criticism, her greatest challenge came from some of the people she trusted most. In February 1937, she became embroiled in a bitter public dispute with her secretary, Ethel Waddell.[50] Born Ethel Hunter in Arkansas sometime around 1906, Waddell relocated to Chicago during the early years of the Great Migration.[51] During the early 1930s, she ran a hair salon from her apartment in Chicago. In 1936, the thirty-year-old beauty shop owner approached Gordon and expressed an interest in joining the organization and serving as one of her private secretaries.[52] Waddell's decision to join the PME marked a shift in her engagement in black nationalist politics. During the mid-1930s, Waddell became a highly visible black nationalist activist, working alongside Gordon and her supporters in Chicago. In addition to accompanying Gordon to several meetings with Liberian officials in the city, Waddell helped Gordon organize a local fundraising drive in 1936, which yielded an estimated $85.00 to support the PME's delegation to Liberia.[53]

In the immediate aftermath of this fundraiser, tensions between Gordon and Waddell reached a boiling point. In a sensationalist account, Gordon claimed that it began when Waddell "went to the homes of [PME] members, telling them I had sent her to get their signatures for a closed door meeting." On December 9, 1936, Gordon noted that Waddell, along with fellow PME member Charles Watkins, "enter[ed] our meeting like gangsters, demanded the delegate money from us under threats." "Had we resented one word," Gordon continued, "we would have been killed like dogs that night."[54] In the months that followed her alleged "gangster" encounter with Gordon, Waddell initiated a number of lawsuits, accusing Gordon of "operating a racket" and misappropriating funds that should have been reserved for emigration plans.[55] In March 1937, Waddell, along with Watkins and three other black nationalists—Cora Berry, Arthur King, and Antonio L. Paez—established a rival organization, the Peace Movement of Ethiopia, Inc. (PME, Inc.), maintaining the same objective as Gordon's PME: "repatriation of the American Negro who desire to go to Africa to work out his own destiny and become self-sufficient."[56]

With the incorporation in place, Waddell and supporters then sued Gordon in an effort to prevent her from using the name, Peace Movement of Ethiopia. When their efforts failed, they attempted to secure support under the disguise of the original PME. In one instance, Waddell and Watkins contacted FDR's secretary asking for federal aid for emigration, claiming to be affiliated with Gordon's organization.[57] In the end, Waddell's lawsuits were all dismissed, and Gordon retained the right to use the name of the organization she had established in 1932. She also managed to hold on to the funds she raised in support of the PME's delegation to Liberia.[58]

Importantly, Waddell's actions shed light on both the political and personal differences among black nationalist women activists during this period. The skirmishes surrounding the PME's fundraising money and the questions surrounding Gordon's right to use the organization's name derived from Waddell's growing dissatisfaction with Gordon's leadership and ideological differences. Later recounting the course of events, Waddell admitted that she "didn't see any need" for sending a delegation to Liberia in the first place. She reasoned that since American citizens—leaders of the

ACS—were responsible for establishing Liberia as a colony for free blacks, the U.S. government should be fully responsible for making arrangements and bearing the financial costs for black Americans desiring to relocate to the country.[59] As a result, she resisted the idea that ordinary black men and women, already struggling to make ends meet, should use their limited funds to help cover relocation expenses. Her frustration over funds and subsequent lawsuit, then, highlighted an underlying disagreement between the two women about how best to facilitate black emigration during an economic crisis.

Moreover, Waddell's decision to establish her own organization was an assertive move—if only to send the message that she would not allow Gordon to dominate the political scene. Not surprisingly, then, she skillfully used the PME, Inc. as a way to bolster her political leverage and visibility in black nationalist circles. While the exact membership figures are unknown, Waddell used her newly established rival organization as a platform for recruiting black nationalists in Chicago. Unlike Gordon, who in the PME's constitution claimed to "freely coincide" with Marcus Garvey, Waddell emphasized her loyalty to Garvey and openly touted the training she received from the charismatic black nationalist leader. Describing the PME, Inc. as an "affiliate of the [UNIA]," Waddell boasted that some of the officers had graduated from the School of African Philosophy.[60] Introduced by Garvey at the 1937 Regional Conference in Toronto, Canada, the school was an intensive month-long course of instruction in Toronto, which Garvey later made available through mail order and provided students with an introduction to a wide range of subjects, including the history of the UNIA and financial success.[61] Waddell was one of ten UNIA leaders, and only four women, who successfully completed the first iteration of the course in 1937.[62]

Under the auspices of the PME, Inc., Waddell pursued alliances with influential white supremacists, maintaining a biological view of race and envisioning these alliances as a viable strategy for securing federal legislation for black emigration.[63] She believed that individuals like Earnest Sevier Cox had greater political capital, including access to state resources, legal support, and financial resources, and the material means to spread these ideas to an even larger audience. Months after establishing the new organization, Waddell reached out to Cox, offering an explanation for why she parted ways with Gordon. "Due to the mishandling of funds, inefficiency of the former officers to carry out intelligently the scheme of the organization, and their attempt to disrupt the [UNIA] and disregard for the Honorable Marcus Garvey," she carefully explained, "we found it necessary . . . to incorporate [the Peace Movement of Ethiopia]." The PME, Inc., Waddell added, had "capable leaders to carry out intelligently the work for the ultimate success of the 'Back to Africa' project."[64] Implying that Gordon was neither "capable" nor "intelligent," Waddell attempted to discount Gordon's activities yet capitalize on some of the networks she had established much earlier. While Waddell's letters threatened to sever Gordon's alliance with Cox and ultimately derail her plans, Gordon managed to maintain her relationship by preemptively warning Cox.[65] In the ensuing years, the two women worked separately with Waddell's PME, Inc., often collaborating with the UNIA on community events.[66]

Theodore G. Bilbo and the Greater Liberia Bill

Determined to make strides with the emigration campaign despite mounting tensions with Waddell and others, Gordon again reached out to Cox in June 1937 to insist that he amplify his efforts to secure federal aid for black emigration. Although Cox's support had resulted in the 1936 congressional resolution, Gordon and her supporters were becoming increasingly frustrated as emigration plans appeared stalled. The Great Depression was in full swing, and despite the implementation of New Deal programs, black Americans remained at the bottom rung of the economic sector, largely excluded from the benefits of these programs.[67] For Gordon, the prospect of remaining in the United States—in a constant state of poverty and what appeared to be a never-ending struggle for civil and economic rights—was no prospect at all. Writing to Cox in June 1936, Gordon noted, "Many times I have gone without food yet traveled on to carry out the work. And I have never received one penny of salary. . . . It will be hard for you to understand the groans coming up from a suffering people, the groans which I face daily."[68] Her strategic alliance with Cox, though a source of contention among many of her counterparts, had certainly yielded some positive result, particularly by drawing national attention to her efforts. In reality, however, Gordon and her supporters were no closer to leaving the country than when they launched the pro-emigration campaign years earlier.

   Though Gordon had turned to Cox three years earlier in a strategic effort to realize her goals, she understood that she could not rely on this one ally. After receiving no favorable response from her letters to FDR, Eleanor Roosevelt, and every member of the Illinois legislature, Gordon reasoned that she needed the backing of an influential white politician who would have the ears of other white politicians and constituents.[69] After carefully expressing thanks to Cox for his unwavering support of her efforts, Gordon made her intentions clear in a 1937 letter, requesting the name of a white politician willing to take a financial bribe to push for legislation. "Can you cite a purchaseable member of either House who is on the market, and try to learn his price?" she asked Cox in no uncertain terms.[70] As she waited for a response, the answer came in the person of Senator Bilbo, apparently without the need for any financial incentive.

An ardent separatist, Bilbo had already begun advocating for black emigration months before introducing the Greater Liberia Bill. In 1938, during a filibuster against the NAACP's proposed federal anti-lynching bill on January 21, the senator recommended racial separation as the only solution. "It is essential to the perpetuation of our Anglo-Saxon civilization that white supremacy in America be maintained," he argued, "and to maintain our civilization there is only one solution, and that is either segregation within the United States, or by deportation or repatriation of the entire Negro race to its native heath, Africa." While he offered no further explanation for how such a plan might be accomplished, Bilbo immediately identified Liberia as the ideal location and referenced the PME's 1933 petition to FDR as evidence that African Americans were ready and willing to leave the country. Arguing that the U.S. government could relocate African Americans just as they did Native Americans, Bilbo rationalized that black emigration to West Africa was not only logical but also feasible.[71]

His controversial comments drew the attention of Cox, who at the time was on the lookout for new political collaborators to assist Gordon and her supporters in the PME. On the same day of Bilbo's filibuster against the NAACP's anti-lynching bill, Cox wrote to the senator, offering a gesture of support and providing Bilbo with information on his speeches and writings on the emigration issue. Clearly enthused by the gesture, Bilbo immediately responded and requested a copy of Cox's pro-emigration article, "The Effort to Colonize Them Will Be Continued."[72] In the weeks to follow, Bilbo requested additional information from Cox, asking for advice on how to advance the emigration of black Americans. "I am anxious to get your plan," Bilbo wrote to Cox, "[in order to] eliminate the NAACP from future efforts related to the anti-lynching bill."[73] Notwithstanding his commitment

FIGURE 11. Senator Theodore Bilbo. Harris & Ewing Collection,
LC-H22-D-10044-X, Library of Congress.

to racial separatism, Bilbo's comments underscore his own efforts to advance an emigration bill for this own political interests—as a way to undermine anti-lynching legislation. Regardless, Cox was anxious to give advice and immediately began laying out plans to advance black emigration through the widespread support of Gordon, Waddell, and other like-minded black nationalist activists.

Meanwhile, Bilbo continued to bring up the issue of black emigration in Senate proceedings, making several proposals and reiterating his earlier stance that racial separatism was the ultimate solution to the nation's racial problems. On May 24, 1938, Bilbo presented an amendment to the work relief bill, calling for the federal government to cover the "transportation and colonization expenses for the almost two million Negroes who have joined in a request to be repatriated to Liberia, Africa." According to Bilbo, "It would be better for [African Americans] and for their own country to use the money that will be spent in their maintenance here . . . in paying their transportation and colonization . . . in Africa."[74] Thus, he proposed that the federal government provide monetary aid for all black Americans, under age forty, willing to leave the country. When it became quite apparent that Liberia could not possibly accommodate the proposed two million blacks willing to relocate, Bilbo then amended his proposal, suggesting that England and France should relinquish control of their West African colonies to provide more physical space for potential black emigrants, in exchange for American forgiveness of their war debts.[75] In true Bilbo fashion, the presentation included a number of overtly racist statements, including Bilbo's crass suggestion that "God created the whites [but] I know not who created the blacks. Surely a devil created the mongrels."[76]

Convinced that Senator Bilbo was a means to an end, black nationalist activists publicly appeared unfazed by the senator's remarks. In a letter to Cox shortly thereafter, Gordon expressed her gratitude for Bilbo's support. "We are inclined to believe we have found a Moses to lead us [through] the Senate," she argued, "and [believe] that our work will become an accomplished fact."[77] "For my part," she wrote to Cox in a subsequent letter, "nothing Senator Bilbo says, or can say, offends me, it does not matter what he says so long as he puts this bill through successfully."[78] Notwithstanding the irony of a black nationalist leader referring to a white supremacist as "Moses," Gordon's comments underscore the activist's dogged determination to realize her political goals irrespective of the questionable nature of her political alliances. Certainly, the activist maintained full knowledge of Bilbo's beliefs about black people—ideas that clearly reinforced the very same ideals she vigorously rejected. However, Gordon's comments also offer a glimpse into the performative nature of her politics. Given the intended recipient of the letter—another white supremacist—it is not surprising that Gordon spoke positively of Bilbo, overemphasizing her gratitude for the senator's help.

Moreover, the activist consciously and strategically described Bilbo as a "Moses" of black people to signify the representative role Bilbo would play in facilitating the Greater Liberia Bill. It is especially striking that Gordon selected Moses—the biblical hero who would lead his people to freedom. In African American folklore, Moses represented "ideal black leadership," and the Hebrews symbolized the experiences of black men and women under slavery.[79] Certainly, Bilbo was no black hero, and his intentions for supporting black emigration had much more to do with his desire to maintain white supremacy than a genuine interest in improving conditions for blacks in the diaspora. However, by evoking the biblical character, Gordon was emphasizing the magnitude of the senator's bill and its ability to significantly alter the lives of people of African descent—using a familiar analogy that her followers and Cox immediately understood. In this way, Gordon's words and acts of performance embodied the traditional stories of the communities in which she came of age.[80] Moreover, by referring to Bilbo as a "Moses," Gordon attempted to situate him within a larger historical trajectory of white political leaders who, in her view, took initiatives that aided black nationalists' political goals. She drew a parallel between Bilbo and U.S. Presidents Thomas Jefferson, James Madison, and Abraham Lincoln; U.S. Senator Henry Clay; and U.S. Congressman Charles Fenton Mercer—all individuals who had supported the idea of relocating black Americans to Africa or the Caribbean. As she explained to Cox, "We see and recognize the spirit of Jefferson, Madison, Clay, Lincoln, and Mercer [in Bilbo]."[81]

In early 1939, Bilbo began drafting the Greater Liberia Bill, drawing on his earlier proposals before the Senate. With the assistance of Puerto Rican attorney Ramon A. Martinez, president of the Detroit-based Negro Nationalist Society of America, Bilbo completed the bill that spring and began circulating copies to Cox, Gordon, and other political collaborators. Similar to the earlier proposals, the Greater Liberia Bill called for the relocation of African Americans to West Africa. In addition to Liberia, the bill stipulated that U.S. officials would obtain additional land throughout West Africa. Reiterating his earlier proposal, Bilbo explained, "We shall buy 400,000 square miles from France and England, the purchase price of which will be credited upon their war debts." He added, "The bill further provides that building materials and supplies necessary for the proper resettlement of the emigrants may be furnished not only by France and England but by any country in Europe which owes us a war debt, and credit will be given for the supplies furnished."[82] Moreover, the bill provided fifty-acre land grants and financial assistance for black Americans between the ages of twenty-one and fifty to relocate to West Africa. It granted each emigrant up to $300 for clothing and household items; $300 for "machinery, tools, implements, and materials of labor"; up to $1 per day for food (50 cents per day for children under age 12); and up to $50 a year for "educational and recreational facilities." It further stipulated that such financial assistance "shall not extend, under ordinary circumstances, for more than 1 year after the migrant and his household shall have settled in their new location, or, under extraordinary circumstances, for more than 2 years."[83] Though Bilbo envisioned the U.S. government providing fifteen to twenty billion dollars over a period of forty years, the Greater Liberia Bill set an initial cap of one billion dollars in federal aid to facilitate black emigration.[84]

The release of the first draft of the Greater Liberia Bill ignited excitement among black nationalist women leaders, who saw it as a tangible step forward in the struggle for black liberation. As Gordon later explained, "[The bill] will determine whether emancipation is to remain half completed or if the freedmen are to be returned to their homeland. . . . It will determine whether the Negro is permitted to work out his own culture."[85] Yet, the bill included a number of unexpected stipulations that Gordon and her supporters rejected, thereby underscoring the ideological tensions between Bilbo and his black nationalist collaborators. The Greater Liberia Bill included a clause that granted the U.S. government military control over the West African territories for a period of two years after emigrants arrived to "preserve public peace and order during the transition." According to the bill, "the President shall immediately provide for and proceed to the military occupation and policing of such territories, which territories shall become one jurisdiction to be known and designated as the United States Territory of Greater Liberia, under a military governor and government, pending the establishment of civil government by Congress."[86] Ironically, though not surprisingly given Senator Bilbo's involvement, the bill that black nationalists envisioned as a step toward securing full economic and political autonomy for black people included a clause that would grant the United States the right to occupy Liberia and other nearby countries. In addition, the Greater Liberia Bill included a proposition that would displace indigenous Liberians. It granted the U.S. president the right to appoint a commissioner "who shall be the custodian of all forests, flora, and fauna" of the proposed United States Territory of Greater Liberia.[87]

Clearly compromising what Gordon and other PME leaders had in mind, these stipulations immediately became a source of contention. In a letter to Bilbo dated March 7, 1939, Gordon, writing on behalf of the PME's executive council, asked the senator to revise the bill, which they believed had deviated far from the original plan. She reminded Bilbo that the purpose of the bill was to ensure that black people would be free from "white boss rule" and thus have the ability to "live in our new country completely independent of such."[88] To that end, she questioned the need for white military officials yet suggested that black men were more than capable to serve in this capacity as needed. She also expressed discomfort in the idea that African American emigration could result in the displacement of indigenous Liberians. "To set the natives aside in a separate corner of the country as the Indians were done in America will create hatred between us and them," she argued. She went on to reflect on the kind treatment the PME delegation received during their earlier visit to Liberia and expressed concern that the Greater Liberia Bill, as drafted, would sever relations between African Americans and Liberians in general. "It is the great hope of the [nationalists] to live together among the natives as one big family," she concluded.[89]

Not surprisingly, her critiques fell on deaf ears. Senator Bilbo refused to oblige, arguing that regardless of the particulars, black nationalists would ultimately accomplish their goals.[90] Gordon eventually acquiesced, recognizing that little could be done to change the specifics of the bill and reasoning that after two years of military rule, nationalists would have full autonomy in West Africa. There is no doubt that Gordon's acceptance of these terms signaled the activist's decision to compromise for the sake of progress, but they also capture the complicated nature of her politics. Though she felt uneasy about white military control or policies that would displace indigenous Liberians, she did not consider the full implications of how an influx of African Americans into Liberia might impact Liberians in general. While deeply committed to anticolonial politics, Gordon, like many other black nationalists and internationalists during this period, was often complicit in promoting imperialist and civilizationist ventures. The complexities surrounding the Greater Liberia Bill underscores how black nationalism and anti-imperialism often stood side-by-side with imperialistic and hegemonic aspirations.[91]

As news of the Greater Liberia Bill spread across the nation, black nationalists from various organizations lent their support for the bill. From their base in Jacksonville, Florida, a group of followers of Laura Adorker Kofey, the former UNIA organizer who had been assassinated in 1928, extended their well wishes in a letter to Senator Bilbo. "Prayerful wishes for your continued interest and courageous efforts in this cause so thoroughly misrepresented by an element of our visionless misleaders," they wrote.[92] Similarly, G. E. Harris, president of the Garvey Club—a New York–based division of the UNIA that remained loyal to Garvey after the contentious

1929 convention in Jamaica—extended his group's support for the Greater Liberia Bill. "Ten thousand Negroes of the Universal Negro Improvement Association," he explained, "assembled in mass meeting, endorse your proposed repatriation bill."[93] While black nationalists certainly supported Bilbo's proposal, some tried to distance themselves from the Mississippi senator. During the summer of 1938, Ethel Waddell, Ethel Collins, and other black nationalist leaders convened at a UNIA convention in Toronto, Canada, where Marcus Garvey insisted that the bill for black emigration should be considered separately from Bilbo the person. "Regardless of how good or how bad a man may be himself," Garvey argued, "whenever he brings something that appeals to a race or group it is up to that particular group to grasp that particular thing and carry it for their own good."[94] Therefore, he and others resolved that the Greater Liberia Bill was far too important to abandon on account of the senator and his many offensive public remarks. Instead, they were convinced that with careful and strategic political organizing, Bilbo's proposal had the potential to improve the socioeconomic conditions of blacks in the United States and across the globe.

As Bilbo prepared to introduce the Greater Liberia Bill before Congress, black nationalist women did most of the legwork, engaging in a nationwide grassroots campaign to promote the bill.[95] In Chicago, Gordon revived a pro-emigration petition in order to secure more signatures of support.[96] Garveyites Peter M. Easley, S. Campbell, and Leroy Edwards followed suit, circulating a pro-emigration petition in favor of the bill.[97] Ethel Waddell and others in the PME, Inc. offered their full support to Bilbo, promising to do "what ever we can do to push the amendment to the Relief bill or whatever steps you think advisable."[98] During a short visit to Clarksville, Tennessee, which coincided with her organizing efforts in Mississippi, PME organizer Celia Jane Allen actively promoted Bilbo's emigration bill. Speaking before a crowd of churchgoers and local community leaders at a local African Methodist Episcopal Zion church, Allen championed the "colonization of American [N]egroes in Liberia."[99] Writing to Bilbo in June 1938—weeks after Gordon had made contact with the senator—Allen insisted, "I want to do all that I can do in the fight" for black emigration.[100]

Allen's correspondence with the senator during this period further exemplifies how women activists often engaged in performative acts aimed at coaxing their white political allies as a strategic effort to attain their goals. Allen, who grew up in the Jim Crow South, fully understood this performative culture.[101] Though Allen was in the process of facilitating a nationalist movement in the Southern region during the late 1930s, the PME organizer skillfully downplayed her political agency and influence in letters to Senator Bilbo. Feigning uncritical admiration, Allen described the senator as the "greatest and strongest friend that the [N]egro has ever had." Seemingly embracing a patriarchal vision of the masculine protector and a paternalistic racial view, Allen added, "I am depending on you to save me."[102] Gordon followed suit, describing Bilbo and Cox as "the greatest friends the Race has, at this time" in a letter addressed to Bilbo. "The membership [of the PME] holds you in the highest place of any white man in this country," Gordon added.[103]

Yet, writing to William Fergerson, a PME leader residing in Florida, Gordon made her intentions quite clear. In a 1939 letter to Gordon, Fergerson had expressed deep frustration over Bilbo's overtly racist comments and questioned the rationale behind an alliance with the senator. After first reminding Fergerson "to be careful" with what he expressed in writing since "letters often go astray," Gordon reminded Fergerson that Bilbo and other white supremacist collaborators were solely a means to an end and nothing more. "When we have to depend on the crocodile to cross the stream," she carefully explained, "we must pat him on the back until we get to the other side."[104] Her comments to Fergerson illuminate the strategic, yet questionable, means by which Gordon maintained her alliances with influential white supremacists like Bilbo. She recognized the need to perform the characteristics of the "Old Negro"—the accommodating and submissive cultural performance—if she hoped to attain her goals. "We have served our purpose as slaves here," she later argued, "[and] the longing for our ancestral country and people have always been prevalent in our minds."[105]

On the afternoon of April 24, 1939, Gordon and her supporters in Chicago set out for the nation's capital in order to witness Senator Bilbo's formal presentation of the Greater Liberia Bill. With limited financial resources, the activist had somehow managed to arrange travel for an estimated five hundred PME supporters to come along.[106] Gordon's initial plans of arranging transportation by bus or train had fallen through due to lack of funds. As an alternative, she coordinated rides for as many supporters as she could accommodate in twenty-one tightly packed trucks and cars—some of which broke down during the ten- to twelve-hour commute.[107]

FIGURE 12. Members of the Peace Movement of Ethiopia emerging from the Capitol building on April 24, 1939. Schomburg Center for Research in Black Culture, Photographs and Prints Division, The New York Public Library.

Despite these challenges, PME members arrived at the Capitol building just in time for Bilbo's presentation. "Mr. President, with the patience and kind indulgence of my colleagues," Bilbo began, "I trust I may be permitted at this time to discuss for a little while what is, in my judgment, the greatest, most important, and far-reaching problem that has ever or will ever confront the American people for solution." "It is important in the highest degree," he insisted, "because it involves the welfare and perpetuity of two races, the white race and the black race, which are now trying to live side by side in the same domain and under the same government." Occupying half of the Senate gallery seats, Gordon and her supporters listened intently to Bilbo for more than three hours as he outlined the terms of his bill, often quoting Thomas Jefferson and Abraham Lincoln. "It is to us of special significance that Thomas Jefferson was the first man of great prominence to be identified with a repatriation movement in this country," Bilbo stated. "This man Jefferson, the father of the party to the principles of which a majority of the Senate subscribes," he continued, "wrote more learnedly and truthfully about the Negro than any other man of his time." With characteristic racist overtones, Bilbo insisted that "without a proper solution both races will be destroyed and will be succeeded by a mongrel race, and . . . the white race will suffer the loss of all that is dear and precious, high and noble in our civilization."[108] It must have seemed like an eternity, and one can easily imagine that Gordon and her supporters were uneasy with the tone of the senator's lengthy speech even though they accepted the basic premise of his message—the need for racial separatism.

Despite his passionate presentation, Senator Bilbo's "Back to Africa bill" received a chilly reception from some of his colleagues. Though it does not appear that most of the Senate walked out, as some newspapers erroneously reported, the critical questions some senators raised after Bilbo's speech suggest that they were not fully persuaded.[109] Senator James Davis, a Republican from the state of Pennsylvania, questioned Bilbo on the specifics of the bill—asking how much land the Liberian government had committed and inquiring about the amount of financial support that black Americans would receive once in Liberia.[110] Though Bilbo had a prompt response—assuring Davis that black Americans would obtain financial support and the basic necessities in Liberia, including land and property—the Greater Liberia Bill failed to receive the support Bilbo, Earnest Sevier Cox, and other white separatists had anticipated.

Moreover, the newspaper coverage, or lack thereof, spoke volumes. In the immediate aftermath, few black newspapers mentioned the controversial senator and his bill—an indication that their editors were unsympathetic to the cause or did not consider these developments newsworthy. In the months leading up to Bilbo's presentation, several race leaders had openly denounced the bill and the black men and women supporting it. Not surprisingly, black media outlets, including the NAACP's *Crisis* and the National Urban League's *Opportunity*, made no mention of the developments—almost certainly intentionally.[111] The few black newspapers that did cover the story emphasized the role of Mittie Maude Lena Gordon, identifying her as the originator of the pro-emigration campaign years earlier.[112] Writers were fascinated by the unlikely alliance between this outspoken black nationalist leader and the notorious white supremacist. Though a few newspaper articles were quite critical of Gordon—in one instance, describing her as "buxom, well-heeled and loquacious" fanatic of Marcus Garvey—she welcomed the public attention, using it as an opportunity to vigorously defend her nationalist views and, to Bilbo's surprise, to openly denounce white supremacy.[113]

In the immediate aftermath of Bilbo's failed presentation, Gordon held an impromptu interview with members of the white press. "You people don't want us," she boldly declared to a group of white reporters, "and we don't want you." Referencing the sexual abuse that black women endured at the hands of white slaveholders, Gordon unapologetically blamed white people for the "problem" of race mixing. "Some day the man you elect [as president of the United States] is going to be a black man because you can't tell the difference," the activist mockingly remarked. "And it's simply going to be the price you're paying for the sins of your forefathers," she continued. Without mincing words, she added, "All of you know—I do, if you don't—that in days gone by your male ancestors used to raise their white children in the front yard and their black children in the back yard."[114]

Gordon's public critique of white people effectively marked the end of her alliance with Senator Bilbo. By one newspaper account, the senator was deeply embarrassed by Gordon's display.[115] Perhaps, in this impromptu moment, driven by anger and frustration, she chose not to perform—as she often did in her earlier writings. No doubt she had already come to the conclusion that her attempt to secure federal legislation through Bilbo's support was now unlikely. Clearly offended by Gordon's expressive display and harsh criticism of white America, especially her blaming of white men for the race problem, Bilbo tried to form his own delegation of black nationalist leaders in the ensuing months, hoping to limit Gordon's influence and also hoping that he might garner more control of the pro-emigration campaign.[116] He turned to a group of male leaders in the fragmented UNIA.[117]

"She's the 1939 Moses"

In the aftermath of Gordon's break from Bilbo, several mainstream civil rights leaders and black journalists criticized the black nationalist woman leader—much as they had done before. Writing to black journalist Lester Walton on the day the bill was introduced, Claude Barnett of the Associated Negro Press criticized Gordon and her supports for traveling to Washington, D.C. in support of the Greater Liberia Bill. "They are a crude, ignorant

lot," he wrote, "reminding one of the early Garvey days."[118] Ralph Matthews, a writer for the *Baltimore Afro-American* newspaper, expressed similar views, comparing Gordon and her followers to those who were involved
in the "Hunger Marches" in cities across the nation and other parts of the
globe during the early 1930s. Initiated by labor organizers and, in many
cases, backed by the Communist Party, the Hunger Marches represented
grassroots efforts among the unemployed to demand government aid following the onset of the Great Depression.[119] In Matthews's view, however,
those who participated in these marches were simply "bedraggled" men and
women begging for food to eat and a place to stay. By comparing Gordon's
PME to the Hunger Marches, Matthews argued that their efforts were
guided solely by economic desperation. No doubt reflecting his own elitism,
Matthews went on to describe Gordon and her mostly working-class supporters as "misfits in a complex economic system." He facetiously concluded that all they wanted was a "pot of gold at the end of the rainbow."[120]

For Gordon, the conflict and subsequent break from Bilbo marked a
pivotal turning point in her political career and public image—despite the
public critiques levied against her by some black journalists and civil rights
leaders. Ironically, the same newspaper that published Matthews's critical
article included another piece, which succinctly captured this change. Shifting focus from "The Man Bilbo," the anonymous writer of the *Baltimore
Afro-American* lauded Gordon as the "1939 Moses" of black people—
ironically evoking the same analogy Gordon once used to describe the senator. Displaying a full-length photo of a smiling Gordon—under the
capitalized words "She's [the] 1939 Moses"—the newspaper story included
a short description of the black nationalist woman leader credited for leading a group of "500 disciples" to D.C. to lobby in support of the Greater
Liberia Bill.[121] Symbolically, the newspaper's declaration underscored a significant shift that was beginning to take place at the national level. Although
Gordon hoped to secure federal legislation through the help of a powerful
white (male) ally, some members of the African American community had,
in essence, selected the leader of their choice. Reminiscent of Harriet Tubman, who led hundreds of enslaved people to freedom through the Underground Railroad, Gordon became a female embodiment of the "Moses"
figure.[122]

Along these lines, many black nationalist activists envisioned Gordon as
a messianic figure who, like the biblical Moses, would lead the way to the
Promised Land. Mrs. Jowers, a member of the PME in Chicago, expressed

FIGURE 13. Mittie Maude Lena Gordon in "She's [the] 1939 Moses," *Afro-American*, April 29, 1939, 24.

this point of view in an original song entitled "You Better Run." "God
called Madam Gordon from the start," Jowers declared, "He stamped His
will upon her heart / He placed his commandments in her mind / And He
told her not to leave his children behind."[123] In a new spin on the American
patriotic song, the "Battle Hymn of the Republic," Juanita Carter, a young
PME member, composed a song that endorsed emigration to West Africa
and praised Gordon's divinely ordained leadership:

> Mine eyes have seen the glory of the returning of Africans
> To the land of Promise for we'll let her will be done.
> All our brother Africans will meet us on the run,
> Mother Gordon will lead us home
>
> Mother Gordon is leading,
> Mother Gordon is leading,
> Mother Gordon is leading, and she will lead us home
>
> Like the Sphinx o'erlooking Egypt tho never a word it speaks
> We'll follow Mother Gordon's footsteps and always be meek
> Mother Gordon will lead us home.
>
> The Rock of [Gibraltar] has through the ages stood,
> The winds and storms about it washed as furiously as they could
> Behind our leader we will stand four million strong,
> For she will lead us home.[124]

Carter's song, along with Mrs. Jowers's comments, repeatedly evoked the
"mother" trope often used in black churches to describe the "primary
matriarchal figure."[125] By emphasizing Gordon's role as "mother" and the
female embodiment of "Moses," members of the African American community sought to authenticate and validate the activist's leadership at the
local and national levels.

Although Gordon did not obtain the congressional support she desired,
her efforts to pass the 1939 Greater Liberia Bill and uncanny political alliances with white supremacists propelled her status among a community of
working-class black nationalists in Chicago. Members and supporters of
the PME showered her with praises and gifts in recognition of her hard
work and dedication. By one account, local residents threw parties for the
black nationalist woman leader, bringing her food, clothing items, and

money.[126] Others expressed their thanks and appreciation through songs and poetry. In a song entitled "The Land for Me," one young activist praised Gordon's vision and unparalleled leadership: "Madam Gordon is leading this Peace Movement Band / To the Bible's much talked about promised land / When I get there, so happy I'll be, / For Mother Gordon said 'it's the land for me.' "[127]

Expressing similar sentiments in a poem, Albert McCall, a PME activist residing in Chicago, underscored Gordon's unwavering commitment to black emigration and credited the activist for her many years of struggle. "To build this Peace Movement club it took a long time," he noted, "But Madam and her helpers did not mind."[128] Re-creating the scene of Gordon at the Capitol building, filled with hyperbolic elements, PME activist J. E. Hart noted, "I saw her running with something in her hand, / T'was a bill made up for the promised land / The news went out from land to land / It seemed to stampede every man." Addressing those who criticized Gordon's actions, Hart warned, "You keep on talking you'd better let her alone / What a wonderful leader has been born." "She stretched her arms across the sea," he continued, "And made this connection for you and me."[129] Hart's statement, along with McCall's, shed light on the respect and popularity Gordon enjoyed among many black nationalist activists in Chicago even as she endured stark criticism from some race leaders and black journalists.

Moreover, these songs and poetry underscore the grassroots appeal of the Greater Liberia Bill among many ordinary black men and women who embraced the idea of emigration. In the aftermath of Senator's Bilbo's presentation, Gordon received a record number of letters from black men and women across the country, inquiring about the PME and their plans to facilitate emigration to West Africa.[130] Even the ACS experienced an increase in letters during this period from black people across the nation inquiring about the "Back to Africa bill."[131] During the summer of 1939, members of the PME in Chicago held a series of public meetings, promoting the Greater Liberia Bill and securing additional signatures from black residents in support of emigration. In October of that year, Gordon issued a call for additional PME organizers to help recruit new members, "arouse the sentiment of the people," and promote the "Back to Africa bill."[132]

*   *   *

During the 1930s, black nationalist women leaders relied heavily on the support of influential white supremacists in order to advance their political goals. These women activists embraced the ideas of biological determinism that dominated the racial discourse of the period. Working within these conceptualizations of race, Mittie Maude Lena Gordon, Ethel Waddell, and others actively pursued alliances with Earnest Sevier Cox and Theodore G. Bilbo. During a period that was particularly marred by racial violence, black disenfranchisement, and Jim Crow segregation, black nationalist women engaged in a series of performative interactions with white supremacists who sought to bolster their political cause. To a large extent, this was certainly the case. However, women's controversial alliances with white supremacists ultimately failed to yield all of the results they expected.

By 1940, the Greater Liberia Bill began to wane as the United States became increasingly embroiled in World War II. In the aftermath of Germany's attack of Poland in September 1939 and the immediate military response from British and French allies, it became quite apparent that the passage of the Greater Liberia Bill would not become a reality.[133] Moreover, as more nations became embroiled in the global conflict, the United States began to mobilize for war and shift focus from national concerns to global ones—including stimulating the economy and lifting the Depression.[134] Reflecting on the war's outbreak, Gordon expressed deep concern for these developments: "Our hearts are broken, our eyes are filled with tears to think that our brothers and sons, weak from hunger and ragged are being recruited to go back to Europe to another war." "We hope that this nation will stay out of this war," she continued, "or at least keep the black man out of it. It is not our war; we have nothing to do with it."[135] While Gordon lamented the outbreak of World War II, other black nationalist women leaders envisioned the war as a moment of opportunity for black activists across the globe.[136] From her base in Jamaica, Amy Jacques Garvey launched an international pro-emigration campaign, calling on black men and women across the African diaspora to seize the moment as an opportunity to secure their individual and collective freedom.

CHAPTER 5

秀

Pan-Africanism and Anticolonial Politics

WRITING IN 1944 to A. Balfour Linton, editor of *The African* newspaper, the Pan-Africanist leader Amy Jacques Garvey laid out a strategic plan for securing the political, social, and economic freedom of black men and women across the globe. "The Redemption of Africa," she insisted, "is a solution for the ills of all Africans, those at home and those abroad, and all people of African descent, the world over." "The nerve center is Africa," she continued, "and unless, and until, this spinal column is put into working order, the limbs cannot function properly; for it is the nerve center—Africa—that we must get our motivating power." "Strengthen that, and you automatically strengthen even the far-flung fingers and toes," she added.[1] Jacques Garvey's statements, which came during a global economic and political crisis of World War II, reflected her unwavering commitment to anticolonialism and Pan-Africanism—the political belief that African peoples, on the continent and in the diaspora, share a common past and destiny.[2] As colonial rule spread throughout Africa, Jacques Garvey emerged as part of a vanguard of black nationalist women leaders at the forefront of black liberatory movements. In the 1940s, she launched an international Pan-Africanist movement from her base in Jamaica, aimed at challenging global white supremacy and securing universal black liberation.

As Jacques Garvey fought to eradicate the global color line from her base in Jamaica, a vast diasporic community of black women from all walks of life, many of them involved in black nationalist organizations, were also engaged in anticolonial and Pan-Africanist politics. Amid the sociopolitical upheavals of World War II, Amy Bailey, Ethel M. Collins, Amy Ashwood Garvey, Una Marson, and many other black women activists and intellectuals of the period challenged global white supremacy through various mediums, including journalism, media, and overseas travel. Recognizing that the challenges facing people of African descent in the United States or any other nation-state were deeply intertwined with the experiences of black people throughout the diaspora, these black nationalist women promoted a global black liberationist vision and added distinctive voices to discourses surrounding Pan-Africanism. Through an array of writings and speeches during the 1940s, they exercised their political agency, affirmed their humanity, and demanded equal recognition and participation in global civil society.

While these women embraced Pan-Africanism and were deeply committed to anticolonial politics, they often embraced imperialist and civilizationist views that paradoxically promoted some of the same ideals they rejected. Likewise, even as they advocated women's rights, many of these women also endorsed a repressive and patriarchal vision of black liberation—one in which men occupied positions of power and authority while relegating women to secondary, subordinate positions. Through their many writings and speeches, which circulated throughout the United States and other parts of the globe, women played a key role in keeping nationalist ideas alive in black public discourse decades after the Universal Negro Improvement Association (UNIA) effectively lost its stronghold. Foregrounding black nationalist women's writings during World War II not only captures the complexities, tensions, and contradictions within nationalist women's political ideas and praxis but also illustrates how these women shaped and were shaped by black internationalist movements and discourses of the period.

Black American Women and Diasporic Politics

The 1940s was an era of significant transformation in the lives of black men and women across the African diaspora. The outbreak of World War II, more than any other development during this period, marked a turning point in global history.[3] Concerned about the future of millions of people of color across the globe whose lives would be greatly impacted by World War II, black activists across the diaspora amplified their efforts to end global racism, imperialism, and colonialism.[4] On the home front, many black Americans were ambivalent about supporting American military aspirations given the persistence of racial violence, disenfranchisement, and Jim Crow segregation. A. Philip Randolph's plan for a March on Washington (1941) and the "Double V" campaign (1942), which called for an end to fascism abroad and Jim Crow at home, exposed the racial grievances concerning U.S. foreign policy.[5] These developments coincided with the formation of the Congress of Racial Equality (CORE), a multiracial political organization that helped to launch the modern Civil Rights Movement and with the second wave of the Great Migration, in which an estimated one million black southerners relocated to the North and West.[6]

For black women, in particular, the 1940s was an era of hope and possibility marred by the persistence of racial and gender inequality. After the United States entered World War II, women joined the labor force in record numbers to replace the men who had gone to battle. Certainly, the rapidly expanding labor force improved socioeconomic conditions for many black women, who constituted 600,000 out of one million black workers during the war.[7] A significant number of black women who entered the army—an estimated four thousand—joined the Women's Army Corps (WAC), and more than three hundred became members of the Army Nurse Corps.[8] Notwithstanding the significance of these opportunities, racial and gender discrimination shaped black women's experiences during the 1940s. On the war front, American WACs were relegated to segregated living quarters and endured, on a daily basis, gender and racial prejudice in an army dominated by white male officers.[9] In the workplace, black women encountered the same racialized and gender-based hierarchy, which consistently placed them at the bottom.[10] In addition to poor working conditions and segregated spaces—including bathrooms and separate water fountains—black working women received inferior earnings that were substantially lower than the salaries paid to white employees.

These historical developments profoundly shaped the political activities of black women in the United States. No doubt many found a space in mainstream civil rights organizations, women's clubs, or leftist groups to challenge racial and gender discrimination and denounce racism and segregation on both national and international levels. For many working-class and impoverished black women, however, grassroots organizations like Mittie Maude Lena Gordon's Peace Movement of Ethiopia (PME) had a particular appeal and thus provided a significant site for political engagement. By the 1940s, the PME had attracted a substantial following in Chicago and across the nation. Frustrated with developments concerning the failed Greater Liberia Bill, Gordon turned her attention to global concerns during this period. Reflecting her commitment to Pan-Africanism and black internationalism, Gordon advocated black unity and emigration to Liberia while agitating for the end of colonialism in Africa. During the 1940s, she joined a diasporic community of black activists committed to these causes. Writing to a political ally in 1942, she expressed frustration over European imperialism, admitting that "speaking of Italy and Germany controlling Africa has left me bewildered." "It is the desire of the Nationalist in America as well as Africa," she added, "that our country be free of all whites."[11]

Gordon's grassroots efforts to build an alliance with Nigerian nationalist Akweke Abyssinia Nwafor Orizu during the early 1940s exemplify her embrace of Pan-Africanism and support for the anticolonial movements of this period. In December 1940, after reading about Orizu in the *Richmond Times*, Gordon invited him to speak before an audience of PME supporters.[12] For ten days in March 1941, Orizu held a series of public meetings with Gordon and her supporters addressing a range of topics, including emigration to West Africa.[13] Born in 1920, Orizu later became acting president of Nigeria in 1966.[14] At the time of his visit in 1941, he was a college student at the Ohio State University with a desire to build alliances with members of the diaspora.[15] He was also a staunch proponent of African liberation from European colonialism, working alongside other African students studying in the United States such as Kwame Nkrumah, future prime minister of Ghana.[16] Orizu's book, *Without Bitterness* (1944), joined a number of other African nationalist works openly condemning European colonialism and calling for self-determination.[17] Gordon's desire to meet with Orizu in Chicago exemplifies her growing interest in the Pan-African struggle to end colonialism.

Throughout the United States, many black nationalist women shared Gordon's political vision, using their writings and speeches to endorse Pan-Africanism and anticolonialism. In 1942, Josephine Moody, a member of the UNIA residing in Cleveland, Ohio, wrote an impassioned article entitled "We Want to Set the World on Fire," which appeared in the *New Negro World*—a Cleveland-based newspaper modeled after the original *Negro World*.[18] In the article, Moody called for an immediate overthrow of the global white power structure in order to achieve universal black liberation. Reflecting the ethos of the "New Negro Movement," the antiracist political and cultural awakening that swept the nation and the world during the

1920s and 1930s, Moody demanded a militant and urgent response to global white supremacy.[19] "The bleeding wound of Africa is wide open," Moody argued, "and the nations of the world keep the wound from healing, and we, the Negro must be our own physician to effect a healing of that wound." The liberation of Africa, Moody continued, would only come by force: "We want to set the world on fire, we want freedom and justice and a chance to build for ourselves. And if we must set the world on fire . . . we will, like other men, die for the realization of our dreams."[20]

During the tumultuous years of World War II, the black press provided a crucial platform for black nationalist women in the United States to articulate global visions of black freedom and call for improved conditions for people of African descent. Reminiscent of nineteenth-century journalist Ida B. Wells, activist Florine Wilkes, a member of the UNIA, advocated the end of lynching in the United States. In a 1943 poem entitled, "My Race," Wilkes expressed deep frustration over the mistreatment of black men and women in the United States:

In the depths of a long dark corridor
Stands the remains of a Noble Race
They've butchered, lynched and hanged us
Because we wanted better place

We've been kicked, shunned and segregated
And looked upon as an outcast,
We've suffered under the foot of the white man
How long will this terror last?[21]

Wilkes's poem captured the mood of frustration that many African Americans felt during the 1940s. As the global war for democracy waged on, these men and women were engaged in a seemingly never-ending struggle for freedom and equality at home. Wilkes's question—"How long will this terror last?"—was certainly one that countless black activists were pondering.

For black nationalist women in the United States, the pervasive acts of racial violence and terror undermined the very notion of democracy. In her article, "The Real Solution," black nationalist writer Theresa E. Young upheld this point of view. An activist from Cincinnati, Ohio, Young served as the UNIA's assistant secretary general and an associate editor of the *New Negro World* newspaper. In her 1943 editorial, Young described white mob violence and racial discrimination as part of the very fabric of American society. "Discrimination has extended to every phase of racial life," she argued, "In every city, state, and town, Negroes are restricted from white residential areas and forced to live in undesirable sections." "Negro children must attend separate and inferior schools," she continued, "and where school opportunities are available nothing of the history of the Black Man is taught, but in every instance the race is reminded that it [cannot] successfully aspire to a social and personal relation on the same level as whites."[22] Young's editorial cited racial prejudice as the ultimate failure of American democracy.

Despite the political gains of the 1940s—most notably, the passage of FDR's Executive Order 8802 in 1941 to prohibit discrimination in the defense industry—many black activists were frustrated with the slow pace of social change in the United States. Similar to black women in U.S. leftist and civil rights groups during this period, black nationalist women used their writings to bring attention to the persistence of racial inequality domestically and abroad.[23] In her 1940 master's thesis at Fisk University, entitled "The Negro Woman Domestic Worker in Relation to Trade Unionism," Communist Party activist Esther Cooper Jackson decried the exploitation of African American women along the lines of race, sex, and class.[24] Cooper Jackson's writings were consistent with those of other black women in the Communist Party, including Claudia Jones and Grace P. Campbell, who framed "black women domestics as the most vulnerable and exploited women and workers in the U.S. political economy."[25]

Although black nationalist women were certainly cognizant of the class dimensions of their political struggle, their writings centered on challenging all forms of racial oppression.[26] In a 1941 poem, one black nationalist woman in the PME—referred to only as "Mrs. Canada"—denounced racism in the United States and emphasized the need for racial equality: "All we want is equal justice / The color of skin doesn't mean a thing." "God created all men equal," she continued, "How dare you discriminate?"[27] Similarly, Ethel M. Collins, the veteran activist from Jamaica who had joined the UNIA during the early 1920s, called on black men and women across the globe to demand their God-given rights in a 1942 editorial. "As far as humanity goes," she wrote, "all men are equal." "It is true," she continued, "that economically and scientifically certain races are more progressive than others; but that does not imply superiority." Rather than sit idly by as the ideology of white supremacy continued to spread throughout the world, Collins appealed to readers to take a definitive stance toward racial progress.

Employing masculine language that underscored the gendered dynamics of black nationalism, Collins declared, "Our appeal to the world today is [this]: Let us have justice, let us have fair play and we shall prove ourselves as real men should."[28]

In another article, Eustance G. Campbell, an activist residing in Newark, New Jersey, decried white supremacy and called for an immediate response from black activists across the globe. "There is no time to lose," she explained in a July 1942 editorial, "There is a lot of work to be done. We can't wait until the War is over to be free; the time is now, right now."[29] Similar to nationalist leaders Marcus Garvey and Edward Wilmot Blyden before him, Campbell drew inspiration from the Zionist movement for Jewish self-determination.[30] During the 1940s, as news of the Holocaust spread across the globe, Zionist groups attempted to secure international support for the creation of a Jewish state. Campbell insisted that black men and women, like Jews, deserved support and, more specifically, an army of their own: "Don't you see what the White Race is doing? He is speaking about giving the Jews an Army in Palestine, then, where will OUR Army be?" Emphasizing the urgency of the situation, Campbell implored "Brothers and Sisters of the African Tribe" to join the struggle for black liberation and political self-determination. "This is the only chance we have," she explained, "and if we let this chance pass us, we will not get it again for a thousand years more."[31] Campbell's editorial underscored the heightened sense of urgency and awareness of global racial politics among people of the African diaspora during this period. It also illustrates how black nationalists constructed a "transnational and racialized 'imagined community.'" Viewing herself as a member of a diasporic community of black activists across the globe, Campbell emphasized the need for sustained political alliances and collaborations across geographical boundaries.[32]

Through their political writings and speeches, black nationalist women grappled with questions about citizenship, identity, and national belonging. At a moment when race leaders like W. E. B. Du Bois were calling on African Americans to join the war effort to improve their political standing in the United States, nationalist women emphasized the need to create a black nation-state elsewhere. These women, from wide-ranging cultural backgrounds, envisioned themselves as members of a diasporic polity and hoped to facilitate the unification of people of African descent.[33] In their view, the black struggle for full citizenship and equal participation under the law appeared futile. "America knows the story of our 300 years of suffering," Ethel Collins explained, "We have watered her vegetation with our tears. We have built her cities and laid the foundations of her materialism with the mortar of our blood and bones. We have fought in all wars, and die[d] courageously." Yet, Collins lamented, the struggle to "solve the race problem" persisted.[34]

Viewing emigration to West Africa as the ultimate solution for eradicating global white supremacy, Collins explained, "We want the right to have a country of our own . . . Africa is the legitimate, moral, and righteous home of the Black peoples of the world." Insisting that people of African descent needed to "create their own destinies" and build the "culture and civilization of their own," she went on to emphasize the importance of reclaiming Africa: "We of the Universal Negro Improvement Association have made up in our minds to work for the restoration of human liberty and the land of our fathers."[35] Elaine Cooper, secretary of the UNIA's division in Montreal, Canada, expressed similar sentiments, arguing that "Negroes should be more determined today than they have ever been, to protect their own interests." Emphasizing the need for black men and women to establish their own nation, Cooper implored black readers to "realize that the time is coming when every man and every race must return to its own 'vine and fig tree.' "[36]

Echoing the sentiments of earlier black nationalist thinkers—Martin Delany, Edward Blyden, and Henry McNeal Turner, among them—black nationalist women writers championed black emigration, arguing that Africa is the homeland for people of African descent. "Africa is calling us Home to our Native Land," Eustance G. Campbell explained, "Africa, where we can enjoy Peace and Happiness for ourselves." Other women writers embraced this point of view. In a 1943 editorial, Theresa Young reasoned that black emigration was a viable response to the persistent challenges of racial segregation, black disenfranchisement, violence, and terror. "The conditions of life that Negroes have faced and are still facing in America," Young argued, "are conducive in the highest degree to a nationalistic spirit." "At every point in their social evolution," she continued, "opposition presents persistent discrimination to show that the Negro . . . will be tolerated only in the capacity of menials." "The Negro must learn," she concluded, "that if he is to take his rightful place, he too must have a government of his own."[37] Without mincing words, activist Edith Allen endorsed this point of view, informing readers that racial acts of violence would only cease to occur if—and when—black people "had a country of [their] own."[38] Writing in a 1942 editorial entitled "Liberty," Jamaican-born activist Ethel Collins asserted, "The Pilgrim and colonists did it for America, and the New Negro can do it for Africa."[39] These statements underscore how the rights of self-determination, belonging, and autonomy were essential themes in black nationalist women's political writings.

Significantly, women's writings during this period also shed light on their contradictory political ideas. While black nationalist women envisioned black emigration as a means of bolstering black political and economic autonomy, they also subscribed to a civilizationist view of Africa that was characteristic of nineteenth-century black nationalist thought.[40] Indeed, these activists laid claim to African land and envisioned relocation to West Africa as an opportunity to control and Americanize native Africans. Their perspectives illustrate the contradictions of black nationalist movements, which emphasized a radical response to white supremacy while propagating conservative and repressive views.[41] On one hand, black nationalists were deeply committed to Pan-Africanism in response to imperialism in Africa and Eurocentric attitudes.[42] On the other hand, they subscribed to a civilizationist view of racial uplift that mirrored the same practices they rejected. Florine Wilkes captured this contradictory impulse when she declared in a poem, "No man shall successfully rule my people, [b]ut a man who looks like me."[43]

Notwithstanding the imperialist undertones that sometimes appeared in their writings, black nationalist women writers rejected the racist belief that black people were devoid of a history. To that end, they centered their writings on acknowledging and celebrating the historical accomplishments of black men and women across the diaspora.[44] Rejecting the negative images and stereotypical depictions of black history and culture that dominated mainstream mass media, these women wrote articles that emphasized African beauty and exalted the nobility of African civilizations. In one editorial entitled "Arise," Adelia Ireland, a black nationalist residing in St. Louis, Missouri, emphasized the rich African heritage of black people: "We are the Sons and our Father left us a great heritage, for in the days of old, there were Kings and Princes. They had a civilization. . . . The City of our Forefathers was traveled by Cesar, and who can forget Hannibal, who scalled [sic] the Alps and marched on Rome. His Nobility shall never die."[45] Subscribing to a romanticized view of precolonial Africa, Ethel M. Collins expressed similar sentiments: "Stand beneath the colossal Pyramid of Egyptian civilization from the books of the dead. Walk along the banks of the

Niger and listen to the solemn voice of Nineveh's ashes and Babylon's decay; they all tell that the Black Sons of Ham gave to the World its civilization."[46]

Similar to earlier black nationalists, women embraced the philosophy of Ethiopianism, evoking biblical verses as a prophetic reminder of inevitable black redemption.[47] Reflecting Ethiopianist discourse of the eighteenth and nineteenth centuries, women writers endorsed the belief that the "redemption" of Africa, the complete liberation of peoples of African descent, was divinely ordained. As one activist woman from Virginia expressed, "Let us ask Him to hasten the day the Princes shall come out of Egypt, and Ethiopia shall stretch forth her hand to God; let us tell Him that we know now that our house is occupied by strangers, but are willing to take a chance to fight, yes even die, for a part of His house that He gave to the Black Race."[48] Collins agreed, urging readers to hold fast to Psalm 68:31: "Princes shall come out of Egypt, and Ethiopia shall stretch out her hands unto God." "We have accomplished much . . . through Unity of purpose," she added, "but we shall not stop . . . for there is much more to be done to reach our objective."[49] These statements illustrate how women drew upon earlier Pan-Africanist traditions to refine their political strategies and ideologies during the 1940s.

The global visions of African redemption that appeared in black nationalists' writings during this period were intertwined with the question of gender roles. Whereas black women on the Communist Left embraced progressive gender politics—by pursuing a "black left feminist" agenda that was attentive to the intersecting dimensions of race, gender, and class—black nationalist women generally endorsed a more conservative point of view.[50] As proto-feminists, they challenged sexism and sought to empower black women globally but walked a fine line between advancing women's opportunities and simultaneously supporting black men's leadership. In July 1941, UNIA activist Adelia Ireland articulated a masculinist vision of black liberation, emphasizing the absolute necessity of strong black male leadership. "Arise Black men," Ireland declared, "and come out in the light and let the world know their sense of duty."[51] Speaking before a crowd of UNIA supporters in 1942, Elinor White, state commissioner for Illinois, elaborated on this point: "If the men of the Black race in Africa, West Indies, South and Central America and the United States of America, would work together on this great program given us by the late honorable Marcus Garvey, there is no reason why we cannot present to the world . . . a race

of self-respecting and able people."[52] Florine Wilkes expressed similar sentiments in a poem, calling on black men across the globe to "wake from
[their] slumber . . . and fight for [the] MOTHERLAND."[53] These examples
reveal how black nationalist women envisioned men's roles in the global
struggle for liberation and within the imagined future black nation-state.
Like Garvey and other black men in the UNIA, nationalist women often
endorsed a masculinist view of leadership.

At the same time, women also found ways to challenge patriarchy. The
actions of Ethel Collins exemplify this point. In 1943, Collins found herself
in a precarious situation when UNIA leader James Stewart openly denounced her in a series of articles published in the *New Negro World*.
Despite her more than twenty years of service to the UNIA, Stewart quickly
dismissed Collins, describing her as "totally disloyal."[54] Collins had exerted
authority by openly challenging Stewart's leadership and questioning his
"executive" decisions.[55] Unwilling to accommodate Collins's defiance,
Stewart went to great lengths to discredit Collins's standing in the movement. Because she was unable to address the issue in the newspaper, Collins
launched a letter-writing campaign shortly thereafter in an effort to defend
her actions and clear her name. Writing on August 15, 1943, Collins
attempted to set the record straight: "No doubt you have read the articles
written by Mr. James R. Stewart, president general of the U.N.I.A. in Cleveland, Ohio; and published in the *New [Negro] World* . . . quoting me and
others as being disloyal to the association. In this act of his, I am compelled
to make a reply and give some enlightenment on the matter." After reminding readers of her twenty-three-year service to the organization, Collins
denounced Stewart's actions, noting that it was "wicked for anyone at this
late hour to style me as being disloyal." "It is too late now for me to
change," she added, "You can count on me to be the same in life and in
death—my work for good shall never cease."[56] Despite her inability to challenge Stewart's leadership directly in the *New Negro World*, Collins's actions
demonstrate her refusal to accept Stewart's behavior and exemplify the
ways in which women articulated proto-feminism by resisting patriarchy
within Pan-Africanist and black internationalist political movements.

Anticolonial Politics in the African Diaspora

If black nationalist women in the United States endorsed a diasporic politics committed to anticolonialism and racial equality, then so did their

counterparts in other parts of the African diaspora.[57] In Jamaica, for example, teacher and social activist Amy Bailey published a plethora of writings, addressing a number of key issues concerning people of African descent on the island and in other parts of the diaspora. Born in Manchester, Jamaica, in 1895, Bailey became one of the most prolific Caribbean women writers of the twentieth century.[58] Like other black women on the island during the early twentieth century, Bailey had limited access to the formal political process in Jamaica—one that was largely dominated by whites and non-white elite men. In 1919, Bailey entered the teaching profession, marking the formal beginning of her public career as a social worker and activist.[59] With the introduction of *Public Opinion* and other progressive black newspapers in Jamaica, Bailey and other black middle-class reformers found an informal yet crucial space in which to engage in Jamaican politics, thereby attempting to influence the direction of public policy.[60] Her writings addressed a range of concerns, including racial discrimination and the marginalization of black women in Jamaican society.

During the 1920s, Bailey began to embrace the teachings of Marcus Garvey. While she did not become a member of the UNIA, Bailey endorsed the key tenets of Garveyism, including racial pride, black political self-determination, and anticolonialism. She also deeply admired Garvey during her lifetime. "As a young enthusiast," she later explained, "I followed Marcus Garvey to every night meeting at Edelweiss Park and to many other meetings that were held in an open space (now a car park) beside Parish Church on Sunday afternoons." She added, "So enthused was I that on reaching home I would write down much of what I had heard. Unfortunately my bookkeeper friends borrowed those exercise books and I lost them but memories linger." According to Bailey, one of the "high spots" of her memories included the UNIA's 1929 procession in downtown Kingston led by Henrietta Vinton Davis and Maymie De Mena, two women pioneers of the Garvey movement. While the 1929 convention marked the effective collapse of the UNIA as an organization, Bailey remained deeply moved by Garvey's teachings and, during the 1930s, went to visit him in London.[61] In the ensuing years, Garvey's ideas continued to inform Bailey's writings as well as her social and political work.

A gifted writer, Bailey found a public platform from which to share her ideas in a range of black newspapers, including the *Jamaica Standard* and the *Kingston Daily Gleaner*. These opportunities helped to catapult Bailey's political career, expanding her visibility and influence in Jamaica. Moreover, these newspapers linked Bailey and many others to black communities in other parts of the diaspora.[62] Writing in *Public Opinion* in 1938, Bailey argued, "The problems of the labouring classes of this country are many, and must be solved; and we who claim to have the milk of human kindness in our breasts must spare no effort to show our dissatisfaction and to see about remedying these conditions. It ought to be done. It can be done."[63]

Like other members of the black middle class in Jamaica, as elsewhere in the diaspora, Bailey advocated for racial uplift and sought to improve the social conditions of the less fortunate.[64] In another article, entitled "Don't Shoot: Educate," Bailey criticized the black middle class and elite Jamaicans who dismissed the working poor and categorized them as uneducated "brutes." Drawing a comparison between Jamaica and the United States, Bailey pointed out the shortcomings of Jamaican educators: "The [United States] can boast of hundreds of schools that have as their aim the educational advancement of the Negroes . . . and vocational schools turn out thousands every year who are fit to take their place in the machinery of the country; alas, no Booker T. Washington sprang up from amidst the people to lay the foundations of a Jamaica Tuskegee."[65] With these words, Bailey implored black educators to acknowledge their complicity in educational inequality and disparity in Jamaica.

Bailey's comments also highlight her diasporic vision. She understood the ways in which the experiences of black Jamaicans were intertwined with those of other people of color across the globe. In 1944, Bailey openly condemned racial prejudice in Jamaica as in the United States: "The USA will not be the great country it is meant to be unless it resolves this [colour] question, and puts in practice the Four Freedoms, as it affects the Negro Race." "Jamaica . . . will be a miserable tragedy," she continued, "if it fails to realize that not only must black, brown, and white sit side by side in the same schools, but they must be given like opportunities when they leave to occupy the positions they deserve, irrespective of class, colour or creed."[66]

Bailey's statements closely mirrored the poetry of fellow Jamaican writer Una Marson. Born in 1905 in St. Elizabeth, Marson relocated to London during the early 1930s and later worked for the British Broadcasting Corporation (BBC). Similar to Bailey, Marson praised Garvey's political strategies and tactics and credited the black nationalist leader for helping to expand her political vision and increase her race consciousness.[67] During the mid-twentieth century, Marson used poetry as one of the literary forms to condemn racial inequality and imagine a better future for people of African descent. In Marson's poem "For There Will Come a Time," for example, she dreams of a world free of racial prejudice:

> For their will come
> A time when all races of the earth,
> Grown weary of the inner urge for gain,
> Grown sick of all the fatness of themselves
> And their boasted prejudice and pride,
> Will see this vision[68]

Marson's poetry and Amy Bailey's voluminous writings exemplify the ways in which black nationalist women creatively used the black press and various literary mediums to condemn the twentieth-century global color line. Importantly, these women's writings also call attention to how black activists articulated the imagined linkages that form a diasporic consciousness—linkages that were not inevitable but carefully constructed.[69]

Like Marson, Bailey, and others, Amy Ashwood was actively engaged in "forging diaspora"—vigorously pursuing relationships with activists in other parts of the globe and creating spaces and mediums through which to engage in global political dialogue and collective political action.[70] During the 1940s, London became one of the key sites from which Ashwood sought to do so. With the influx of black intellectuals and activists from various parts of the diaspora during the early twentieth century, Britain—despite its status as an "empire state"—had become the epicenter of Pan-Africanist movements.[71]

Black men and women from the United States, the Caribbean, and Africa—Paul Robeson, Claudia Jones, and Jomo Kenyatta, among them—found in Britain a crucial space in which to engage in critical dialogue and political organizing. The majority of these individuals relocated from Britain's four West African colonies—Nigeria, the Gold Coast, Sierra Leone, and the Gambia.[72] By relocating to Britain during this period, these men and women were in a unique position from which to challenge colonialism and lobby for the rights of colonized peoples in British territories.[73] For similar reasons, many black activists from British colonies in the Caribbean relocated to Britain during the late nineteenth and early twentieth centuries. In 1900, for example, Trinidadian Henry Sylvester Williams and his colleagues convened the first Pan-African conference in London. In several other cities, including Liverpool and Edinburgh, black activists established various organizations that helped to heighten race consciousness and champion anticolonial and black radical politics.[74]

Like many of these individuals, Amy Ashwood Garvey found a political home in London, where she had relocated in 1922—three years after her marriage to Garvey ended. Shortly after her arrival, Ashwood had joined forces with Nigerian activist Ladipo Solanke to establish the Nigerian Progress Union (NPU) in 1924.[75] Reflecting some of the same objectives of Garvey's UNIA, including political self-determination and self-sufficiency, the NPU drew a modest following of mostly Nigerian students. During this period, Ashwood traveled to New York, where she produced several plays including *Hey Hey*, a musical comedy, which debuted at the Lafayette Theater in 1926. The play, which received widespread acclaim, featured a diverse cast of black performers, including Ashwood's business partner, Trinidadian calypsonian Sam Manning, and well-known actress Alberta Pryme.[76] Based on a catchphrase from the Harlem Renaissance, *Hey Hey* told the story of two African American men who traveled to Africa in search of their true soulmates after their wives evicted them out of their homes.[77] A subsequent play entitled *Brown Sugar*, released one year later, told the story of a brown-skinned girl being pursued by an American mechanic and an Indian prince.[78] While Ashwood left Britain for a short period during the mid-1920s, she returned in the mid-1930s, when she opened up the International Afro Restaurant and then the Florence Mills Social Parlour, which both provided significant spaces for black activists and intellectuals to socialize and forge political alliances in London.[79] During this period, Ashwood worked closely with several black intellectuals, including Trinidadian journalists and activists George Padmore and C. L. R. James, in the International African Service Bureau (IASB), a revolutionary black organization that advocated for anticolonialism, political self-determination, and racial equality.[80] In 1935, when Italy invaded Ethiopia, Ashwood joined other IASB leaders at London's famous Trafalgar Square, where she delivered a rousing speech in support of Ethiopia.[81] Articulating a commitment to anticolonialism, she boldly declared, "We will not tolerate the invasion of Abyssinia. . . . You said you brought us from Africa to Christianize us, but the only Christianity you gave us was three hundred and more years of enslavement." Further critiquing white imperialists, Ashwood added, "You have talked of 'The White Man's Burden.' . . . Now we are carrying yours and standing between you and fascism."[82] Her statements succinctly capture

FIGURE 14. Amy Ashwood and the Friends of Ethiopia organization at a demonstration in Trafalgar Square (London), to protest Italy's Invasion of Ethiopia in 1935. Bettmann/Contributor via Getty Images.

the black nationalist woman leader's anticolonialist stance and her fearless commitment to advancing this cause.

This unwavering commitment to securing universal black liberation would continue to inform Ashwood's political work during the 1940s. Though Ashwood spent much of her time in London during the 1940s, she also traveled extensively to Africa, the United States, and the Caribbean. In April 1944, she attended the Africa—New Perspectives Conference by the Council of African Affairs (CAA) at the Institute for International Democracy in New York City. Established in 1937 by celebrity-activist Paul Robeson and Max Yergan, one-time secretary of the Young Men's Christian Association (YMCA) in South Africa, the CAA became one of the leading Pan-Africanist and anticolonial organizations of the twentieth century, providing a bridge between people of African descent in the United States and Africans on the continent. The organization's 1944 conference on Africa underscores its leaders' commitment to advancing black liberation in Africa and other parts of the globe. In her public remarks at the CAA's 1944 conference, Ashwood emphasized the significance of Africa in struggles for universal black liberation and praised the council's focus on the continent. "My thoughts go back . . . to 25 years ago and the difficulty of getting people in the United States to think of the word Africa," she noted. "And when we gather here to endorse the program of this Council, I feel honored and privileged," she admitted.

Endorsing black internationalism, Ashwood argued that black people needed to "broaden our vision and broaden our policy to include other groups of people who have been suffering as we have suffered." Maintaining the belief that interracial political unity was a necessary step toward ending colonial rule, Ashwood added, "I see no ill in finding white allies."[83] Ashwood's statements exemplify how the activist departed from Marcus Garvey's "race first" political views and certainly marks a shift in her own ideological trajectory.[84] Similar to Mittie Maude Lena Gordon, Ashwood championed Pan-Africanism and black nationalism as political strategies to combat racial oppression yet also adopted an interracialist perspective that allowed for greater collaboration with white allies.[85] In her travels abroad, Ashwood continued to pursue new political alliances, often crossing racial, geographical, and gender lines. In 1944, she became president of Jamaica's "Jag-Smith Party," a progressive political party founded by J. A. G. Smith, a Jamaican attorney and planter.[86] Describing the motivations behind her involvement in the party, Ashwood suggested that black women's leadership in mainstream political parties was inevitable: "The rapid forward movement of the Negro woman in Jamaica was bound to bring her within the ambit of politics."[87]

Ashwood's statements underscore how she combined her interests in women's rights with Pan-Africanism and black nationalism. In April 1944, she traveled to the United States, where she sought out new political alliances, attempted to organize black women workers, and publicly championed black labor rights. In a public statement during her visit, Ashwood demanded that Caribbean women working in the United States receive wages comparable to those of white men.[88] Her unwavering commitment to advancing women's rights and opportunities served as a driving force behind her decision to announce plans to launch an international women's magazine in 1944. She envisioned the magazine as a means to "bring together the women, especially those of the darker races, so that they may work for the betterment of all."[89] Although Ashwood never managed to publish the women's magazine, her plans reflected her continued efforts to advance women's rights and black internationalist politics during the 1940s.

Ashwood's diasporic political activities mirrored those of Maymie De Mena, who continued to champion black nationalist and internationalist politics on the local and national levels. After relocating to Jamaica from the United States during the early 1930s, De Mena married Percival Aiken, a Garveyite activist from Kingston, and quickly became involved in local and national politics. In a 1942 letter, De Mena pledged her unwavering commitment to black nationalist politics and reaffirmed her desire to help improve conditions for black men and women in Jamaica. "I shall always be a member of the [UNIA]," she assured a fellow Garveyite leader. "I am not as young as I used to be," she explained, "but I am still doing my best to help Jamaica, the home of my adoption."[90] In February 1942, she launched a women's column in the *New Negro Voice*—a Garveyite newspaper based in Kingston.[91] Reminiscent of Amy Jacques Garvey's earlier women's page of the *Negro World* and similar to Ashwood's plans for a women's magazine, De Mena's column in the *New Negro Voice* highlighted the writings of black nationalist women and showcased the significant contributions of black women across the globe.

In deciding to launch a women's newspaper column in Jamaica, De Mena continued her efforts to advance proto-feminist politics. Indeed, during the duration of her political career, De Mena often challenged male chauvinism in black nationalist movements and called for more opportunities for women in the ranks of leadership. In September 1942, De Mena held the first of several "women's nights" in Kingston, which drew a diverse group of black women intellectuals, including Jacques Garvey, writer Amy Bailey, and labor organizer Adina Spencer.[92] These gatherings, held monthly from 1942 to 1943, drew both men and women and provided opportunities for black nationalist women leaders to address crucial issues of the day. Not surprisingly, they offered platforms for these women to articulate proto-feminism, calling for expanded opportunities for black women in black nationalist movements and in Jamaican society at large. In one meeting, held in December 1942, Jacques Garvey delivered a rousing speech entitled "Women's Place in the World." In another session, held in June 1943, Bailey passionately appealed to black men in the audience to respect and honor black women, arguing that "whatever a woman's station is in life, she should be treated with respect."[93]

Similar to Ashwood, De Mena also became active in Jamaica's labor movement and worked closely with a number of black women activists in Jamaica entering the realm of formal politics. In the late 1940s, she ran for a position on the legislative council in East St. Andrew's, Jamaica. Although she did not win the seat, De Mena's run for office provides yet another example of the range of political strategies black nationalist women employed in their efforts to expand rights and opportunities for people of African descent during this period.[94]

Amy Jacques Garvey and the Greater Liberia Bill

As Maymie De Mena fought for black rights in Jamaica and Amy Ashwood engaged in black internationalist politics moving from locale to locale, Amy Jacques Garvey was at the forefront of an unprecedented diasporic movement for black self-determination. An influential and long-time proponent of black emigration, Jacques Garvey relocated to Jamaica with her husband, Marcus Garvey, in the aftermath of his 1927 deportation. Determined to reinvigorate the UNIA and thereby continue the fight for black liberation in Jamaica and across the globe, Garvey relocated to London in 1935. Meanwhile, Jacques Garvey chose to stay in Jamaica to raise their two sons: Marcus Garvey Jr., born in 1930, and Julius Garvey, born in 1933.[95] When Garvey passed away in June 1940, Jacques Garvey played a key role in the continued dissemination of black nationalism throughout the African diaspora, writing for various newspapers in Jamaica and later completing the important text *Garvey and Garveyism* in 1958 (published in 1963).[96]

During World War II, Jacques Garvey amplified her efforts to improve the lives of black men and women in Jamaica and across the African diaspora. Social conditions in Jamaica had improved little since she left for the United States in 1917. Similar to other Anglophone Caribbean countries during this period—including Trinidad, Grenada, and Barbados—Jamaica remained under British colonial rule. Despite representing the majority of the population in Jamaica, the lives of black men and women were circumscribed by a racial hierarchy in which whites and nonblack ethnic groups—such as the Chinese and those classified as "colored"—controlled much of the island's domestic economy. Within this context, black Jamaicans found limited job and educational opportunities in a repressive colonial system designed to "keep them in their place" at the bottom of the social and economic ladder. Against this backdrop, black men and women on the island were actively engaged in the struggle for labor rights in the face of violent opposition and state repression. While much of the labor unrest in Britain's Caribbean colonies, which erupted during the mid-1930s, had subsided by the start of World War II, circumstances in Jamaica were growing increasingly unstable. Tensions between Jamaican politicians Alexander Bustamante and Norman Manley, combined with interparty conflicts and the colonial authority's divisive strategies, created a violent political atmosphere in Jamaica during the 1940s.[97]

Jacques Garvey was deeply concerned about these developments taking place in Jamaica. Yet, she understood that the national concerns were linked to global ones, and while she became increasingly involved in Jamaican politics, she was also engaged in a larger struggle for global black liberation. During the early 1940s, she turned her attention to the Greater Liberia Bill, which she envisioned as a vehicle for advancing the cause of "African redemption" and improving the future of black men and women across the African diaspora. In her view, the Greater Liberia Bill was a viable solution to the social and economic challenges facing people of African descent by making it possible to establish an autonomous black nation-state during a historical moment of political and economic uncertainty. Following U.S. Senator Theodore Bilbo's unsuccessful presentation before Congress in April 1939 and the start of a war in Europe in December of that year, the bill had quickly become a nonissue. However, when Jacques Garvey learned of Senator Bilbo's desire to reintroduce the bill in 1944, she launched an international pro-emigration campaign, calling on black men and women across the diaspora to support the bill.[98]

By that time, Mittie Maude Lena Gordon of the PME had suspended her emigration campaign, shifting her focus to more pressing personal concerns. Her efforts to collaborate with Japanese activists in the years leading up to and during World War II had drawn the attention of federal officials, who had begun to build a case against the black nationalist leader during the early 1940s. After the Japanese attack on Pearl Harbor in December 1941, federal authorities began to crack down on black activists like Gordon who seemed to justify Japan's actions. According to one FBI informant who discreetly attended one of Gordon's meetings in Chicago in 1941, the black nationalist leader had not only dissuaded her supporters from serving in the U.S. Army but also offered a positive outlook on Pearl Harbor, arguing that "on December 7th, 1941, one billion black people struck for freedom."[99] Gordon later denied making this statement, but her earlier letters

MITTIE MAUD LENA GORDON

FIGURE 15. Mittie Maude Lena Gordon's arrest photo. *Afro-American*, October 7, 1942.

to Japanese activists provided the FBI officials with sufficient evidence to bolster their case. Moreover, several black activists in Chicago shared accounts of Gordon endorsing Afro-Asian solidarity and dissuading her members from fighting in the U.S. military with FBI officials.

On September 20, 1942, Gordon was arrested in Chicago, along with her husband, William, and two PME leaders—David Logan and Seon Jones—and charged with the crimes of sedition and conspiracy.[100] Their arrests coincided with the FBI's crackdown on over eighty black activists, including several members of the Nation of Islam (NOI). After making various appearances at the PME's public meetings, FBI officials later raided Gordon's home and confiscated the organizational records, including hundreds of letters sent to Gordon and other leaders in the movement. Many of these items were used as evidence in the subsequent trial that began on January 25, 1943. Unable to afford the costs of litigation, PME leaders filed a motion to appeal in *forma pauperis* and were represented by Chicago attorney Lloyd T. Bailey. During the trial, which lasted three weeks, the prosecution displayed letters from PME leaders and other writings in an attempt to highlight the organization's support for Japan and resistance to military service. Several witnesses, including Gordon's archrival Ethel Waddell—who by that time was busy helping revive UNIA chapters in the U.S. Midwest—testified in support of the prosecution.[101] Despite an appeal in the months that followed, the court maintained Gordon's guilt, sentencing her to two years in prison.[102] Her colleague, Seon Jones, received the same sentence while her husband was given three years of probation and David Logan was found not guilty. On January 17, 1944, the court ordered Gordon to enter the Federal Reformatory for Women in Alderson, West Virginia.

As Gordon sat in a prison cell for almost two years, Amy Jacques Garvey began to use her networks and political savvy to help revive the Greater Liberia Bill. There is no evidence to suggest that the two women were in contact with each other, but Jacques Garvey certainly admired Gordon's leadership and praised her efforts to pass the Greater Liberia Bill.[103] In March 1944, Jacques Garvey wrote a detailed letter to Bilbo, attempting to forge an alliance with the senator based on their mutual interests in "race integrity" and black emigration. "I feel that we are both sincerely interested in the success of the Repatriation Bill," she wrote to Bilbo. "In view of our interest," she continued, "I am sure you will welcome suggestions." Reminding Bilbo about her years of extensive travel, political activism, and international influence, Jacques Garvey proceeded to lay out a number of suggested changes to the bill—including changing its name. "The word Repatriation, to many of my people is misinterpreted to mean forcing them out of America," she carefully pointed out. Thus, she advised Bilbo to rename the Greater Liberia Bill to "A Bill to Establish an Independent Democratic Nation in Africa for people of African descent." "The name is long," she admitted, "but it implies the purpose of the bill." After suggesting more than twenty changes to the bill, Jacques Garvey expressed optimism about its future, insisting that the world war strengthened, rather than hampered, the proposal. With a "publicity campaign" and a "brand new name," Jacques Garvey optimistically predicted that all "oppositionist[s] [would] fall for it."[104]

As she waited for a response from Bilbo, Jacques Garvey began using her global networks to garner support for the Greater Liberia Bill. In April 1944, she wrote to Harold Moody, a Jamaican doctor and civic leader who served as president of the League of Colored Peoples, a London-based Pan-Africanist organization.[105] Detailing her multiple efforts to improve the lives of black men and women in the diaspora through a myriad of initiatives, Jacques Garvey laid out her arguments in support of Bilbo's bill. She described the bill as "the best plan" that would "ease the . . . problems" of black Americans and other people of African descent. She also requested Moody's help to obtain data on "the emasculation of our Race."[106] "Thirteen million African-Americans lynched, ostracized, and frustrated," Jacques Garvey argued, "would find an outlet for their professionals, skilled experts and industrious and intelligent members in a country, in which they can . . . rise to the highest posts within the government." Therefore, the prospect of relocating to West Africa, she insisted, provided a viable means for black men and women both to escape the harsh realities of life in the United States and to have economic and political autonomy.

Moreover, she envisioned the bill as an opportunity for the United States to "develop West Africa from Gambia to Equatorial Africa . . . [and] send experts in all branches of government and for security, to teach and train Africans and Colonists from America to take over their country eventually." Ultimately, Jacques Garvey believed that skilled black emigrants from the United States would play a crucial role in making West Africa "a progressive, Democratic nation."[107] Her comments revealed her civilizationist views toward indigenous Africans—ideas that were characteristic of other black nationalists, including her late husband, Marcus Garvey. Not long after writing to Moody, Jacques Garvey reached out to C. V. Jarrett, editor of the *African Standard* in Freetown, Sierra Leone, expressing a sense of optimism about the future of people of African descent. "For a solution of the conditions of our people in America," she wrote, "I present the Greater Liberia Bill, sponsored by an American Senator."[108]

Significantly, Jacques Garvey also used this opportunity to present her proposal for an amendment to the Atlantic Charter. Introduced in August 1941 by Franklin D. Roosevelt and Winston Churchill, the Atlantic Charter represented one of the most significant World War II documents, laying out a set of principles that would ultimately guide the Allied powers toward peace and stability.[109] Among the charter's stipulations was its emphasis on political self-determination. The document declared that Roosevelt and Churchill "respect the right of all peoples to choose the form of government under which they will live." For people of color, including millions living under the heel of colonialism in Africa, Asia, and the Caribbean, the charter's introduction in 1941 was a pivotal development. Not surprisingly, it became a significant organizing tool, galvanizing activists across the African diaspora and resulting in the resurgence of Pan-Africanist sentiments.[110]

While the charter symbolized the United States' and Britain's commitment to human rights, freedom, and justice, it ultimately excluded people of color.[111] In the immediate aftermath of the charter's debut, Churchill publicly declared before the British Parliament that it was not "applicable to colored races in colonial empire." Though Roosevelt later argued that the charter's provision should include colonized nations, the lack of consensus on the issue underscored the persistence of the twentieth-century global color line that ultimately marginalized the needs and concerns of people of color.[112] During this period, activists in various civil rights organizations, including the National Association for the Advancement of Colored People (NAACP) and the National Negro Congress (NNC), agitated for the inclusion of colonized nations in the Atlantic Charter. In a 1943 speech, NAACP leader Channing Tobias passionately argued that the charter was a monumental development—so significant that black people would be willing to "live, work, fight and, if need be, die for."[113] Jacques Garvey certainly embraced this point of view, calling on Roosevelt and Churchill to recognize the rights and liberties of colonized peoples across the diaspora. In July 1944, three months after contacting C. V. Jarrett, she drafted *A Memorandum Correlative of Africa, the West Indies and the Americas*, a crucial Pan-Africanist document that identified the loopholes in the Atlantic Charter and called for the creation of an African Freedom Council—comprising both African and European leaders—to oversee African colonies.

Among the many stipulations of the *Memorandum*, which included a call for the unification of "Africans the world over," Jacques Garvey also promoted the Greater Liberia Bill.[114] She envisioned the bill as a significant part of the "rehabilitation of Africa." In her view, Bilbo's proposal for voluntary emigration signified a larger commitment to securing black political and economic self-determination.[115] Though she fully understood the controversies—and certainly the contradictions—associated with promoting the senator's bill, Jacques Garvey attempted to convince other black leaders to rally around it. Writing to Hilbert Keys, a Garveyite residing in Delaware, Jacques Garvey explained her position on the issue: "Senator Bilbo's bill is the happy solution to the problem of the conditions of our people in the United States of America" and "would bring about a practical effort . . . [to establish an] independent, Democratic Nation on the West Coast of Africa."[116] Though she lauded the Greater Liberia Bill, which would help to establish "an Independent Democratic Nation for Negroes," Jacques Garvey offered a scathing critique of the bill's sponsor in her letter to Keys. "I do not know if you quite understand," she wrote to Keys, "[Bilbo] is very unpopular, every speech of his is more rabid anti-Negro, even if he does not realize it." Conceding that "it is [still] his bill," Jacques Garvey laid out a strategic plan for promoting it but cautioned, "Connecting him with the bill . . . is hopeless. . . . We must be diplomatic . . . in the way we present [it]."[117]

Jacques Garvey continued to galvanize support for the Greater Liberia Bill by advising Keys to organize black activists from his base in Delaware and encouraging him to revive *The African* magazine in order to promote the bill.[118] "You must be diplomatic," she cautioned, "and act as a real statesman for Africa."[119] She also wrote to members of the Garvey Club in New York, reiterating her favorable position on the Greater Liberia Bill. Though members of the club supported the basic principles of her *Memorandum*, they unequivocally resisted Jacques Garvey's decision to support the senator's bill. Writing to Jacques Garvey in August 1944, James A. Blades Jr., one of the leaders of the club, challenged Jacques Garvey's position in no uncertain terms. "As a good Christian would you accept a plan from the devil as to how you may get to heaven?" he asked rhetorically. "To put it another way," he added, "would you appeal to the devil for a solution as to how to solve your problems?" "That is what you are asking the Garvey Club to do when you suggested the insertion of the Bilbo Bill in the Africa Freedom Charter," Blades concluded. Recounting Bilbo's controversial political career and his virulent racist comments and reminding Jacques Garvey of her late husband's commitment to black self-sufficiency, Blades contended that any connection to the Greater Liberia Bill would ultimately undermine black nationalists' efforts. In Blades's view, Jacques Garvey's decision to link herself—and, by extension, the "movement and [Garveyite] philosophy"—with an avowed white supremacist was entirely wrong-headed and counterproductive.[120] Ironically, Blades overlooked Marcus Garvey's own early efforts to court white supremacists to advance his political goals.

With her characteristic tact, Jacques Garvey sent a carefully crafted four-page response to her critic. "You seem to have gotten quite a load off your chest in the one letter," she began, "too bad we could not meet personally." "But it is for this and other important reasons," she continued, "why my movements are so much hampered." After briefly summarizing Blades's points of contention, Jacques Garvey reminded Blades that she advocated the *bill*—not the bill's sponsor. Moreover, she disputed Blades's assertion that she was "looking to Bilbo for a solution to our problem." "I regard his Bill," she clarified, "as fashioned by him as a means to induce our people in America to build their future in Africa." "Yes, Mr. Blades," she responded to Blades's curt question, "if the Devil, in trying to rid himself of those who stand in his way, send them to purgatory; it is for wise men to use the free transportation and other subsidies, and make purgatory a real Heaven."[121]

Jacques Garvey's response to Blades captures the complexity of her political ideas and the extent of her pragmatic political strategizing during this era. Like Gordon, Waddell, and other black nationalist women activists, Jacques Garvey was not oblivious to Bilbo's underlying goals or the inherent contradictions of such an alliance, but she also reasoned that in the fight for universal black liberation, allies might come from the most unlikely places. Thus, she expressed a willingness to "use the free transportation and other subsidies" from white supremacist collaborators, who, irrespective of their ulterior motives, could serve a far greater purpose.

Although Jacques Garvey adamantly supported the Greater Liberia Bill, which she viewed as a culmination of her late husband's efforts, she began to feel disheartened following her tense exchange with Blades and other Garveyite leaders.[122] Mirroring her earlier critiques of male Garveyites in the women's page of the *Negro World*, Jacques Garvey expressed frustration about "our [Black] men" in a letter to Keys.[123] She declared, "They are breaking my body by being dead-weight to carry all the time. So selfish, self-seeking, so slow, so lazy, I chafe under restraint, that I cannot use some kind of superhuman effort to kick them into action." "My men!" she lamented, "I weep to think, what an apology they are for real, strong, self-asserting men." Reassuring Keys that he was an exception to the rule, Jacques Garvey enthusiastically encouraged him to "go forward" with the important task of promoting the Greater Liberia Bill and thereby advancing "race freedom."[124]

Despite Jacques Garvey's vigorous defense of Bilbo's Greater Liberia Bill, she never actually received a response from the senator. Her earlier letter, dated March 26, 1944, along with a follow-up letter requesting copies of his bill, went unanswered. The senator's silence may have been a result of his increasing health-related issues during this period—Bilbo would undergo a medical operation in August of that year. However, it is also likely that he was put off by the assertive tone of Jacques Garvey's letter—or simply resistant toward the idea of associating with the Jamaican activist in crafting U.S. legislation.[125] Though he welcomed new black supporters, Bilbo certainly preferred to ally himself with individuals who appeared to acquiesce with, rather than challenge, his proposals. Moreover, his earlier experiences with Gordon might have fueled some misgivings about forging an alliance with another assertive black nationalist woman activist.

Whatever the reason for Bilbo's silence, Jacques Garvey was undeterred in her stance on the bill. She acknowledged that Bilbo failed to respond to her letters but continued to emphasize her political support, attempting to draw a distinction between the bill and its sponsor. In a letter to Keys in June 1944, Jacques Garvey carefully advised, "All your comments and arguments . . . must confine itself with the text of the Bill . . . make no mention of Bilbo's name."[126] Jacques Garvey's advice to Keys underscores how the activist hoped to capitalize on the bill without evoking its sponsor. Unlike Mittie Maude Lena Gordon, who had publicly lauded the senator's proposal in an effort to attain her goals, Jacques Garvey employed a "new [covert] strategy" that aimed to "swing [the bill] entirely out of the atmosphere of Southern prejudice and hate." By the act of concealing or, at the very least, downplaying the connection between the bill and the white supremacist senator, Jacques Garvey hoped to garner widespread support from blacks in the diaspora. She also reasoned that if the bill were implemented, it would serve as a "small amount in recompense for services rendered under slavery."[127] From her vantage point, then, the Greater Liberia Bill, which would allocate federal funds to establish a black nation-state in West Africa, represented a small yet significant step toward redressing hundreds of years of racial and economic exploitation.

By August 1944, the growing tensions surrounding Senator Bilbo's bill began to weigh heavily on Jacques Garvey. Though she had vigorously defended her decision to include the bill in her *Memorandum*, she ultimately decided to remove it, recognizing that it would only fuel more conflict and division.[128] She was not, however, willing to break ties with white supremacist collaborators. Maintaining essentialist and biologically based views on race—despite shifting perceptions on race in mainstream black thought during this period—Jacques Garvey continued to pursue collaborations with ardent white separatists. In subsequent years, Jacques Garvey reestablished contact with Earnest Cox, who remained committed to the cause of black emigration from his base in Richmond, Virginia.

Black Nationalist Women and Pan-Africanist Discourses

For black activists who viewed Jacques Garvey's focus on the emigration bill as a significant distraction or even departure from her Pan-Africanist and anticolonialist politics, her involvement in the Fifth Pan-African Congress would have dispelled any concerns. Indeed, as she worked to revive the Greater Liberia Bill, Jacques Garvey was also working to bring the Fifth Pan-African Congress to fruition, using her diasporic networks and skills as a writer. The congress, held in Manchester, England, in 1945, was arguably the most significant of the series of Pan-African events held during the twentieth century. After the first 1900 Pan-African Conference led by Trinidadian lawyer Henry Sylvester Williams in London, four Pan-African Congresses followed between 1919 and 1927—three held in Europe and one held in the United States. The Fifth Pan-African Congress, scheduled for 1945, was organized by Trinidadian journalist George Padmore with the assistance of Kwame Nkrumah and W. E. B. Du Bois.[129] During World War II, Du Bois invited Jacques Garvey to serve as the Congress's co-convener, a position she eagerly accepted. Although she could not afford travel expenses to England, she did much of the legwork for planning the event in the months preceding it. Among other things, Jacques Garvey offered detailed suggestions on crafting the invitation letter for the significant gathering and insisted that black women be included in the program.[130] On October 15, 1945, the Fifth Pan-African Congress began at the Chorlton Town Hall in Manchester with Jacques Garvey still in Jamaica.

Her archrival Amy Ashwood, however, attended the event as one of only two women speakers at the Fifth Pan-African Congress. In addition to chairing the Congress's first session, Ashwood provided a report to attendees in which she reinforced her commitment to anticolonalism and feminist politics. "Very much has been written and spoken of the Negro," she remarked, "but for some reason very little has been said about the black woman." "She has been shunted into the social background to be a child-bearer," Ashwood added, "This has been principally her lot."[131] Her comments resembled those of Jacques Garvey, who had also written at length about the unique challenges facing black women in the diaspora. Though disheartened that she could not be there in person, Jacques Garvey none-theless extended her full support for the gathering: "You know my heart is with you all," she reminded Padmore.[132]

While Amy Jacques Garvey was physically absent from the Fifth Pan-African Congress, she was certainly not absent from the discourse sur-rounding Pan-Africanism, anticolonial politics, and black women's rights. Jacques Garvey put pen to paper to address the concerns facing people of African descent across the globe. From 1944 to 1948, she found a public platform from which to articulate these ideas in *The African: A Journal of African Affairs*, the official periodical of the Harlem-based organization called the Universal Ethiopian Students Association (UESA). Established sometime during the early 1930s, the UESA was a Pan-Africanist organiza-tion composed mostly of student-activists from various parts of the globe, including historian John Henrik Clarke, African nationalist Nnamdi Azik-iwe, high school history teacher Willis N. Huggins, and journalist David Talbot.[133] Inspired by the UNIA, the leaders of the UESA, many of whom were former Garveyites, articulated a commitment to Pan-Africanism, black nationalism, and anticolonial politics.

In the aftermath of Garvey's 1927 deportation, leaders of the UESA sought to build upon Garveyism even as they articulated a distinct political vision for the new organization and its members. Similar to the UNIA, the UESA called for the complete liberation of Africa from white colonial rule and emphasized the significance of education as a means of improving the lives of black men and women across the globe. During the thirties, mem-bers of the UESA led a series of campus protests across the United States and held community debates on colonialism and imperialism in Africa. Reminiscent of the UNIA's School of African Philosophy, the UESA also held evening summer courses for members of the community on African history and culture.[134] Even as the organization drew inspiration from Gar-vey's UNIA, the UESA certainly reflected the time period in which it gained political traction. Against the backdrop of the 1935 Italo-Ethiopian Crisis, members of the UESA endorsed modern Ethiopianism and joined a range of other black organizations in defense of Ethiopia.[135] In a booklet entitled "The Truth of Ethiopia," published in 1936, members of the UESA outlined the history of the conflict and called on people of African descent to join forces in opposition to European powers.[136] Huggins, who facilitated much of the UESA's educational ventures, lectured frequently on African history and colonialism and raised funds for the Friends of Ethiopia, an organization he founded to aid Ethiopia during the 1935 crisis.[137]

During the 1940s, Amy Jacques Garvey and a cadre of black nationalist women found a space in the UESA's *The African* newspaper to engage in national and political discourses of the period.[138] In 1944, at the same moment in which she was promoting the Greater Liberia Bill, Jacques Garvey joined the editorial board of *The African*, thereby expanding her political influence in the Black diaspora. By the time Jacques Garvey began writing for the newspaper, it had acquired international prominence and had been circulating in black communities across the globe, including Nigeria, Ethiopia, Djibouti, and the Gold Coast. In 1937, the year of its debut, *The African* attracted a significant readership of more than 30,000. No doubt some of these readers included individuals who once read Marcus Garvey's *Negro World* and *The Blackman* during the 1920s and early 1930s. In one letter to the editorial board, for example, Stanley Davis, an activist residing in Harlem, described *The African* as "the only thing which seems to satisfy my soul in the form of Journalism since the *Blackman* magazine by the late Hon. Marcus Garvey."[139] Given the overlapping publication dates and similarities between *The African* and the UNIA's *New Negro World*, it is also likely they attracted some of the same readers—black men and women who embraced the newspapers' anti-imperialist, nationalist, and anticolonial bent. In the case of *The African*, colonial authorities went to great lengths to ban (or delay) the circulation of the newspaper in various places, including the Congo, South Africa, and Trinidad.[140] Despite their efforts, *The African* remained in consistent circulation in communities across the African diaspora until 1948—four years after the *New Negro World* folded. From 1944 to 1948, Jacques Garvey contributed articles to *The African* on a range of issues affecting black men and women.

Alongside an impressive group of black writers—including Liberian Victoria Johnson Schaack and African American Gladys P. Graham and well-known activists George Schuyler, J. A. Rogers, and George Padmore—Jacques Garvey openly endorsed Pan-Africanism and emphasized a commitment to ending colonialism and imperialism.[141] In a 1945 article entitled "Africans at Home and Abroad," Jacques Garvey argued that the "ties of blood that bind us transcends all national boundaries." "The differences of languages and dialects," she continued, "are being overcome as all of us are learning the language of freedom."[142] In "The Coming Era," Jacques Garvey condemned global white supremacy and called on black men and women across the diaspora to help liberate Africa from the grip of European colonialism. "Thirteen million people of African descent in the United States of America," she lamented, "[are] denied their manhood rights by a government representing the will of the majority view with interest in the evolutionary drift of civilization." Drawing a link between people of African descent and those of Asian descent, Jacques Garvey went on to condemn the exploitation of both racial groups, arguing that "the wealth and resources of their lands are also being used [by whites] to the fullest extent." "Indians have been promised self-government when the war is over," she added, "[while] India's manpower is being used as soldiers on the ground and in the air, and her fields and ammunition plants are in full swing on the Indian home front."[143] Jacques Garvey's comments resembled those of Mittie Maude Lena Gordon, who also emphasized the common experiences of people of African descent and those of Asian descent. At the time of Jacques Garvey's writing, Gordon remained in a prison cell, where she would serve out her prison sentence until August 1945.[144]

Jacques Garvey, therefore, used her writings to endorse anticolonial politics and challenge global white supremacy—outside of the grasp of U.S. officials who had managed to silence some black nationalist activists while intimidating others. She appealed to blacks under colonial rule to "be prepared educationally and scientifically to strike a blow for their own freedom."[145] Writing in 1944, Jacques Garvey condemned the ideology of white supremacy, reminding readers that "even [so-called] 'backward peoples' have minds . . . and sooner or later these primitive minds . . . will rise to superhuman strength, and build for themselves a 'Heaven of Hell.' "[146] While acknowledging the challenges facing people of African descent across the globe—who were "treated as serfs, second rate citizens and objects of exploitation"—Jacques Garvey expressed optimism that "these sacrifices . . . will be compensatory in the perennial struggle of Africa's people, at home and abroad, for the right to rise without hindrance to their full stature as men, and to control and direct their own destiny."[147] Echoing the rhetoric of self-determination, Jacques Garvey expressed similar sentiments in an article entitled "The Language of Freedom": "Liberty is a synonym of independence and self-government. And only when we too have created the states, built the nations and erected the governments comparable to those of other men, can we honestly hope to erase the stigma of inferiority."[148] Her words captured the essence of Pan-Africanist thought—an incisive critique of imperialism and demand for black political rights. These demands, however, often stood side-by-side with civilizationist and even imperialist views. Endorsing racial uplift ideology, Jacques Garvey called on skilled black men and women in the diaspora to "answer [Africa's] crying needs by taking advantage of every opportunity in the Western World to fit yourself for service in her rehabilitation." "'To thine own self be true. Enlist now for service," she added.[149]

The complexities and contradictions that characterized black nationalist women's ideas also extended to issues of gender and women's rights. In one 1945 article, Jacques Garvey advocated an expansion of women's leadership opportunities while also endorsing traditional ideas concerning gender roles. "Men build houses," Jacques Garvey explained, "[and] women make homes."[150] Her comments mirrored those of Victoria Johnson Schaack, another black woman writer affiliated with the UESA. Born in Monrovia, Liberia, in 1909, Schaack was the granddaughter of Hillary Johnson, the first native-born president of Liberia.[151] Her father, F. E. R. Johnson, Chief Justice of the Supreme Court in Liberia, served as a delegate to the 1900 Pan-African Conference in London.[152] A highly educated and well-traveled black woman, Schaack attended Monrovia College in Liberia and completed advanced study in various schools across Europe and the United States. An ardent African nationalist and Pan-Africanist, Schaack advocated black unity and implored black men and women to take a stance to prevent "the white man" from "steal[ing] our land and everything else we hold dear."[153] In September 1946, while residing in Boston where she attended a music school, Schaack began writing for UESA's *The African* newspaper. A wife and mother, Schaack often penned articles addressing gender roles, women's rights, and women's efforts to balance their personal and political commitments.[154] Describing them as the "head of the family," Schaack emphasized black men's roles as breadwinners and decision makers while describing black women as "mother[s] and home makers." Yet, Schaack also called on black women to expand their visions beyond the duties of home and family: "To protect primary interest, women must be prepared to correct evils in Community and State. To mend and make over a world out of repair is the major talk of women today."[155] Her comments, like those of Jacques Garvey, shed light on the complexities and contradictions of black nationalist women's views on gender and women's rights during the twentieth century.

*   *   *

Against the backdrop of World War II, a vanguard of black nationalist women leaders in the United States, Europe, and the Caribbean were at the forefront of an international Pan-Africanist movement aimed at eradicating the global color line. Maintaining a commitment to anticolonialism and Pan-Africanism, these women, from all walks of life, employed a range of political strategies and tactics in their efforts to secure universal black liberation. Through various mediums including journalism, media, and overseas travel, Amy Bailey, Ethel M. Collins, Amy Ashwood Garvey, Una Marson, and many other black women activists and intellectuals fought to advance anticolonial and Pan-Africanist politics while articulating proto-feminism. Reflecting the richness and complexity of their political thought and praxis, black nationalist women's anticolonial visions often stood side-by-side with imperialist and civilizationist discourses. Likewise, their views on women's rights and gender roles reflected the diversity of black feminist thought at the time, which was by no means monolithic or always progressive.[156]

Significantly, these women helped to sustain black nationalist politics, endorsing racial pride, African heritage, black political and economic autonomy, and Pan-Africanism during the tumultuous years of World War II. In the postwar era, black nationalist women in the United States and in other parts of the diaspora amplified their efforts to obtain human rights. In the absence of crucial diasporic newspapers like *The African* and the *New Negro World*, black nationalist women remained steadfast in their resolve to disrupt the global color line and found new avenues from which to articulate their views. Moreover, they continued to build transnational alliances, recognizing that their struggles for black rights on the local and national levels were deeply connected with struggles for freedom all across the globe. As many of these women grew older in age, some with failing health, they actively mentored a younger generation of black women who would be ready to carry on the work in their physical absence. Moreover, the global visions of freedom black nationalist women promoted in their writings and speeches during the 1940s remained salient in the decades to follow—no doubt providing a source of inspiration for black activists and intellectuals during the 1950s and 1960s.

CHAPTER 6

⇥

Breaks, Transitions, and Continuities

IN A 1956 letter to a political ally, sixty-seven-year-old Mittie Maude Lena Gordon, the founder of the Peace Movement of Ethiopia (PME), insisted that the fight for universal black liberation was far from over. "It seem[s] that all our work is in vain, [b]ut we shall continue as long as we live," she explained.[1] Gordon's comments captured black nationalist women's unwavering determination to improve conditions for black men and women throughout the diaspora. During the postwar era, Gordon and other veteran black nationalist women leaders, including Amy Ashwood Garvey, Maymie De Mena, and Amy Jacques Garvey, continued to pursue a host of causes, including black emigration, anticolonialism, and black internationalism. Against the backdrop of the modern Civil Rights and Black Power movements in the United States, rapid decolonization in Africa, and a surge of liberation movements in Latin America, the Caribbean, and across the globe, these women continued to build transnational alliances and employed a range of strategies and tactics in their struggles for civil and human rights.

As veteran women activists grew older, they sought to maintain their political work, inspiring and mentoring a younger generation of black men and women who attempted to carry on the work in the decades to follow. In the United States, Gordon relaunched a grassroots emigration campaign during the postwar era, working alongside younger women activists in the PME. In London, Monrovia, and other locales, Ashwood, in her late fifties, continued the fight against racism and discrimination, forging transnational networks with a diverse group of black activists and intellectuals.

From her base in Kingston, Jamaica, Jacques Garvey, also in her late fifties, advocated African liberation and black emigration to Liberia while also attempting to preserve and popularize the ideas of her late husband. Her colleague Maymie De Mena, who by this time was in her early seventies, supported these efforts, working with members of the Harmony Division of the Universal Negro Improvement Association (UNIA) in Kingston. Together, these women worked tirelessly to advance black nationalist and internationalist politics, unwilling to relent during a period of significant political change.

These women laid the groundwork for a new generation of black activists and intellectuals during the 1950s and 1960s.[2] In many ways, the Civil Rights–Black Power era represented an extension of the political work that women like Ashwood, Jacques Garvey, De Mena, Gordon, and others had begun several decades prior. Ideological and organizational links tied new black nationalist and internationalist groups to older organizations established during the first half of the twentieth century such as the UNIA, the PME, and the Universal Ethiopian Students Association (UESA). Indeed, a new generation of black activists would draw upon the ideas and legacies of earlier black nationalist women leaders who preceded them. The emphasis on grassroots political organizing, the commitment to Pan-African politics, and the ideals of black political self-determination, racial pride, African redemption from European colonization, and economic self-sufficiency underscore how a diverse group of black activists and intellectuals during the 1950s and 1960s—Ella Baker, Fannie Lou Hamer, Mary McLeod Bethune, Robert F. Williams, Mabel Williams, Mae Mallory, Malcolm X, and Stokely Carmichael, among them—drew on the ideological foundations and political strategies employed by earlier black nationalists and internationalists.[3] Yet the organizational and ideological breaks between older and younger generations of activists were also evident. While younger black activists shared veteran black nationalist women's anticolonial and anti-imperialist visions, many rejected the call for racial separatism, maintaining the belief that racial equality in the United States was achievable. The historic *Brown v. Board of Education* ruling (1954) and the Montgomery bus boycott (1955–56) signaled to many black activists and intellectuals— including those closely aligned with the National Association for the Advancement of Colored People (NAACP)—that change was not only possible but also imminent. Moreover, veteran black nationalist women's particular focus on black emigration and their unwavering interest in Liberia

marked a significant departure from the priorities of several black nationalist groups of the period. Rather than endorsing black emigration, black
nationalist groups such as the Nation of Islam (NOI) and the Republic of
New Afrika (RNA) advocated territorial separatism—the establishment of
autonomous black communities within the United States.[4] While black
activists in these groups sought to advance economic self-sufficiency and
political self-determination, they lacked the strong inclination to relocate
to West Africa. Instead, they set out to empower black communities
through various means, including religious expression, armed self-defense,
and cultural nationalism.[5]

During the Civil Rights–Black Power era, Gordon, Ashwood, Jacques
Garvey, and De Mena continued to fight for the rights and dignity of black
people in the diaspora—until they could physically fight no longer. In their
absence, a diverse group of civil rights and Black Power activists and intellectuals emerged to lead the battle for universal black liberation, articulating
visions of freedom that built upon yet also departed from earlier expressions of black nationalist and internationalist thought. Black nationalist
ideas, made popular by earlier groups such as the UNIA and the PME,
outlived and outgrew these organizations and their leaders—even despite
the assault on black radical political activity during the early Cold War.
Black nationalism not only survived but also thrived during the postwar
era—taking on new shapes and expressions in a range of black political
organizations in the United States and across the globe.

Rebuilding the PME After World War II

The end of World War II in 1945 ushered in a period of significant change
in the United States and across the globe. Many African Americans in the
military who traveled abroad during the war returned to the United States
radicalized. Yet these men and women would find the same challenges in
the United States they left behind during the war. Across the country, black
men and women continued to face pervasive acts of racial violence and
discrimination, a reality that underscored the hypocrisy of U.S. leaders who
fought to dismantle fascism abroad while maintaining white supremacy at
home. With a profound sense of urgency, many of these individuals became
involved in race organizations of the period. With the surge of black political activity, they found a wealth of political groups from which to choose.
Indeed, the postwar era in the United States witnessed the proliferation of

black political groups. In addition to older groups like the NAACP and the National Urban League (NUL), activists during the postwar era found crucial spaces in which to agitate for black political rights in reformist groups such as the National Negro Labor Congress, the Civil Rights Congress, and the Council on African Affairs.[6]

After her release from prison in August 1945, Mittie Maude Lena Gordon attempted to rebuild the networks she had established through the PME prior to World War II. This was no easy task. Black activists across the country, including some who had previously supported the black nationalist woman leader, grew distant from Gordon. In one instance, Benjamin Jones, a Garveyite residing in Harlem, expressed concerns about working with Gordon because of her prior troubles with the FBI. In a detailed letter to Jones, white separatist Earnest Sevier Cox, who remained unwavering in his support of Gordon, immediately came to her defense: "In relation to the great petition prepared by the [PME] and used in support of the Greater Liberia Bill, Mrs. Gordon was imprisoned, charged with seditious utterance. The petition itself cannot be tainted by her imprisonment for it explicitly states its purpose and a vast number who signed it did not even know Mrs. Gordon."[7] His comments reflected his relationship with Gordon, which by this time had evolved from that of a political alliance to a friendship. By the mid-1940s, the white supremacist and the black nationalist were in contact on a weekly basis and even exchanged Christmas cards and presents. Interestingly enough, Gordon would often send Cox words of encouragement written on Afrocentric cards.[8] These gestures shed light on the complex relationship between two vastly different individuals who were united by similar political interests. During Gordon's imprisonment, Cox wrote often to the black nationalist woman leader and also remained in close contact with her spouse, William. Cox's letters revealed what appeared to be his genuine concern for her physical health and well-being.[9] It is not surprising, then, that he took Jones's critiques to heart and attempted to lessen the blow to Gordon's reputation, emphasizing her tireless efforts to advance black emigration.

In reality, Jones's misgivings about Gordon had little to do with his worries about her imprisonment; instead, they represented longstanding tensions between the PME and the UNIA and struggles over power and control. Still, Jones's comments also underscore how Gordon's arrest and imprisonment undermined her political work. It was no coincidence that many of her letters to activists across the globe went unanswered during the postwar era. Certainly, some potential allies were unwilling to collaborate with an activist who had been arrested for "seditious activities." Moreover, by the time Gordon returned home from prison in 1945, many of the PME's chapters had completely dissolved while others were struggling to stay afloat.

Though the exact membership figures of the PME during this period are uncertain, the organization was a far cry from what it was before the war. By 1946, many of the organization's key organizers and recruiters, including activists like Celia Jane Allen and Thomas Bernard, who played key roles in building and leading PME chapters in the U.S. South, were no longer active in the movement—partly as a result of the FBI's crackdown.[10] The vast majority of the PME's political organizing during the postwar period took place in the U.S. Midwest with Gordon facilitating the activities with the assistance of a few other women leaders. The members of the organization continued to meet weekly to strategize about how to advance black emigration to West Africa. Morale was low because many of the members were frustrated with their inability to secure federal funding or pass legislation. "We are becoming disgusted over this matter, after so many years of hard work and suffering for this cause," Gordon complained in 1949.[11]

During the mid to late 1940s, a younger generation of black nationalists emerged as leaders in the PME—endorsing black emigration, racial pride, political self-determination, and economic self-sufficiency. Many of these individuals were black working-class women who had joined the movement during the 1930s and early 1940s. Rosie Lee Gearring, a black nationalist from Indiana, was among them. Born Rosie Lee Williams in Arkansas on April 19, 1922, Gearring resided in East Chicago, Indiana, where she became an active member of the PME, most likely as a result of her grandfather, Jacob Hart, who served as a member of the PME's board of directors.[12] Petite and dark-skinned with short black hair, Gearring was a quiet woman who was described by her associates as a passionate activist. Her former classmates at Washington High School in East Chicago, where Gearring was enrolled from 1932 to 1940, remembered her as a "crusader type of person" who was especially interested in black nationalist politics.[13] Rejecting the classification "Negroes," Gearring maintained the belief that black people ought to be described as people of "African descent," thereby emphasizing connections to the continent and ties to black men and women throughout the diaspora.[14] In 1939, Gearring had joined hundreds of PME activists who journeyed to Washington, D.C. to witness the late Mississippi Senator Theodore Bilbo's presentation of the Greater Liberia Bill.

For the young activist, the PME offered a space to engage in black nationalist politics while also providing a sense of community. On July 28, 1940, Gearring—then Rosie Lee Williams—married classmate John W. Gearring at the PME's central meeting place in East Chicago.[15] Surrounded by friends and loved ones in the PME, including her grandfather, Gearring exchanged vows on the site where she and others engaged in much of their political work. In the months following her nuptials and even after the birth of her daughter, Jeanette Olivia, in December 1940, Gearring remained actively involved in the PME from her base in East Chicago, Indiana. On Sunday evenings, she joined hundreds of black men and women, sometimes including PME members from Chicago, who gathered at a community hall along the Indiana harbor to strategize and discuss future plans for the movement.[16] During the years after World War II, Gearring worked to rebuild a record of the group's supporters, including those who had lost contact with the organization's headquarters in Chicago.[17]

Despite the significant age difference between the two women, Gordon and Gearring maintained a close relationship on the basis of their mutual interest in black nationalism. "I am young in years," the twenty-one-year-old Gearring told one political ally in 1944, "but I have the same spirit our leader [Mittie Maude Lena Gordon] has—a nationalist one."[18] By Gearring's own account, Gordon mentored her closely, teaching her the ins and outs of the movement and connecting her with some of the organization's contacts across the country.[19] In 1944, Gordon appointed Gearring as first assistant president general of the PME, a formal title that recognized her collaborative work with Gordon.[20] On the surface, this small gesture demonstrated Gordon's investment in nurturing and mentoring younger black women.

However, Gordon's actions also reveal how the black nationalist leader fought to maintain full authority of the organization she founded even as she recognized the leadership potential of others. During the period in which Gearring served as first assistant president general, Gordon endured significant health problems, including arthritis and an ailing heart.[21] Rather than identifying a new president general for the organization, Gordon chose to hold on to the position until she could physically serve no longer. Her actions may have been guided by selfish ambitions or an inability to fully trust others—perhaps as a result of her earlier experiences with individuals like Ethel Waddell, her former secretary turned archrival. Regardless, these shortcomings eventually caused Gearring to drift away from the PME. "It has been so difficult for me," Gearring admitted in a letter to a political ally. "Being young in years has its disadvantages," she explained, "because the older ones are inclined to believe that they aren't competent because of their youth."[22]

Gearring's difficulties in the PME during the 1940s shed light on some of the internal challenges in the organization. However, they were not representative of all black women's experiences in the PME. Alberta Spain, an activist from Chicago who had joined the movement during the early 1930s, maintained a close relationship with Gordon and continued to work on the organization's behalf during the postwar era. Moving up the ranks—first as a secretary and then as a member of the organization's executive council—Spain became increasingly involved in PME activities.[23] In February 1948, when Gordon's husband, William, passed away following a brief illness, Spain not only took on a greater role in the organization but also was responsible for planning William's memorial service, perhaps because Gordon was too overcome with grief to do so.[24] The very fact that she was able to facilitate the memorial service suggests that Spain was especially close to Gordon. Spain would later describe Gordon as a close confidant and mentor who taught her how to run the affairs of the organization and introduced her to several of the PME's political contacts.[25] Gordon's relationship with Spain highlights some of the positive intergenerational exchanges between veteran black nationalist women and a younger generation of activists during the Civil Rights–Black Power era.[26]

The Persistence of Liberian Dreams

During the postwar era, veteran black nationalists advocated black emigration to Liberia—a political strategy that had largely fallen out of favor with a younger generation of black nationalist activists and intellectuals. Instead, younger black nationalists advocated African liberation and supported black separatism (to varying degrees), while black emigration to Liberia was not a pressing concern for them. Yet veteran activists held fast to the belief that black emigration—and relocation to Liberia, in particular—remained a viable option. Despite Liberia's economic challenges, veteran black nationalists continued to view relocating to Liberia as a unique opportunity to advance African liberation and Pan-Africanism.[27] Reminiscent of earlier black nationalists, including African American minister Alexander Crummell and educator Edward Wilmont Blyden of St. Thomas, these men and women envisioned Liberia—one of only two independent African states at the time—as the ideal location for uniting people of African descent in the diaspora.[28]

Activists in the PME continued to endorse this point of view, emphasizing the significance of black emigration as an avenue for political self-determination and economic empowerment. During the mid to late 1940s, Gordon, Spain, and other PME activists refocused their efforts on black emigration to Liberia, strategically steering clear of any other political issue. "We will not be decoyed away from our repatriation plan; for Africa for the Africans," Gordon insisted. "Our cause is [now] a one-point program; we are not interested in anything else," she claimed.[29] Although an attempt to revive the Greater Liberia Bill was unlikely—Theodore Bilbo, its controversial author, had passed away in 1947—Gordon and her supporters in the PME were hopeful that they could secure federal funds for relocation to some part of Africa. During the late 1940s, as civil rights leaders in the NAACP turned to the United Nations (UN) to agitate for human rights, Gordon toyed with the idea of going to the UN to obtain support for her emigration plans.[30] However, she ultimately decided to focus her energies on securing a new pro-emigration U.S. congressional bill. In 1948, she wrote a letter to President Harry Truman asking for his support, but the administration dismissed it.[31] In October 1948, Gordon visited Cox in Richmond, Virginia, to strategize plans for securing a new sponsor to introduce a pro-emigration bill to Congress—one that would closely mirror the Greater Liberia Bill. She also traveled to Washington, D.C. to meet with Liberian officials who were visiting the United States in hopes of convincing them to support her new emigration campaign.[32]

Gordon received hopeful news when Cox informed her about a new emigration bill, introduced by Republican Senator William Langer from North Dakota.[33] Unbeknown to Gordon, while she was busy seeking a sponsor for a new emigration bill, members of the Universal African Nationalist Movement (UANM), a black nationalist organization led by Benjamin Gibbons, managed to secure a sponsor for a bill to provide federal support for black men and women desiring to relocate to West Africa. Established by Gibbons during the mid-1940s, the Harlem-based UANM was an outgrowth of Garvey's UNIA.[34] Prior to establishing the UANM,

Gibbons had been active in the UNIA and, during the early 1940s, served as president of the Harlem-based Garvey Club.[35] In 1947, Gibbons traveled to Liberia, where he stayed for several months in order to build political networks and become better acquainted with the region. Upon his return to the United States, Gibbons expanded his efforts to secure federal legislation for black emigration. In a letter to the *Philadelphia Tribune*, he assured readers that members of the Liberian government fully supported his plans. According to Gibbons, "The government and people of Liberia welcome such a plan of industriously minded people of U.S. African stock who wish to come over to help advance the country."[36]

In 1949, Gibbons received support from Senator Langer, who made plans to introduce an amended version of the Greater Liberia Bill to the U.S. Senate.[37] This new bill was much more modest than Bilbo's earlier proposal. Langer's amended bill called for negotiations between the U.S. president and Liberian officials, thereby allowing for greater flexibility on the terms. Langer's version of the Greater Liberia Bill also called for the creation of a commission to oversee the process of black emigration—requesting individuals to apply for the opportunity to relocate and deciding what kind of support they would receive once in Liberia. In Langer's proposal, black emigrants would be granted loans—up to one hundred thousand dollars based on the commission's discretion—from the U.S. government.[38]

Much like the earlier Greater Liberia Bill, Langer's new bill received a chilly reception. U.S. senators not only doubted the feasibility of the bill but also worried it would taint the United States' public image. Texas Senator Tom Connally, chairman of the Senate Foreign Relations Committee, refused to support the bill, arguing that it would be an act of injustice to encourage black emigration to Liberia—especially in light of Liberia's economic instability. Not surprisingly, many civil rights leaders, including members of the NAACP, publicly denounced the bill, arguing that African Americans were citizens of the United States and should not be relocated elsewhere. Writing to black nationalist leader Benjamin Jones in 1949, Madison S. Jones Jr. of the NAACP expressed his disapproval of the emigration bill along these lines and made it clear that the NAACP would not support it in any way. Liberian officials also rejected the proposal on the basis that they had not been fully consulted before Langer drafted the bill. They also pointed out that Liberia could not accommodate the large-scale migration that Langer envisioned. Moreover, Langer struggled to obtain white support for the bill—his letters to several prominent white politicians asking for their support went unanswered.[39]

Black nationalists, however, were undeterred. After learning about Langer's new emigration bill, Gordon reached out directly to the senator to offer her support.[40] With Cox's prodding, she attempted to forge an alliance with the UANM, though she did not hide her belief that Gibbons and his supporters had slighted her by intentionally leaving her out of planning meetings. As she explained in a 1949 letter to Cox, "It is not fair to shut the door in my face after I have given my life to help the white race as well as my own—without one penny salary." "If I committed a crime so did Jesus Christ. He only asked for the freedom of his people and so did I," she added.[41] Notwithstanding the hyperbolic overtones, Gordon's comments capture the depth of pain and disappointment she felt as she tried unsuccessfully to gain recognition for a movement she once led. "No one in this country in our race . . . [has] worked as hard for the [culmination] of this cause as we have," Gordon argued.[42] While Gordon despised Gibbons and his supporters for failing to include the PME in their planning, she remained hopeful that the Langer Bill might finally make it possible for her to relocate to Liberia. In reality, the Langer Bill would meet the same fate as Bilbo's earlier proposal. It never passed.

While Gordon's desire to advance black emigration to Liberia appeared anachronistic, it reflected an aspect of black nationalist thought that remained prominent among a cohort of older activists and intellectuals during the 1950s. In the United States, other veteran black nationalists, including longtime UNIA activist Ethel M. Collins, supported black emigration to Liberia. Under the auspices of the Rehabilitation Committee—a group established in 1943 for the purpose of reviving the UNIA and advancing Marcus Garvey's mission—Collins and other UNIA activists organized mass community meetings in Detroit in which they emphasized the need and significance for blacks to relocate to the West African nation.[43]

In the late 1940s, members of an offshoot of the PME also supported the Langer Bill. Chicago-based black nationalist activist Lucreacy (Lucrecia) Rockmore, the wife of former PME leader Joseph Rockmore, supported efforts to relocate to Liberia and publicly backed efforts to pass the Langer Bill. Lucreacy had been a member of the PME during the 1930s along with her husband, Joseph Rockmore—a member of the organization's 1938 delegation to Liberia. Along with David Logan, Joseph had traveled to Liberia on behalf of the PME to observe conditions on the ground in preparation for relocation plans. In the months following the trip to Liberia, the relationship between Rockmore and Gordon grew sour after Gordon caught wind of his efforts to launch his own organization. Other PME members alleged that Rockmore stole some of the funds the PME had raised for emigration plans.[44]

During the early 1940s, he and his wife had launched their own black nationalist organization in Chicago called the Sons and Daughters of Africa, Inc. to facilitate plans for relocation to Liberia on their own terms. Relying on some of the contacts Rockmore had made during his 1938 visit to Liberia, the Sons and Daughters of Africa, Inc. hoped to hasten black emigration to Liberia during the Great Depression. While the specific membership numbers are unclear, the Sons and Daughters of Africa, Inc. attracted a following of mostly disaffected members of the PME who were frustrated with the slow pace of progress toward realizing emigration plans. In April 1941, during a heated argument over Rockmore's alleged theft, a PME organizer in Chicago fatally shot Rockmore and injured his wife, Lucreacy.[45] Determined to advance the cause of emigration in her husband's absence, Lucreacy launched a new organization in the late 1940s—now called America's Sons and Daughters Association, Inc.[46]

Similar to the PME, America's Sons and Daughters Association, Inc. publicly endorsed black emigration. However, unlike the PME, the organization focused on identifying and training skilled workers who might be able to help improve Liberia's destabilized economy. "In our organization we have skilled people in agricultural and building construction," Lucreacy explained in a 1949 letter to Cox. "We [are] preparing to have those skilled in their respective trades to teach those who desire to learn," she continued. Relying on an earlier promise by former Liberian President Edwin Barclay—who claimed he would back African American relocation to Liberia during the 1930s if prospective emigrants had certain skills and capital—Lucreacy Rockmore held fast to Liberian dreams.

From her base in Kingston, Jamaica, Amy Jacques Garvey followed suit. Like Lucreacy Rockmore, Jacques Garvey imagined the postwar era as an opportune moment to revive efforts to advance black emigration to Liberia. While Rockmore worked diligently to build a base of support for her cause in the United States, Jacques Garvey made one last-ditch effort to revive Theodore Bilbo's original Greater Liberia Bill.[47] During the late 1940s, she launched yet another letter-writing campaign, seeking to convince others to back the bill in an effort to improve the lives of black men and women in the diaspora. Moreover, she saw racial separatism—by way of emigration to Liberia—as a practical way to remedy many of the social challenges facing people of African descent in the United States and on the African continent. "Both materially and spiritually (meaning racially and socially)," she insisted, "black and white will benefit [from emigration]."[48] Once again, her appeal fell on deaf ears.

Although most veteran black nationalists advocated black emigration without ever setting foot on the African continent, some managed to relocate to Liberia during the postwar era. Amy Ashwood was among this cohort of black nationalist activists and intellectuals. In 1946, with the help of her old friend Lapido Solanke from the West African Students' Union (WASU), Ashwood relocated to Monrovia, where she developed a close relationship with Liberian President William V. S. Tubman.[49] In a 1946 letter to Tubman, she emphasized the longstanding pride and respect she had for Liberia, describing it as "the only Black republic in Africa."[50] Ashwood was so excited about Liberia that she made attempts to become a Liberian citizen, emphasizing her pride and her desire to help improve the nation's political standing and image on the international stage.[51] "I have read many books [and] newspaper articles published on Liberia," Ashwood explained to President Tubman, "and noticed that the trend has invariably been to degrade, expose the country to ridicule and make capital out of any deficiencies from which all countries founded on similar grounds must struggle to fulfill their destiny."

"Because of the pride I now feel in becoming a Liberian citizen," she continued, "and because I know of the aims, aspirations and hope of millions of denationalized Blacks who look with jealous pride to [Liberia]; I not only beseech or recommend, but I demand that [a] Cultural Relations Department be established." This Cultural Relations Department would be responsible for disseminating accurate information on Liberia's history and culture to various publicity outlets. Moreover, this proposed department would create "libraries, women's voluntary services . . . recreation camps, playgrounds, parks, old folks homes [and] social clubs" in an effort to counter public criticisms of Liberia as being underdeveloped. In so doing, Ashwood insisted that these developments would attract "qualified and ambitious and well trained people of African descent from all over the world." She envisioned that a Cultural Relations Department would help to "promote a better understanding between Liberians and other races [and] encourage and inspire National patriotism in the hearts of the people."[52]

On the surface, Ashwood's suggestions appear to be well-meaning attempts to improve conditions in Liberia. Yet, her recommendations shed light on Ashwood's civilizationist outlook—one that was characteristic of other black nationalists during this period. Her statements offer a glimpse into how black nationalists often viewed Liberia as a symbol of hope and freedom while embracing a civilizationist impulse of racial uplift.[53] Rather than addressing the economic and political challenges that Liberia was facing during this period, Ashwood appeared to be far more concerned with enhancing Liberia's image abroad. She was also deeply concerned about the kind of people Liberia might attract, emphasizing the need for "qualified and ambitious and well trained people" who would help to modernize the country. These statements underscore how Ashwood's engagement with Liberians was very much circumscribed by Western ideas and attitudes about modernity.[54] In this way, Ashwood's perspectives stood in direct contrast to those of civil rights activists and intellectuals such as Paul Robeson, chairman of the Council of African Affairs (CAA), who eschewed racial uplift ideology and argued that Africans would liberate themselves.[55]

From 1946 to 1949, Ashwood resided in Liberia, traveling across the country to meet with African officials and other leaders in an effort to forge new political connections.[56] Much like she had done before World War II, she also spoke before audiences of black women, addressing the need to expand the rights and opportunities for women of African descent on the continent and throughout the diaspora. Her manuscript, *Mother Africa*, which she began writing while in Liberia, discussed her admiration for Liberia—and the African continent as a whole—as well as her concerns about the unique challenges facing West African women.[57] Ashwood's sojourn to Liberia and the time she spent residing in Monrovia underscore the place of prominence Liberia held among veteran black nationalists in the postwar era.

Significantly, Ashwood's experiences mirrored those of James R. Stewart—Marcus Garvey's successor in the UNIA. In 1949, Stewart relocated to Monrovia with his family after several years of leading the new UNIA headquarters from Cleveland, Ohio. Determined to advance the cause of "African redemption," Stewart established a new home in Liberia and worked to revive a local UNIA chapter. There he led a chapter of the UNIA in Monrovia from the late 1940s to 1964, working alongside local activists committed to advancing African nationalism.

In 1949, Stewart, with the assistance of President Tubman, established a UNIA settlement called "Liberty Farm" on 200 acres of land in the remote community of Gbandela. The commercial farm in Liberia, which featured an elementary school and several modern buildings, provided a space for Stewart and other UNIA members to advance the goals of racial separatism, black political autonomy, and economic self-sufficiency. Several UNIA activists from the United States relocated to Liberia to join Stewart on "Liberty Farm" during the late 1940s.[58] Similar to Ashwood, Stewart and his supporters maintained a civilizationist outlook, desiring to improve conditions in Liberia largely on their own terms. To that end, they envisioned their efforts as crucial steps toward civilizing Liberians—often cloaked in the language of "modernization."[59]

Veteran black nationalists, including James Stewart, Amy Ashwood, and Lucreacy Rockmore, maintained the belief that Liberia provided the ideal site from which to advance black liberation and nation building. While the challenges facing Liberia during the 1940s were not remarkably different from the 1930s—the nation was still steeped in debt, and tensions between elite Americo-Liberians and indigenous groups persisted—these men and women continued to view Liberia as a source of hope and opportunity. This particular stance underscored one key distinction between an older generation of black nationalists and younger activists. By and large, a new generation of black nationalists in the postwar era had little interest in Liberia—even as they were committed to African liberation and engaged with activists on the continent.

Black nationalists, old and young, believed that black people would never be able to experience full equality in the United States. In their view, efforts to advance citizenship rights were meaningful but failed to overturn a system of white supremacy that shaped the very foundations of the United States. From the vantage point of many older black nationalists, emigration was still a relevant and even necessary response to white supremacy. Even as the United States underwent an unprecedented period of social change during the 1950s, Gordon insisted that a black nationalist agenda was one that fully embraced black emigration to West Africa. "We are strictly nationalist," she argued, "and [therefore] we want our own nation in our own country, Africa."[60] Despite her assertion, this matter remained a fraught issue among those who embraced black nationalism.[61] For many younger black nationalists, the liberation of Africa and the establishment of black governments would end colonialism, prove black capability, and provide a figurative and actual homeland for black people.

If black nationalists could not agree on the specific terms of racial separatism, domestic civil rights activists were certainly unsympathetic to that
cause. During the 1950s, black political leaders in mainstream organizations
such as the NAACP continued to resist black emigration as a political strategy. Gordon categorically dismissed these individuals as "intellectuals,"
underscoring what she perceived as their disconnect with the black masses.
Referencing the biblical Christmas story, Gordon argued, "It is a strange
thing to us that history fails to teach people anything. Don't they know it
was the shepherd boys that saw the star of Bethlehem? The intellectuals of
our race will never support a back to Africa program [because] they fail to
see the star."[62] In a letter to George W. Armstrong, a white supremacist
judge residing in Mississippi, PME activists pointed out that there were
"many self-respecting people of African descent, who have been working
for many years trying to go back to Africa, where we were kidnapped from
and brought here against our will."[63] Their emphasis on "self-respecting
people of African descent" alludes to the class tensions at the center of
much of these public debates on black emigration. In effect, by employing
this phrase, PME members were sending the clear message that black people who desired to leave the United States—regardless of their educational
background or socioeconomic status—equally deserved to be recognized
and respected.

During the 1950s, Gordon and her supporters attempted to draw a clear
line between their political work and the efforts of mainstream civil rights
leaders. Even as both groups were united by a common desire to liberate
black people, differences in approaches and political strategies rose to the
surface. Reflecting their commitment to black separatism and economic
self-sufficiency, PME activists argued, "We want a free independent nation
of our own in Africa where we can build our own military [academies] and
such other institutions as we as a nation see fit."[64] Emphasizing distinctions
between some of her political interests and those of civil rights activists,
Gordon criticized efforts to integrate schools and other public spaces.
Although many black activists celebrated the Supreme Court's 1954 decision in *Brown v. Board of Education* to integrate public schools, Gordon
saw the development as a pointless feat: "Suppose we do mix the schools,
don't you still have the race problem? It is a waste of time and many inno-
cent lives [lost] to try to mix the schools."[65] "We have mixed schools in the
North and here in the [Midwest] and it does not help the race issue [one]
bit," she added. Appealing directly to white Americans, Gordon argued,

"We [know] that we are no longer wanted in the United States . . . [therefore] assist us in getting federal aid to send us to all parts of Africa; instead of resorting to bloodshed; as is going on in Alabama, Florida, and Tennessee." Alluding to the Montgomery bus boycott, Gordon maintained, "We [would] rather be in Africa riding in an ox wagon, rather than being in America fighting the White man about his bus."[66] Though her comments were meant to shed light on the limitations of the Civil Rights Movement, they also reflected her image of Africa as a relatively backward place.

Despite the problematic way she defended her commitment to black emigration in this instance, Gordon tried to help others understand the practicality of her proposal. Beyond a utopian ideal of constructing an independent black nation in Africa, Gordon envisioned relocation as a solution to addressing the social ills facing people of African descent during the 1950s. She pointed to an overcrowded job market and housing discrimination as factors that contributed to African Americans' inability to experience upward social mobility: "We are being pushed around worse now than ever due to the displaced persons of Europe being brought into this country. It is impossible to get a place to live with money. There are just no houses for us and something must be done."[67] "All decent houses and jobs are being provided for the white people . . . the white people coming in here from Europe are crowding us out," Gordon added.[68] Therefore, she insisted that relocating to Africa would help lift black people out of the depths of poverty.

More specifically, she imagined finding a wealth of job opportunities on the continent: "We hope to make our own jobs . . . we first want farms to produce our own food. Then we will be able to build any kind of industry that we can get facilities to build."[69] With these goals in mind, she pointedly and passionately asked, "How long shall we have to wait for something to be done for the poor black peoples of this country? We should have been in Africa long ago," she reasoned.[70] While few black Americans disagreed with Gordon's perspectives on the challenges facing people of African descent in the United States, most rejected Gordon's proposed solution to leave the country. Despite Gordon's best efforts, many continued to dismiss her views. By her own account, several mainstream black newspapers refused to publish any of her articles on the issue of emigration.[71]

By the mid-1950s, the prospects of securing federal assistance to relocate to Africa were rapidly disappearing. And as the modern Civil Rights Movement gained increasing momentum, Gordon and her supporters found themselves grasping at straws. Senator Langer's bill, much like Bilbo's, never moved any further than the Senate floor. "The condition of the world is so dark for black people," Gordon painfully observed in 1954, "it is hard to believe that our government will do anything for us. They seem to have forgotten all about the suffering slaves in America."[72] In one instance, she tried to obtain support from the American Colonization Society (ACS), but the organization's leaders were no longer interested in black emigration. Naturally, Gordon grew discouraged, recognizing that her efforts would not yield the immediate and tangible results she desired. At the same time, she maintained a glimmer of hope as she witnessed conditions improving for people of African descent across the globe. In one of the last letters she wrote before her passing, Gordon expressed a profound of sense of joy over victories gained in African liberation struggles: "We are so grateful to [know] there are . . . colonies [in Africa] free now."[73]

If the wave of independence victories on the African continent signaled to black activists that global black liberation was imminent, then it signaled to veteran black nationalists that black emigration was perhaps more likely than ever before. No doubt it was an indication that there were now more options available beyond Liberia as a potential site for black relocation. These new potential sites included Ghana, which became a new prospect for emigration following the nation's independence in March 1957. Indeed, by the late 1950s, Ghana emerged as a symbol of triumph and hope for black men and women everywhere.[74] Liberia, which had long occupied the black nationalist imagination, gradually became less significant for many veteran black nationalists desiring to witness firsthand the unraveling of colonial rule in Africa. In the late 1950s, Benjamin Gibbons, who had been a passionate champion for emigration to Liberia, identified Ghana along with Guinea and Nigeria as new prospects for black relocation.[75] Even Gordon lost the passion for Liberia in the late 1950s, viewing Ghana and other African nations as new viable options.[76]

These changes in perspective underscore how historical developments on the African continent had a profound impact on black Americans' political vision.[77] As individuals like Gordon and Gibbons began to embrace Ghana, so too did a cadre of civil rights activists across the country who saw the appeal of relocating to Africa following Ghana's independence in 1957. During the early 1960s, several well-known black activists and intellectuals, including poet Maya Angelou, W. E. B. and Shirley Du Bois, and writer Julian Mayfield, relocated to the newly independent nation.[78] There, these men and women supported President Kwame Nkrumah's antiracist platform and Pan-Africanist vision of a unified Africa. They also witnessed the process of nation building for one of the first African nations to break free from the grip of European colonialism.[79]

Ruptures and Disruptions

During the 1950s, black women throughout Latin America and the Caribbean were actively engaged in black nationalist politics—promoting racial pride and unity, economic self-sufficiency, and political self-determination. From her base in Jamaica, Maymie De Mena continued to advance the work of the UNIA despite growing fragmentation, scant resources, and limited support from the organization's male leaders. Her efforts coincided with the significant growth of the Rastafarian movement, which had begun in Jamaica in the 1930s. Maintaining the belief that Africans were one of God's chosen people, Rastafarians became increasingly popular during the 1950s and appealed to thousands of black men and women in Jamaica and in other parts of the Caribbean. The core tenets of Rastafarianism—including the emphasis on black pride, African heritage, and Ethiopianism—closely mirrored Garvey's black nationalism and no doubt resonated with the black masses in Jamaica and other parts of the Caribbean.[80] As Rastafarianism and other new expressions of black nationalism dominated black political discourse, De Mena's efforts to revive the UNIA as an organization—to the place of prominence it once had—appeared futile.

Still, the veteran black nationalist leader persisted. Despite failing health, De Mena utilized several strategies and tactics that she hoped might draw new UNIA members in Jamaica and throughout Latin America and the Caribbean. Writing to UNIA President Thomas W. Harvey in 1953, she emphasized her efforts to raise funds specifically for this purpose: "I am back on the warpath for our organization along the Caribbean Seaboard where we once reigned strongly. From Cuba down to Panama and Costa Rica, our membership have all scattered and have gone into all sorts of things . . . I am trying to gather up the threads, and resuscitate the [UNIA] membership."[81] She went on to describe efforts to raise money and her decision to organize mass meetings in various locales to attract new members in areas where the UNIA once boasted a large following.

In her efforts to revive the UNIA, De Mena turned to other veteran black nationalist women for assistance. To that end, she solicited advice

from Amy Jacques Garvey, who was also residing in Kingston.[82] During
the 1950s, Jacques Garvey actively supported De Mena's efforts as she
maintained a busy schedule of her own, raising her teenage sons while
continuing to write for several newspaper outlets, including the South
African newspaper, the *Drum*.[83] In addition to her own writings that
emphasized the core tenets of black nationalism—black pride, African
heritage, Pan-Africanism, black political self-determination, and economic self-sufficiency—Jacques Garvey tirelessly promoted the writings
and teachings of her late husband and even defended them when others
critiqued them.[84] Recognizing De Mena's crucial role in supporting the
UNIA, Jacques Garvey provided support and offered advice when needed.
Other black nationalist women provided support for De Mena during this
period. In 1952, De Mena reached out to U.S.-based activist Ethel Collins
for assistance in reviving local chapters in Kingston. Collins had left the
UNIA during the mid-1940s after a falling out with James Stewart, Garvey's successor in the UNIA, but remained in close communication with
De Mena during the years. In 1952, Collins made a visit to her native
Jamaica, where she delivered speeches before crowds of local residents in
Kingston. According to De Mena, Collins's visit to Jamaica ignited a "new
awakening" in the movement and provided a catalyst for drawing new
members to the organization.[85]

In the months after Collins's departure, De Mena amplified her efforts
to help revive the Garveyite movement in Jamaica. In addition to opening
up a new office on Hanover Street in Kingston in 1952, the seventy-two-
year-old activist spent much of her time speaking to activists in St. Andrew
and other parts of the island. By her own admission, she also attempted to
track down old UNIA members in chapters that were no longer active.
Desiring to do much more, De Mena asked UNIA leaders in the United
States to help her purchase a car to make it easier to travel: "I am compara-
tively invalided and cannot walk very far or stand on the streets waiting for
[buses]. I will have to get some sort of transportation to do this work, and
I am of the opinion that the general Organization could supply a small car
in Jamaica."[86] In reality, the UNIA was in no position to provide a car for
De Mena or offer any amount of financial support. However, De Mena's
request underscores her unwavering commitment to help the movement
despite her failing health.

Although De Mena did not succeed in reviving the UNIA or attracting
scores of new members as she had hoped, her political activities were not

in vain. Indeed, De Mena helped to sustain black nationalist politics during the 1950s—popularizing the ethos of black political self-determination, racial pride, economic self-sufficiency, anticolonialism, and Pan-Africanism. These ideas held broad appeal for black men and women in Jamaica and in other parts of the diaspora—even as UNIA membership varied from locale to locale. Indeed, black freedom fighters deployed black nationalism during this period even if they were unassociated with the UNIA. Many would credit Marcus Garvey, in particular, for shaping their political consciousness. This was certainly the case for Eugenie Bailey, a black woman residing in Havana, Cuba, during the early 1950s. "The sound of Garvey's voice has awaken[ed] me," she acknowledged, "though I never go to sleep."[87] Describing the racial and ethnic tensions in Cuba during this period, Bailey lamented that black laborers on the island were being pushed out of the workforce. "Our service[s] are no longer needed here in Cuba," she explained, "all you can hear is *Cuba por los Cubanos* [Cuba for Cubans]."[88] Her comments, though brief, alluded to the antiblack racism and segregationist practices in Cuba that marginalized people of African descent in the workforce. By evoking Garvey, Bailey underscored the significance and utility of black nationalism as a viable political response— and, indeed, challenge—to white supremacy. Not surprisingly, Bailey emphasized the need to keep these ideas alive in mainstream political discourse.

In October 1953, within a year of Ethel Collins's visit to Kingston, De Mena passed away at the age of seventy-three.[89] She had traveled to the United States only a month earlier for medical treatment when she learned that she had cancer, for which she had received treatment years earlier but had recovered. This time, however, the veteran black nationalist leader succumbed to the disease. The obituary that appeared in the *Daily Gleaner* shortly after her passing captured the spirit and vision of the black nationalist freedom fighter:

The late [Madame De Mena] had rare courage and strength of will. She was identified with causes that needed fighters and nothing deterred her from fighting. . . . She did not, like many reformers, regard social work as a "palliative" something that enabled a crippled society to continue crawling along: it seemed to her an essential function of leadership to bring practical aid to the poor, and she was long amongst the few figures that commanded respect in certain "tough" areas of the city. . . . Her personality will be greatly missed in the island's life.[90]

Writing to William Sherrill, one of the UNIA's leaders based in Detroit, Michigan, Amy Jacques Garvey reinforced these views, noting that "the death of [Madame De Mena] is quite a loss out here." "Please do not make any hasty selection, for her successor," Jacques Garvey advised Sherrill.[91] Further revealing De Mena's legacy and the significance of women leaders in the movement in general, Jacques Garvey advised Sherrill to select a woman to lead the UNIA on the island. "A woman is preferable," Jacques Garvey explained, "as she may not be so much watched politically; but she must be internationally informed, alert, and diplomatic."[92]

Amy Jacques Garvey's desire to find a replacement for De Mena never materialized. Though Jacques Garvey failed to see it at the time, De Mena's death signified the end of one chapter in the movement's history. Within ten years, several key women leaders who had once dominated the black nationalist scene passed away. On August 6, 1956, Ethel M. Collins, the veteran black nationalist woman who had traveled to Jamaica to assist De Mena only a few years prior, died around the age of sixty. On the afternoon of October 14, 1956, members of the Garvey Club gathered together at a memorial service in Harlem to honor Collins's life and memory. Bishop Fred Toote, who had been at the center of the conflict at the UNIA's Sixth International Convention in 1929 in Jamaica, delivered the eulogy.[93]

Four years later, on June 16, 1961, Mittie Maude Lena Gordon died of heart failure at the age of seventy-one. Her husband, Moses Gibson, who she had quietly married after William Gordon passed away in 1948, struggled to provide details of his wife's life—a likely indication that Gordon withheld crucial information from her new spouse. He did not know her actual date of birth or the specific location of her birth. For this reason, her death certificate indicated that she was ten years younger than her actual age and listed the city of her birth as "unknown."[94] Unlike Maymie De Mena, who had been eulogized in Jamaican newspapers after her death, there is no record of a public announcement of Gordon's death in the United States. And oddly enough, it does not appear that the men and women with whom she collaborated in the PME organized any public memorial services or meetings in her honor.

Perhaps at Gordon's instruction before her passing, Gordon's mentee, Alberta Spain, tried to take up Gordon's work, seemingly without much time for mourning. On June 19, 1961, she wrote a short letter to Earnest Sevier Cox alerting him of Gordon's passing without providing much detail on the matter. "The Peace Movement of Ethiopia [is] very sad," she wrote, "[because] our leader, Mrs. M.M.L. Gordon passed away Friday evening at 5 o'clock." After briefly mentioning the date of Gordon's funeral, Spain went on to ask for Cox's help with several initiatives, including their efforts to leave the country. "The Peace Movement members and the Executive Council hopes we will continue to have your cooperation and help in our effort to go to Africa," she explained.[95] Spain's comments reflected her dogmatic political approach—one that closely mirrored her mentor's.

Transitions

The world in which Spain emerged as the PME's de facto leader was unlike the one Gordon had navigated before her passing. Spain's newfound leadership position coincided with a period of radical political transformation in the United States as in other parts of the globe. In 1957, following the successful Montgomery bus boycott, Rev. Martin Luther King Jr. established the Southern Christian Leadership Conference (SCLC), an organization largely made up of African American ministers. Emphasizing the use of nonviolent tactics, SCLC would go on to play a critical role in organizing mass protests in Birmingham and Selma, Alabama, during the 1960s.[96] The year of SCLC's debut, Little Rock, Arkansas, took center stage as President Dwight D. Eisenhower sent troops to enforce the admittance of nine black students into the all-white Central High School. Little Rock would represent only one of many battlegrounds during this period as tensions between the federal government and state governments boiled to the surface.

Within the Civil Rights Movement itself, a strain of black nationalism coupled with armed self-defense efforts arose. Events such as Little Rock reinforced many black activists' belief that armed self-defense was a viable political strategy—necessary for the protection of black communities against racial violence and terror. While not a new political strategy in African American communities, armed self-defense became increasingly popular in black nationalist discourse during this era. Robert F. Williams, leader of the NAACP branch in Monroe, North Carolina, was arguably the most vocal proponent of armed self-defense during the late 1950s.[97] His wife, Mabel Williams, an activist in her own right, also endorsed the tradition of self-defense—a topic she frequently addressed in her writings.[98] She

and her husband embraced black nationalism and maintained an uncom-
promising stance on armed self-defense—a decision that ultimately led to
Robert's dismissal by the national NAACP chapter.[99] In 1961, Mabel and
Robert fled to Cuba, where they ran a popular radio station called "Radio
Free Dixie." Their close associate, Mae Mallory, an activist from Harlem
who was incarcerated in 1961 after she was falsely accused of kidnapping a
white couple in Monroe, demonstrated a commitment to black nationalism. To that end, Mallory also endorsed black political self-determination
and economic self-sufficiency. Significantly, she embraced the view that
black people needed to take up arms to protect themselves from southern
white violence.[100]

These core tenets were also popularized by members of the Louisiana-
based Universal Association of Ethiopian Women (UAEW). Established in
New Orleans in 1957 by Audley "Queen Mother" Moore—a former member
of the UNIA who joined the Communist Party during the 1930s—the UAEW
emerged as a crucial site for black women to advance black nationalist and
internationalist politics.[101] The organization represented the blending of various strands of black nationalism and the convergence of both older and
newer nationalist expressions.[102] Central to the UAEW's platform was an
emphasis on reparations, welfare rights for black women, and providing legal
aid for black men who had been wrongly accused of rape.[103] The organization
drew support from a diverse group of black women activists in Louisiana—
including local activists Dara Abubakari (formerly Virginia Collins), Alma
Dawson, Bessie Phillips, and Moore's younger sisters, Eloise and Loretta.
These women articulated proto-feminism, challenging patriarchy and advocating black women's rights and leadership opportunities. Maintaining an
internationalist vision, UAEW members situated the experiences of black
men and women in the United States within a global context and sought to
forge transnational networks with activists across the diaspora.[104]

In addition to advocating black internationalism, social justice, reparations, and black feminism, the UAEW reflected Moore's black nationalist
politics.[105] In all likelihood, Moore's decision to integrate the words "Universal" and "Ethiopian" in the organization's name was influenced by the
Garvey movement as well as the earlier Ethiopianist movements from
which Garvey drew.[106] Viewing her political work as an extension of Garvey's, Moore framed her discussion about black rights within the discourse
of Pan-Africanism. Moore's UAEW, therefore, emphasized the need to
secure freedom for "Africans everywhere at home and abroad," employing

a phrase that was reminiscent of the Garvey movement.[107] Echoing some of the same goals as earlier black nationalists, Moore vowed that the UAEW would "uplift and inspire the oppressed, secure justice for those denied constitutional rights," and bring awareness to African Americans of their "correct status" as Africans in the United States.[108] By emphasizing the organization's core mission as one that would help African Americans understand their "correct status . . . based on origin and national inspiration," Moore articulated her commitment to the nationalist principles of race pride and African heritage.[109]

As Moore and countless other black men and women in the United States denounced white supremacy and advocated civil and human rights, black activists across the diaspora were also fighting against racism, discrimination, and imperialism. Several years before Moore established the UAEW in the United States, armed militants rose up en masse against British colonial rule in Kenya. Referred to as the "Mau Mau" by British colonialists, these militant fighters denounced years of exploitation and disenfranchisement, including the loss of land and lack of political representation. From 1952 to 1960, "Mau Mau" rebels waged a decisive assault on British colonial forces and white settlers, helping to dismantle colonialism on the African continent.[110] In the neighboring Belgian Congo (now the Democratic Republic of the Congo), tensions were brewing as organizer Patrice Lumumba and other activists in the Congolese National Movement (CNM) began agitating for Pan-African unity and black liberation. In December 1958, Lumumba attended the All-African People's Conference in Accra, Ghana, where he met with a diverse group of black activists and intellectuals, including activist Eslanda Robeson, the wife of singer and civil rights activist Paul Robeson, and Kwame Nkrumah, prime minister of Ghana. At the conference, attendees called for the immediate end of colonialism in Africa.

The liberation of former colonies in Africa inspired and coincided with a new wave of black radical protest—the impact of which could be felt in every corner of the globe. The Cuban Revolution was perhaps the most significant of these developments in Latin America and the Caribbean, representing a triumph in mass political activism. Led by Fidel Castro, the revolution succeeded in toppling U.S.-supported dictator Fulgencio Batista in 1959 with the help of Afro-Cuban fighters and activists. Amid diasporic efforts to challenge imperialism, the Cuban Revolution and the unprecedented transformations that followed—including the elimination of racial segregation policies on the island—served as an inspiration for people of African descent across the globe.[111] Not surprisingly, Cuba became a haven for black activists, including black nationalists Robert and Mabel Williams, escaping racial injustice in the United States.

Amid these key historical developments, Spain and other leaders of the PME attempted to forge ahead in Gordon's absence, maintaining the belief that the organization might still be able to draw new supporters interested in black nationalist and internationalist politics. In the months following Gordon's passing, PME members elected veteran activist Edmond Holiday as the new president—making him the first male activist to lead the organization since its establishment in 1932.[112] It is unclear why Alberta Spain did not assume the position as president general—as Gordon had envisioned. Perhaps she chose not to assume the position or perhaps others in the organization preferred Holiday because he was more senior. It is also likely that members preferred Holiday on account of his sex, reflecting the black nationalist-masculinist tradition, especially during a period in which black charismatic male leaders dominated mainstream media.[113]

Regardless of the circumstances, Spain and Holiday worked closely together during the 1960s—intent on popularizing their collective political vision and broadening their base of support in Chicago and other parts of the country. For Spain, the national struggles over the issue of integration only served to bolster her view that black emigration was absolutely necessary. In 1962, only two years after four black college students in Greensboro, North Carolina, staged a sit-in at a segregated F. W. Woolworth's lunch counter, Spain passionately argued that "there will be no need for segregation" if African Americans relocated to Africa. "The time has come for separation," she explained in a letter addressed to senators across the United States, "for [African Americans] will never live peacefully in the same country [with whites]." Her comments mirrored those of earlier black nationalists—and even white separatists—who justified black emigration on the basis that it would guarantee peace and stability in a nation divided along racial lines. Reinforcing her black nationalist vision, Spain went on to argue that "the [black] race is tired of being pushed around and they want to develop their own culture built for themselves that they can be proud of."[114] Similar to Gordon, Spain's writings reflected her skepticism toward civil rights gains in the United States. Indeed, Spain saw the wave of sit-ins and other developments across the country as evidence that the idea of black emigration to Africa was just as relevant in the 1960s as it was in years prior.

During this period, Spain and her colleagues in the PME attempted to broaden their base of support by reaching out to other black nationalist organizations in Chicago and other parts of the country. They first made efforts to collaborate with Benjamin Gibbons and the UANM, but the organization had dissolved after Gibbons suffered a debilitating stroke in 1962.[115] As new expressions of black nationalism reverberated across the nation and other parts of the diaspora, Spain and Holiday began to reach out to new allies, including members of the Nation of Islam (NOI). Established in Detroit in 1930 by street peddler Wallace D. Fard, the NOI encouraged followers to embrace an alternative religious racial identity. Promoting a syncretic version of Islam, Fard instructed black residents to abandon Christianity for a more "authentic" religious practice. By the 1960s, the religious organization was one of the leading black nationalist groups in the nation. Under the leadership of Elijah Muhammad, who assumed control of the NOI after Fard mysteriously disappeared, the organization denounced white people as "devils" and emphasized black pride and racial separatism.[116]

During the 1960s, the NOI became one of the most popular and influential black nationalist organizations of the period. Its rapid growth was largely attributed to Malcolm X, a follower of Muhammad, who became the national spokesman of the NOI. Born Malcolm Little in 1925, Malcolm X grew up in a Garveyite household in Michigan. His parents had been active in the Garvey movement, laying the ideological foundations for Malcolm's turn to black nationalism and internationalism later in life. Malcom's mother, Louise Little—who had joined the UNIA in Montreal, Canada, and went on to serve as an organizer in the local UNIA chapter in Omaha, Nebraska—played a significant role in shaping her son's political ideas even at a young age.[117] After Malcolm's father, Earl Little, was murdered by local Klansmen, Louise struggled to care for her son while dealing with the trauma of her husband's tragic death. After being imprisoned for robbery, Malcolm converted to the Nation of Islam in 1948, marking a turning point in his life. Following his release, Malcolm became Muhammad's protégé, working as a local NOI minister in Harlem.

Like the PME, leaders in the NOI endorsed the core tenets of black nationalism, including racial pride, political self-determination, and economic self-sufficiency. Muhammad, Malcolm X, and other NOI leaders embraced the idea of racial separatism, but their vision was more conservative than the PME leaders' views on the issue. While Spain, Holiday, and other PME leaders continued to advocate black emigration to West Africa, NOI leaders called for the establishment of separate black communities within the United States. Reminiscent of earlier black nationalists, including Marcus Garvey and Mittie Maude Lena Gordon, Muhammad envisioned racial separatism as a viable response to racism and racial violence in the United States: "Since we cannot get along with [whites] in peace and equality after giving them 400 years of our sweat and blood . . . we believe our contributions to this land and the suffering forced upon us by white America justifies our demand for complete separation in a state or territory of our own." [118]

Like Gordon and many other black nationalists before her, Muhammad insisted that the U.S. government was responsible for advancing these efforts as reparations for past exploitation. "The former slave-masters are obligated to provide such land and that the area must be fertile and minerally rich," he argued. "We believe that our former slave masters are obligated to maintain and supply our needs in this separate territory," he continued, "until we are able to produce and supply our own needs." [119] Reiterating Muhammad's message, Malcolm X also endorsed territorial separatism, arguing in a 1963 speech that the U.S. government needed to provide "some states" and "everything we need to start our own independent civilization." "It's time to get a divorce and we want a property settlement," Malcolm passionately argued before a crowd of an estimated four thousand black people in Harlem. [120]

This message resonated with many black men and women across the country, including those who were not directly affiliated with the NOI. Certainly, the idea of racial separatism—whether black emigration to West Africa or the establishment of separate communities in the United States—had deep roots in black political discourse. Amid the political upheavals of the period, Muhammad's ideas held sway in black communities—especially among the black working class. In July 1962, Muhammad spoke before an estimated three hundred people in Chicago in which he reinforced his position on territorial separatism. By one account, the black nationalist leader argued that he was not opposed to going to Africa but would only do so if they were unable to create a separate community for black people in the United States. The very reference to Africa caught the attention of PME leaders and some of their political allies, including Earnest Sevier Cox, who sent a note to Spain inquiring as to whether or not she had reached out to the black nationalist religious leader. Cox emphasized the fact that Muhammad would make a good ally for PME leaders not only because of his mutual stance on black separatism but also because of the widespread popularity of the NOI.[121]

Spain's reply to Cox revealed her enthusiasm for collaborating with the NOI—a strategy that marked a departure from Gordon's approach. During her lifetime, Gordon had resisted efforts to collaborate with the NOI, arguing that they were not authentic black nationalists on account of their religious rituals and practices.[122] For Gordon, the distinctions between the PME and the NOI seemed to be more salient than the similar platforms of both groups. In Gordon's absence, however, the new PME leaders attempted to forge an alliance with Elijah Muhammad on the basis of their mutual interests in racial separatism and black political determination. In a letter to Cox, Spain expressed her optimism that the NOI leader "with all his thousands that follow him" would join forces with the PME to help advance a bill that would provide funding for black relocation to West Africa.[123] To that end, she and other PME leaders sent letters to Muhammad and even asked Cox to do the same. "I hope you can make him understand that unity in this program . . . is strength," she explained.[124] There is no evidence to suggest that Elijah Muhammad or any other leader in the NOI responded or even entertained the PME's request to collaborate. However, Spain's attempt to forge this alliance symbolizes the intellectual links between earlier black nationalist groups and new formations. Even when individual efforts to collaborate failed to materialize, ideas connected black activists during an era of significant political transformation.

* * *

The surge of black nationalist activity in the United States during the mid-1960s coincided with the gradual demise of the PME. In 1965, Alberta Spain launched another letter-writing campaign in an attempt to secure support for a new emigration bill. Reminiscent of Gordon's earlier activities, Spain sent out copies to U.S. senators with a detailed explanation as to why emigration was the best response for African Americans in the face of segregation and racial violence and terror. "We are tired of being pushed around, segregated and what not," Spain argued. "We want to develop our own culture, and live in a nation built by black men, for we are proud of our ancestry."[125]

Although Spain sent copies of the letters to U.S. senators across the country, they received little coverage in the mainstream media. While

black-owned newspapers across the country largely ignored the PME—
focusing instead on more popular black nationalist groups—the PME
received some coverage in Southern white newspapers during the 1960s. In
1963, the *Richmond Times-Dispatch* featured an article on the "Back to
Africa" movement, highlighting the efforts of Alberta Spain in the PME.
Including several direct quotes from Spain's letter to the newspaper, the
editors provided a sweeping overview of black emigrationist movements in
the United States and took a neutral approach to the issue. "Should they be
given an opportunity to emigrate to Africa?" the editors asked. "It is an
interesting sociological question," they concluded.[126] In September 1965,
the *State* newspaper in Columbia, South Carolina, included a full-page
story on black nationalist efforts to relocate to West Africa, highlighting the
work of the PME.[127] Clearly sympathetic to the group's cause, the editors
credited the PME for reviving an issue that had long fallen out of favor in
mainstream political discourse and recounted PME leaders' efforts to pass
several bills over the years. Although they acknowledged that most black
activists would not "show much interest in any resettlement program," the
editors insisted that the PME should forge ahead with their plans. "If there
are, in fact, American Negroes who have the capacity, the desire, and the
racial pride to work towards establishing a homeland in Africa, then the
United States government should look carefully into the matter." "After
all," they concluded, "Uncle Sam is spending millions of dollars in far less-
worthy projects with far less prospect of materially aiding in a solution of
the racial problem."[128]

Despite the backing of these newspapers, the PME could not sustain
widespread interest in light of the political transformations taking place
nationally and internationally. The focus on black emigration and continued efforts to seek federal aid to advance these efforts found little appeal
among a new generation of black activists caught up in the wave of black
radical internationalism of the period. Not surprisingly, the PME lost many
of its members during the mid-1960s as they found themselves on the margins of the Civil Rights–Black Power era. The passing of Earnest Sevier Cox
in 1966 also dealt a severe blow to the organization's leaders, who lost one
of their most avid (if controversial) supporters and political allies. Inter-
nally, the organization also underwent more leadership changes. Although
the details remain unclear, Spain vanished from extant organization
records—perhaps an indication that she parted ways with the PME. A. B.
Baker, an activist who had been a member of the organization in Chicago

FIGURE 16. Amy Jacques Garvey with Minister Edward Seaga, Eustace Whyte, and Martin Luther King Jr. at Marcus Garvey Shrine. *The Gleaner*, June 1965. Universal Negro Improvement Association Records, Box 19, Folder 6, 1916, 1921–1989, Stuart A. Rose Manuscript, Archives & Rare Book Library, Emory University.

since the 1930s, emerged as the new president general. Under his leadership, the PME continued to hold meetings on Sunday evenings in Chicago until the 1970s.[129] While much smaller in size than in prior years, the organization continued to be a platform from which local activists could engage in black nationalist and internationalist politics. Baker's writings during this period underscore the same ideals Gordon had emphasized in the organization's founding meeting in Chicago in 1932—a commitment to universal black liberation, racial pride, black internationalism, political self-determination, and economic self-sufficiency.

All of these ideas provided the ideological bedrock for a range of new black nationalist organizations established during the 1960s and 1970s. A new generation of black nationalists would not only find appeal in earlier organizations like the UNIA, but in turn, these younger activists would help to renew public interest in these earlier movements.[130] Not surprisingly, Amy Jacques Garvey would be at the center of these discussions, using her writings during this period to draw the links between Garveyism and Black Power. Her 1966 article, "The Source and Course of Black Power in the United States," which appeared in the Jamaican *Star* newspaper, set out to explain the theoretical foundations upon which new expressions of black nationalism were built.[131] "[Garvey] paved the way for all local leaders who have emerged since his death," she argued. "Most of them," she continued, "were his under-studies or followers, who were inspired by his dynamic leadership, and the universality of his appeal for justice, equality and independence for the Negro peoples of the world." After recounting her late husband's efforts, Jacques Garvey briefly mentioned Mittie Maude Lena Gordon's political work as evidence of her late husband's influence. By framing Gordon's political ideas and praxis as solely an extension of Garveyism, Jacques Garvey overlooked the profound complexity of a movement that built on yet also expanded far beyond Garvey's teachings.

Yet Jacques Garvey's essay included an even more glaring omission: it failed to acknowledge the significant part that she and other black women had played in sustaining black nationalist politics. Absent from Jacques Garvey's essay was a discussion of black women who, regardless of their organizational affiliation, had played a fundamental role in shaping black nationalist movements and discourses in the absence of Garvey's dominant presence. In an effort to defend her late husband's ideas and underscore the relevance of Garveyism during the era of Black Power, Jacques Garvey had, in effect, replicated masculinist narratives of black nationalism that had long dominated public discourse. The essay's deficiencies, however, could never overshadow the robust historical record, filled with the stories—some triumphant, some tragic—of how black nationalist women during the twentieth century vigorously fought to eradicate global white supremacy.

Epilogue

꒰

IN 1951, EARNEST SEVIER COX, the white supremacist from Virginia who had collaborated with the Peace Movement of Ethiopia (PME) for decades, wrote a letter to Mittie Maude Lena Gordon, the PME's founder, to assure her that her political work was not in vain. Cox's letter, which arrived on Gordon's desk ten years before her passing, offered words of encouragement during a period in which Gordon lamented her inability to yield any tangible results. Almost twenty years after establishing the PME, she was no step closer to realizing any of her political goals. According to Gordon, many of her supporters had "become disgusted" because of her failed attempts to secure funding for relocation to West Africa—a significant step that she believed was necessary to bolster black political and economic power.[1] Encouraging Gordon to look beyond her current realities, Cox praised the black nationalist leader for the "great service you have done for [your] race and country." "The giant petition prepared by you and your co-workers of the [PME]," he concluded, "will be discussed by the historians of the future."[2] In some ways, he was right. It was, in fact, the giant emigration petition that first piqued this historian's interest in Gordon and the other like-minded black activists who passionately supported it during the turbulent years of the Great Depression.

Yet the significance of the petition extends far beyond the actual document itself. For many, the petition tells a story of a failed political movement—an unsuccessful effort by a group of black activists to relocate to West Africa. What few historians have considered, however, is the meaning of the petition for the hundreds of thousands of black men and women who enthusiastically signed their names. Even fewer have considered the

central role black women played in order to make the petition possible—
with limited economic resources during a tumultuous period of U.S. and
global history. In its pages, the PME's massive emigration petition with an
estimated 400,000 names holds a complex and complicated story about
social justice, black politics, citizenship, identity, and national belonging. It
tells a story of the global black freedom *struggle*—filled with moments of
triumph and hope yet also filled with pain and disappointment, missteps
and errors in judgment, and human foibles and imperfections. It tells a
story of how a vanguard of black nationalist women fought to eradicate the
global color line.

During the Great Depression, World War II, and the early Cold War
years, Mittie Maude Lena Gordon, Amy Ashwood Garvey, Ethel Waddell,
Maymie De Mena, Amy Jacques Garvey, and other black women leaders
dominated the black nationalist scene. These women, from various socioeconomic backgrounds and in various locales, were united in their political view
that people of African descent constituted a separate group on the basis of
their distinct culture, shared history, and experiences.[3] They agitated for the
rights and dignity of black men and women in the diaspora, endorsing Pan-
African unity, anticolonialism, racial separatism, black pride, political self-
determination, and economic self-sufficiency. In the absence of a strong and
centralized Universal Negro Improvement Association (UNIA) and Marcus
Garvey's domineering presence, these women engaged in black nationalist
politics through new, innovative, idiosyncratic, and more creative ways. They
employed a range of protest strategies and tactics, drew on numerous religious and political ideologies, and forged alliances with a diverse group of
men and women, crossing racial and ethnic, socioeconomic, geographic, and
even political lines. Despite their best efforts, however, the women featured
in this book did not live to witness the goals they hoped to attain. But long
after they were gone, the ideas they promoted and the ideals for which they
were fighting persisted. Indeed, new generations of black activists would take
up the mantle of the women in this book, often unaware of these women's
courageous—if complex—stories.

Developments taking place in Chicago, where Gordon once dominated
the black political scene, underscore the continuum of nationalist and
internationalist thought and praxis in black political movements. During
the 1960s and 1970s, local black activists, including some who had been
inspired by Gordon's PME, worked to popularize black nationalist and
internationalist politics in the city. For example, A. B. Baker, a local activist

who had joined the PME under Gordon's leadership, continued to hold weekly PME meetings in the city in an effort to advance many of the unfulfilled goals of the organization. Through his weekly column in the *New Crusader*, a newspaper published in Chicago, Baker promoted black emigration, universal black liberation, Pan-African unity, economic self-sufficiency, and self-determination. Perhaps unbeknown to Baker, federal officials were closely monitoring his activities when they caught wind of the popularity of his weekly column.

While A. B. Baker worked under the auspices of the PME, other black activists in the city were attempting to advance black nationalist and internationalist politics through various groups—old and new. In the late 1960s, a cadre of black nationalists in Chicago, including UNIA leaders James A. Bennett and Elinor White, continued to push for black emigration to West Africa.[4] White, with the assistance of Jean Slappy, a Garveyite based in Philadelphia, provided assistance to Rev. Clarence W. Harding Jr., a UNIA official from Chicago who spearheaded the organization's activities in Monrovia, Liberia.[5] During this period, a younger generation of black nationalists found a space in various new groups in which to advance their political goals. For example, a chapter of the Black Panther Party (BPP) emerged in Chicago in 1968 under the leadership of Fred Hampton.[6] Originally established by college students Huey P. Newton and Bobby Seale in Oakland, California, in 1966, the BPP was the largest black revolutionary organization of the period.[7] During the late 1960s, thousands of young black men and women joined the BPP, dedicating their lives to protecting black communities and combating police brutality. While the BPP was by no means identical to groups like the PME or UNIA, their political goals certainly mirrored those of earlier black nationalists and internationalists. Similar to the PME and the UNIA (which both had militia units), the BPP advocated for armed resistance as a viable response to racial oppression. And like earlier groups like the PME and the UNIA, the BPP provided a platform for black activists to agitate for universal liberation, economic power, community control, and political self-determination.

In this way, the passing of influential women leaders like Mittie Maude Lena Gordon, Ethel Waddell, and Amy Ashwood certainly could not squelch the powerful ideas that undergirded their political activism during their lifetime. Through organizations like the BPP, black nationalist and internationalist ideas remained salient in public discourse during the twentieth century. Far beyond political ideas and strategies, however, the black

women profiled in this book left behind a spirit of hope. Indeed, these
women dared to dream of a better future and sought to "set the world on
fire"—to eradicate global white supremacy and to (re)awaken the political
consciousness of black men and women in the United States and across the
African diaspora. They did not accomplish all of their political goals, and
in fact, some of their actions, in hindsight, undermined the same goals they
fought so vigorously to achieve. But the "freedom dreams" they envisioned
propelled them to create new spaces and opportunities for people of color
to openly confront racial and sexual discrimination and assert their political
agency.[8] In so doing, these women left an indelible mark on the lives of
countless black men and women in the United States and across the globe.
No doubt they will inspire generations of activists for many years to come.

NOTES

࿐

Introduction

1. Tony Martin, *Race First: The Ideological and Organizational Struggles of Marcus Garvey and the Universal Negro Improvement Association* (Dover, Mass.: Majority Press, 1976); Adam Ewing, *The Age of Garvey: How a Jamaican Activist Created a Mass Movement and Changed Global Black Politics* (Princeton, N.J.: Princeton University Press, 2014).

2. Peace Movement of Ethiopia, *One God, One Country, One People; also, a Brief History, Memorial to President, Funeral Oration and Burial Ceremonies, Battle Hymn of the Peace Movement* (United States: s.n., 1941), 14 [Peace Movement of Ethiopia Constitution].

3. Peace Movement of Ethiopia Constitution; Gunnar Myrdal, *An American Dilemma: The Negro Problem and Modern Democracy* (New York: Harper & Row, 2009; orig. ed., 1944), 813; Michael Fitzgerald, "'We Have Found a Moses': Theodore Bilbo, Black Nationalism, and the Greater Liberia Bill of 1939," *Journal of Southern History* 63 (1997): 293–320; Ethel Wolfskill Hedlin, "Earnest Cox and Colonization: A White Racist's Response to Black Repatriation, 1923–1966" (Ph.D. diss., Duke University, 1974).

4. Michael O. West, "'Like a River': The Million Man March and the Black Nationalist Tradition in the United States," *Journal of Historical Sociology* 12, no. 1 (March 1999): 81–100; Wilson Jeremiah Moses, *The Golden Age of Black Nationalism* (New York: Oxford University Press, 1978).

5. Moses, *The Golden Age of Black Nationalism*.

6. Moses, *The Golden Age of Black Nationalism*; Essien Udosen Essien-Udom, *Black Nationalism: A Search for an Identity in America* (New York: Dell, 1964); William L. Van Deburg, *Modern Black Nationalism* (New York: New York University Press, 1997); Alphonso Pinkney, *Red, Black, and Green: Black Nationalism in the United States* (New York: Cambridge University Press, 1976); John T. McCartney, *Black Power Ideologies: An Essay in African-American Political Thought* (Philadelphia: Temple University Press, 1992).

7. Douglass Flamming, *Bound for Freedom: Black Los Angeles in Jim Crow America* (Berkeley: University of California Press, 2005), 193.

8. Joe William Trotter Jr., *From a Raw Deal to a New Deal? African Americans, 1929–1945* (New York: Oxford University Press, 1996); Harvard Sitkoff, *A New Deal for Blacks: The Emergence of Civil Rights as a National Issue* (New York: Oxford University Press, 1978), 34–35.

9. Carol Anderson, *Eyes Off the Prize: The United Nations, and the African American Struggle for Human Rights, 1944–1955* (Cambridge: Cambridge University Press, 2003); Penny Von

Eschen, *Race Against Empire: Black Americans and Anticolonialism, 1937–1957* (Ithaca, N.Y.: Cornell University Press, 1997); Thomas Borstelmann, *The Cold War and the Color Line: American Race Relations in the Global Arena* (Cambridge, Mass.: Harvard University Press, 2001); Kate A. Baldwin, *Beyond the Color Line and the Iron Curtain: Reading Encounters Between Black and Red, 1922–1963* (Durham, N.C.: Duke University Press, 2002).

10. Hilary Beckles and Verene Shepherd, eds., *Caribbean Freedom: Economy and Society from Emancipation to the Present* (Kingston: Ian Randle, 1993).

11. Paul Kramer, *The Blood of Government: Race, Empire, the United States and the Philippines* (Chapel Hill: University of North Carolina Press, 2006); Michael Hunt, *The American Ascendancy: How the United States Gained and Wielded Global Dominance* (Chapel Hill: University of North Carolina Press, 2009); Mary Renda, *Taking Haiti: Military Occupation and the Culture of U.S. Imperialism, 1915–1940* (Chapel Hill: University of North Carolina Press, 2001); Julie Greene, *The Canal Builders: Making America's Empire at the Panama Canal* (New York: Penguin, 2009).

12. Dennis Merrill, *Negotiating Paradise: U.S. Tourism and Empire in Twentieth Century Latin America* (Chapel Hill: University of North Carolina Press, 2009), 1.

13. West, "Like a River"; Moses, *The Golden Age of Black Nationalism*; Essein-Udom, *Black Nationalism*; Theodore Draper, *The Rediscovery of Black Nationalism* (New York: Viking, 1970); Harold Cruse, *The Crisis of the Negro Intellectual* (New York: Morrow, 1967); Pinkney, *Red, Black, and Green*; Rodney Carlisle, *The Roots of Black Nationalism* (Port Washington, N.Y.: Kennikat, 1975); John H. Bracey Jr., August Meier, and Elliot Rudwick, *Black Nationalism in America* (New York: Bobbs-Merrill, 1970); Nikhil Singh, *Black Is a Country: Race and the Unfinished Struggle for Democracy* (Cambridge, Mass.: Harvard University Press, 2004).

14. Kari Palonen, "Four Times of Politics: Policy, Polity, Politicking, and Politicization," *Alternatives: Global, Local, Political* 28, no. 2 (2003): 171–86.

15. Ewing, *The Age of Garvey*; Erik S. McDuffie, "Chicago, Garveyism, and the History of the Diasporic Midwest," *African and Black Diaspora: An International Journal* 8, no. 2 (2015): 1–17; Daniel Dalrymple, "Reclaiming the Fallen: The Universal Negro Improvement Association Central Division, New York, 1935–1942," *Journal of Black Studies* 45, no. 1 (2013): 19–36; Asia Leeds, "Toward the 'Higher Type of Womanhood': The Gendered Contours of Garveyism and the Making of Redemptive Geographies in Costa Rica, 1922–1941," *Palimpsest: A Journal on Women, Gender, and the Black International* 2, no. 1 (2013): 1–27.

16. Carole Boyce Davies, *Left of Karl Marx: The Political Life of Black Communist Claudia Jones* (Durham, N.C.: Duke University Press, 2007); Erik S. McDuffie, " 'I Wanted a Communist Philosophy, but I Wanted Us to Have a Chance to Organize Our People': The Diasporic Radicalism of Queen Mother Audley Moore and the Origins of Black Power," *African and Black Diaspora: An International Journal* 3, no. 2 (2010): 181–95; McDuffie, *Sojourning for Freedom: Black Women, American Communism, and the Making of Black Left Feminism* (Durham, N.C.: Duke University Press, 2011); Dayo F. Gore, *Radicalism at the Crossroads: African American Women Activists in the Cold War* (New York: New York University Press, 2011); Gregg Andrews, *Thyra J. Edwards: Black Activist in the Global Freedom Struggle* (Columbia: University of Missouri, 2011); LaShawn Harris, "Running with the Reds: African American Women and the Communist Party During the Great Depression," *Journal of African American History* 94, no. 1 (2009): 21–43.

17. Craig Calhoun, *The Roots of Radicalism: Tradition, The Public Sphere, and Early Nineteenth-Century Social Movements* (Chicago: University of Chicago Press, 2012), 4.

18. Michael O. West, William G. Martin, and Fanon Che Wilkins, eds., *From Toussaint to Tupac: The Black International Since the Age of Revolution* (Chapel Hill: University of North Carolina Press, 2009), xi.

19. James Meriwether, *Proudly We Can Be Africans: Black Americans and Africa, 1935–1961* (Chapel Hill: University of North Carolina Press, 2002); Brent Hayes Edwards, *The Practice of*

Diaspora: Literature, Translation, and the Rise of Black Internationalism (Cambridge, Mass.: Harvard University Press, 2003); West, Martin, and Wilkins, *From Toussaint to Tupac*; Minkah Makalani, *In the Cause of Freedom: Radical Black Internationalism from Harlem to London, 1917–1939* (Chapel Hill: University of North Carolina, 2011).

20. Joy James, *Shadowboxing: Representations of Black Feminist Politics* (New York: St. Martin's, 1991), 41.

21. Ula Y. Taylor, *The Veiled Garvey: The Life and Times of Amy Jacques Garvey* (Chapel Hill: University of North Carolina Press, 2002), 2; Ula Y. Taylor, "'Negro Women Are Great Thinkers as Well as Doers': Amy Jacques-Garvey and Community Feminism, 1924–1927," *Journal of Women's History* 12, no. 2 (Summer 2000): 104–26.

22. Linda Gordon, "What's New in Women's History," in *Feminist Studies, Critical Studies*, ed. Theresa de Lauretis (Bloomington: Indiana University Press, 1986), 29.

23. Joy James, *Seeking the Beloved Community: A Feminist Race Reader* (Albany: State University of New York Press, 2013), 41.

24. See Deniz Kandiyoti, "Nationalism and Its Discontents: Women and the Nation," *Dossier* 26, no. 45 (October 2004): 45–58.

25. On the discourse of manliness, manhood, and masculinity, see Gail Bederman, *Manliness and Civilization: A Cultural History of Gender and Race in the United States, 1880–1917* (Chicago: University of Chicago Press, 1995); Martin Anthony Summers, *Manliness and Its Discontents: The Black Middle Class and the Transformation of Masculinity, 1900–1930* (Chapel Hill: University of North Carolina Press, 2004); Michelle Ann Stephens, *Black Empire: The Masculine Global Imaginary of Caribbean Intellectuals in the United States, 1914–1962* (Durham, N.C.: Duke University Press, 2005). On black nationalism and masculinism, see E. Frances White, "Africa on My Mind: Gender, Counter Discourse and African-American Nationalism," *Journal of Women's History* 2, no. 1 (1990): 73–97.

26. bell hooks, *Feminist Theory: From the Margin to the Center* (Cambridge, Mass.: South End Press, 2000).

27. W. E. B. Du Bois, *Souls of Black Folk* (New York: Dover, 1994); Manning Marable and Vanessa Agard-Jones, eds., *Transnational Blackness: Navigating the Global Color Line* (New York: Palgrave Macmillan, 2008).

Chapter 1

1. Eunice Lewis, "The Black Woman's Part in Race Leadership," *Negro World*, April 19, 1924. On the "New Negro Woman," see Deborah Gray White, *Too Heavy a Load: Black Women in Defense of Themselves, 1894–1994* (New York: W. W. Norton, 1999), chap. 4; Erin D. Chapman, *Prove It on Me: New Negroes, Sex, and Popular Culture in the 1920s* (Oxford: Oxford University Press, 2012).

2. Nathan Irvin Huggins, *Harlem Renaissance* (London: Oxford University Press, 1971); David Levering Lewis, *When Harlem Was in Vogue* (New York: Penguin, 1979); Houston A. Baker, *Modernism and the Harlem Renaissance* (Chicago: University of Chicago Press, 1987); Davarian L. Baldwin, *Chicago's New Negroes: Modernity, the Great Migration, and Black Urban Life* (Chapel Hill: University of North Carolina Press, 2007); Davarian L. Baldwin and Minkah Makalani, eds., *Escape from New York: The New Negro Renaissance Beyond Harlem* (Minneapolis: University of Minnesota Press, 2013).

3. E. Frances White, "Africa on My Mind: Gender, Counter Discourse and African-American Nationalism," *Journal of Women's History* 2 (1990): 76–97.

4. Martin Anthony Summers, *Manliness and Its Discontents: The Black Middle Class and the Transformation of Masculinity, 1900–1930* (Chapel Hill: University of North Carolina Press, 2004), 8, 26. On the discourse of "manliness and civilization" and its relationship to imperialism,

see Gail Bederman, *Manliness and Civilization: A Cultural History of Gender and Race in the United States, 1880–1917* (Chicago: University of Chicago Press, 1995).

5. Barbara Bair, "True Women, Real Men: Gender, Ideology and Social Roles in the Garvey Movement," in *Gendered Domains: Rethinking Public and Private in Women's History*, ed. Dorothy O. Helly and Susan M. Reverby (Ithaca, N.Y.: Cornell University Press, 1992); Beryl Satter, "Marcus Garvey, Father Divine and the Gender Politics of Race Difference and Race Neutrality," *American Quarterly* 48, no. 1 (March 1996): 43–76; Asia Leeds, "Toward the 'Higher Type of Womanhood': The Gendered Contours of Garveyism and the Making of Redemptive Geographies in Costa Rica, 1922–1941," *Palimpsest: A Journal on Women, Gender, and the Black International* 2, no. 1 (2013): 1–27.

6. Joy James, *Shadowboxing: Representations of Black Feminist Politics* (New York: St. Martin's, 1991), 41.

7. Theodore Vincent, *Black Power and the Garvey Movement* (San Francisco: Rampart, 1972); Adriane Lentz-Smith, *Freedom Struggles: African Americans and World War I* (Cambridge: Harvard University Press, 2009); Chad Williams, *Torchbearers of Democracy: African American Soldiers in the World War I Era* (Chapel Hill: University of North Carolina Press, 2010).

8. Winston James, *Holding Aloft the Banner of Ethiopia: Caribbean Radicalism in Early Twentieth-Century America* (New York: Verso, 1998), 50–91.

9. Martin, *Race First*; Vincent, *Black Power and the Garvey Movement*; Rod Bush, *We Are Not What We Seem: Black Nationalism and Class Struggle in the American Century* (New York: New York University Press, 1998). On UNIA membership, see Martin, *Race First*, 11–12, 14.

10. Erez Manela, *A Wilsonian Moment: Self-Determination and the International Origins of Anticolonial Nationalism* (New York: Oxford University Press, 2007).

11. Martin, *Race First*; Amy Jacques Garvey and Marcus Garvey, eds., *The Philosophy and Opinions of Marcus Garvey or, Africa for the Africans* (Dover, Mass.: Majority Press, 1986); Colin Grant, *Negro with a Hat: The Rise and Fall of Marcus Garvey* (Oxford: Oxford University Press, 2008); Adam Ewing, *The Age of Garvey: How a Jamaican Activist Created a Mass Movement and Changed Global Black Politics* (Princeton, N.J.: Princeton University Press, 2014).

12. Robert A. Hill, *Marcus Garvey and the Universal Negro Improvement Association Papers* (Berkeley: University of California Press, 1983), I:5.

13. Beckles and Shepherd, *Caribbean Freedom*; Thomas Holt, *The Problem of Freedom: Race, Labor, and Politics in Jamaica and Britain, 1832–1938* (Baltimore: Johns Hopkins University Press, 1992).

14. Amy Ashwood, "The Birth of the Universal Negro Improvement Association," in *The Pan-African Connection: From Slavery to Garvey and Beyond*, ed. Tony Martin (Dover, Mass.: Majority Press, 1983), 223.

15. Quoted in Nadia Swaby, "Woman Radical, Woman Intellectual, Woman Activist: The Political Life of Pan-African Feminist Amy Ashwood Garvey" (M.A. thesis, Sarah Lawrence College, 2011), 15.

16. Ashwood, "The Birth of the Universal Negro Improvement Association," 221.

17. Grant, *Negro with a Hat*, 49.

18. Ashwood, "The Birth of the Universal Negro Improvement Association," 225.

19. Lionel Yard argues that Ashwood was cofounder of the UNIA while historian Tony Martin insists that Ashwood's account was "probably fictional." See Lionel Yard, *Biography of Amy Ashwood, 1897–1969: Co-founder of the Universal Negro Improvement Association* (Washington, D.C.: Associated Publisher, 1990); Tony Martin, *Amy Ashwood Garvey: Pan-Africanist, Feminist and Mrs. Garvey Number 1* (Dover, Mass.: Majority Press, 2008), 2.

20. See Yard, *Biography of Amy Ashwood*.

21. Martin, *Amy Ashwood Garvey*, 37.

22. Ula Taylor, "Street Strollers: Grounding the Theory of Black Women Intellectuals," *Afro-Americans in New York Life and History* 30, no. 2 (July 2006): 153–71. For an excellent overview

of black women's intellectual history, see Mia Bay, Farah J. Griffin, Martha S. Jones, and Barbara D. Savage, ed., *Toward an Intellectual History of Black Women* (Chapel Hill: University of North Carolina Press, 2015).

23. Hill, *Marcus Garvey and the UNIA Papers*, XI:115.

24. Taylor, "Street Strollers," 159.

25. Taylor, "Street Strollers," 158; Taylor, *The Veiled Garvey*, 44. Bair, "True Women, Real Men"; Satter, "Marcus Garvey, Father Divine," 43–76; Honor Ford-Smith, "Women and the Garvey Movement in Jamaica," in *Garvey: His Work and Impact*, ed. Rupert Lewis and Patrick Bryan (Trenton, N.J.: Africa World Press, 1991).

26. On respectability, see Evelyn Brooks-Higginbotham, *Righteous Discontent: The Women's Movement in the Black Baptist Church, 1880–1920* (Cambridge, Mass.: Harvard University Press, 1993); Victoria Wolcott, *Remaking Respectability: African American Women in Interwar Detroit* (Chapel Hill: University of North Carolina, 2001); Cheryl Hicks, *Talk with You Like a Woman: African American Women, Justice, and Reform in New York, 1890–1935* (Chapel Hill: University of North Carolina Press, 2010).

27. Martin, *Amy Ashwood Garvey*, 74; Marc Matera, *Black London: The Imperial Metropolis and Decolonization in the Twentieth Century* (Berkeley: University of California Press, 2014), 100–144.

28. Matera, *Black London*, 28–29, 105–7; Hakim Adi, "Amy Ashwood and the Nigerian Progress Union," in *Gendering the African Diaspora: Women, Culture, and Historical Change in the Caribbean and Nigerian Hinterland*, ed. Judith A. Byfield, LaRay Denzer, and Antea Morrison (Bloomington: Indiana University Press, 2010).

29. Martin, *Race First*, 15–16.

30. McDuffie, "'I Wanted a Communist Philosophy,'" 184.

31. Queen Mother Moore, "The Black Scholar Interviews: Queen Mother Moore," *Black Scholar* 4, nos. 6–7 (March–April 1973): 47–55. Moore recounts this story on various occasions and offers slightly altered versions. See Brian Lanker, *I Dream a World: Portraits of Black Women Who Changed America* (New York: Stewart, Tabori and Chang, 1989), 106–7; Cheryl Townsend Gilkes, "Interview with Audley (Queen Mother) Moore," in *The Black Women Oral History Project*, ed. Ruth Edmonds Hill (London: Meckler, 1991), 8:111–201.

32. Moore, "The Black Scholar Interviews," 52. Jahi Issa's study indicates that Marcus Garvey visited Louisiana in 1922, not in 1920, as Moore recalled. See Issa, "The Universal Negro Improvement Association in Louisiana: Creating a Provisional Government in Exile" (Ph.D. diss., Howard University, 2005), 122.

33. Dionne Brand, ed., *No Burden to Carry: Narratives of Black Working Women in Ontario, 1920s to 1950s* (Toronto: Women's Press, 1991), 37–50.

34. Brand, *No Burden to Carry*, 40–41, 44.

35. "Mrs. Lucy Lastrappe's History," *New Negro World*, October 1942.

36. Martha Vicinus, ed., *Suffer and Be Still: Women in the Victorian Age* (Bloomington: Indiana University Press, 1972); Nancy Cott, *The Bonds of Womanhood: 'Women's Sphere' in New England, 1780–1835* (New Haven, Conn.: Yale University Press, 1977); Glenna Matthews, *Just a Housewife: The Rise and Fall of Domesticity in American Society* (Oxford: Oxford University Press, 1987).

37. Rosalyn Terbog-Penn, *African American Women and the Struggle for the Vote, 1850–1920* (Bloomington: Indiana University Press, 1998).

38. Paula Baker, "The Domestication of Politics: Women and American Political Society, 1780–1920," *American Historical Review* 89, no. 3 (June 1984): 620–47. On black women's political involvement in black women's clubs and other religious and fraternal community associations and organizations, see Paula Giddings, *When and Where I Enter: The Impact of Black Women on Race and Sex in America* (New York: Morrow, 1984); White, *Too Heavy a Load*.

39. Lee Sartain, *Invisible Activists: Women of the Louisiana NAACP and the Struggle for Civil Rights, 1915–1945* (Baton Rouge: Louisiana State University Press, 2007); Merline Pitre, *In Struggle Against Jim Crow: Lulu B. White and the NAACP, 1900–1957* (College Station: Texas A&M University Press, 1999).

40. James, *Holding Aloft the Banner of Ethiopia*, 138.

41. Rosalyn Terbog-Penn, *African American Women in the Struggle for the Vote* (Bloomington: Indiana University Press, 1998), 100.

42. Quoted in Julie A. Gallagher, *Black Women and Politics in New York City* (Urbana: University of Illinois Press, 2012), 34.

43. Gallagher, *Black Women and Politics in New York City*, 33; Hill, *Marcus Garvey and the UNIA Papers*, XI:796.

44. Quoted in Gallagher, *Black Women and Politics in New York City*, 33.

45. Hill, *Marcus Garvey and the UNIA Papers*, X:658; New York, Naturalization Records, 1897–1944, National Archives, Washington, D.C.; Petitions for Naturalization from the U.S. District Court for the Southern District of New York, 1897–1944, Series M1972, Roll 530, Ancestry.com subscription database, http://www.ancestry.com (accessed July 8, 2013); Collins migrated to the United States in 1919. See 1930 U.S. Census Records, Manhattan, N.Y., Ancestry.com subscription database, http://www.ancestry.com (accessed July 8, 2013).

46. Irma Watkins-Owens, *Blood Relations: Caribbean Immigrants and the Harlem Community, 1900–1930* (Bloomington: Indiana University Press, 1996); James, *Holding Aloft the Banner of Ethiopia*.

47. James, *Holding Aloft the Banner of Ethiopia*, 12.

48. James, *Holding Aloft the Banner of Ethiopia*, 49; Mae Ngai, *Impossible Subjects: Illegal Aliens and the Making of Modern America* (Princeton, N.J.: Princeton University Press, 2004).

49. James, *Holding Aloft the Banner of Ethiopia*, 12.

50. Hill, *Marcus Garvey and the UNIA Papers*, X:685.

51. On the Black Star Line, see Ramla M. Bandele, *Black Star, African American Activism in the International Political Economy* (Urbana: University of Illinois Press, 2008).

52. Hill, *Marcus Garvey and the UNIA Papers*, X:685; Tiffany Gill, *Beauty Shop Politics: African American Women's Activism in the Beauty Industry* (Urbana: University of Illinois Press, 2010), 57–58.

53. Hill, *Marcus Garvey and the UNIA Papers*, X:685. The Garvey Club of New York was a division of the UNIA that remained loyal to Garvey after the organizational split of 1929. See Hill, *Marcus Garvey and the UNIA Papers*, VII:19.

54. See Huggins, *Harlem Renaissance*; Lewis, *When Harlem Was in Vogue*; Baker, *Modernism and the Harlem Renaissance*.

55. On Black Harlem during the 1920s, see Shannon King, *Whose Harlem Is This Anyway? Community Politics and Grassroots Activism During the New Negro Era* (New York: New York University Press, 2015); LaShawn Harris, *Sex Workers, Psychics, and Numbers Runners: Black Women in New York City's Underground Economy* (Urbana: University of Illinois Press, 2016).

56. Taylor, *Veiled Garvey*, 27.

57. Amy Jacques Garvey, ed., *The Philosophy and Opinions of Marcus Garvey, Part I* (Patterson, N.J.: Frank Cass and Company Limited, 1923), xxxiii.

58. Karen Adler, " 'Always Leading Our Men in Service and Sacrifice': Amy Jacques Garvey, Feminist Black Nationalist," *Gender and Society* 6 (1992): 354.

59. Taylor, *Veiled Garvey*, 64–90; Mark D. Matthews, " 'Our Women and What They Think': Amy Jacques Garvey and the Negro World," *Black Scholar* 10, nos. 8–9 (1979): 2–18.

60. Monroe Alphus Majors, *Noted Negro Women: Their Triumphs and Activities* (Chicago: Donohue and Henneberry, 1893), 102; William Seraile, "Henrietta Vinton Davis and the Garvey Movement," *Afro-Americans in New York Life and History* 7, no. 2 (July 1983): 7–24; Natanya

Duncan, "If Our Men Hesitate Then the Women of the Race Must Come Forward: Henrietta Vinton Davis and the UNIA in New York," *New York History* 94, no. 1 (Fall 2015): 558–83.

61. Eric Yellin, *Racism in the Nation's Service: Government Workers and the Color Line in Woodrow Wilson's America* (Chapel Hill: University of North Carolina Press, 2013).

62. Majors, *Noted Negro Women*; Seraile, "Henrietta Vinton Davis and the Garvey Movement."

63. Seraile, "Henrietta Vinton Davis and the Garvey Movement," 9.

64. Seraile, "Henrietta Vinton Davis and the Garvey Movement," 7–24.

65. Barbara Bair, "Renegotiating Liberty: Garveyism, Women, and Grassroots Organizing in Virginia," in *Women of the American South: A Reader*, ed. Christie Farnham (New York: New York University Press, 1997), 228.

66. Courtney Morris, "Becoming Creole, Becoming Black: Migration, Diasporic Self-Making, and the Many Lives of Madame Maymie Leona Turpeau de Mena," *Women, Gender, and Families of Color* 4, no. 2 (Fall 2016): 171–95; Author's interviews with Mwariama Kamau, January 16, 2013, and July 28, 2013; David Dewitt Turpeau Sr., *Up from the Cane Breaks: An Autobiography* (Cincinnati, Ohio: D. D. Turpeau, 1942); 1880 U.S. Census Records, 1st Ward, St. Martin, La. (Enumeration District 033), Ancestry.com subscription database, http://www.ancestry.com (accessed April 10, 2014).

67. Turpeau, *Up from the Cane Breaks*, 19; 1880 U.S. Census Records, 1st Ward, St. Martin, La. (Enumeration District 033), Ancestry.com subscription database, http://www.ancestry.com (accessed April 10, 2014).

68. Turpeau, *Up from the Cane Breaks*, 14.

69. Turpeau, *Up from the Cane Breaks*, 18.

70. 1912, New Orleans, Passenger Lists, 1813–1963, Ancestry.com subscription database, http://www.ancestry.com (accessed April10, 2014); Morris, "Becoming Creole, Becoming Black."

71. Lara Putman, *Radical Moves: Caribbean Migrants and the Politics of Race in the Jazz Age* (Chapel Hill: University of North Carolina Press, 2013), 37.

72. Bair, "True Women, Real Men," 162.

73. Hill, *Marcus Garvey and the UNIA Papers*, XI:117.

74. Bair, "Renegotiating Liberty," 226, 228–30.

75. Rina Okonkwo, "Adelaide Casely Hayford: Cultural Nationalist and Feminist," *Phylon* 42, no. 1 (March 1981): 41–51; Barbara Bair, "Pan-Africanism as Process: Adelaide Casely Hayford," in *Imagining Home: Class, Culture, and Nationalism in the African Diaspora*, ed. Sidney J. Lemelle and Robin D. G. Kelley (London: Verso, 1991); Adelaide M. Crawford, *An African Victorian Feminist: The Life and Times of Adelaide Smith Casely, 1868–1960* (London: Routledge, 1986).

76. Quoted in Okonkwo, "Adelaide Casely Hayford," 43.

77. Quoted in Okonkwo, "Adelaide Casely Hayford," 44

78. Quoted in Okonkwo, "Adelaide Casely Hayford," 46.

79. Adelaide Casely Hayford to Margaret Murray Washington, November 28, 1922, Papers of Mary Church Terrell, Moorland Springarn Research Center, Washington, D.C., Box 102–12, Folder 240. On racial uplift, see Kevin Gaines, *Uplifting the Race: Black Leadership, Politics, and Culture in the Twentieth Century* (Chapel Hill: University of North Carolina Press, 1996).

80. Ford-Smith, "Women and the Garvey Movement in Jamaica"; Bair, "True Women, Real Men."

81. Barbara Bair, "'Ethiopia Shall Stretch Forth Her Hands unto God': Laura Kofey and the Gendered Vision of Redemption in the Garvey Movement," in *A Mighty Baptism: Race, Gender, and the Creation of American Protestantism*, ed. Susan Juster and Lisa MacFarlane (Ithaca, N.Y.: Cornell University Press, 1996); Bair, "True Women, Real Men"; Satter, "Marcus Garvey, Father Divine."

82. Natanya Duncan, "The 'Efficient Womanhood' of the Universal Negro Improvement Association, 1919–1930" (Ph.D. diss., University of Florida, 2009), 125; Bair, "True Women, Real Men," 157. Also see Anne Macpherson, "Colonial Matriarchs: Garveyism, Materialism and Belize's Black Cross Nurses, 1920–1952," *Gender and History* 15, no. 3 (November 2003): 507–27; Leah Michelle Seabrook, "Service in Green and White: The Activity and Symbolism of the Universal African Black Cross Nurses" (M.A. thesis, University of California Irvine, 2006).

83. Bair, "Renegotiating Liberty," 226.

84. Claudrena Harold, *The Rise and Fall of the Garvey Movement in the Urban South, 1918–1942* (New York: Taylor and Francis, 2007), 37.

85. Bair, "True Women, Real Men," 157.

86. Phillip A. Howard, *Black Labor, White Sugar: Caribbean Braceros and the Struggles for Power* (Baton Rouge: Louisiana State University, 2015), 187–90.

87. MacPherson, "Colonial Matriarchs," 508–10, 517. On materialist politics, see Linda Gordon, "Black and White Visions of Welfare: Women's Welfare Activism, 1890–1945," *Journal of American History* 78, no. 2 (September 1991): 559–90; Seth Koven and Sonya Michel, eds., *Mothers of a New World: Maternalist Politics and the Origins of the Welfare States* (New York: Routledge, 1996).

88. Bair, "True Women, Real Men," 157.

89. Rupert Lewis, *Marcus Garvey: Anti-Colonial Champion* (London: Karia, 1987), 68.

90. Bair, " 'Ethiopia Shall Stretch Forth Her Hands unto God,' " 39–45; Lewis, *Marcus Garvey*, 68.

91. Bair, " 'Ethiopia Shall Stretch Forth Her Hands unto God,' " 45.

92. Hill, *Marcus Garvey and the UNIA Papers*, IV:1037.

93. Hill, *Marcus Garvey and the UNIA Papers*, IV:1037.

94. Hill, *Marcus Garvey and the UNIA Papers*, IV:1037.

95. James, *Holding Aloft the Banner of Ethiopia*, 138–40.

96. Hill, *Marcus Garvey and the UNIA Papers*, IV:1037.

97. Taylor, *Veiled Garvey*, chap. 4; Matthews, "Our Women and What They Think."

98. Saydee Parham, "The New Woman," *Negro World*, February 2, 1924.

99. Blanche Hall, "Woman's Greatest Influence Is Socially," *Negro World*, October 4, 1924.

100. Hill, *Marcus Garvey and the UNIA Papers*, VI:418.

101. Carrie Mero Leadett, "The Negro Girl of Today Has Become a Follower—Future Success Rests with Her Parents and Home Environment," *Negro World*, February 2, 1924.

102. Florence Bruce, "The Great Work of the Negro Woman Today," *Negro World*, December 27, 1924.

103. Martin, *Race First*, 14.

104. Amy Jacques Garvey, "No Sex in Brains and Ability," *Negro World*, December 27, 1924.

105. Amy Jacques Garvey, "Black Women's Resolve for 1926," *Negro World*, January 9, 1926.

106. Taylor, *Veiled Garvey*, 2.

107. "The Ideal Wife," *Negro World*, April 5, 1924.

108. Barbara Welter, "The Cult of True Womanhood: 1820–1860," *American Quarterly* 18, no. 2 (Summer 1966): 151–74; Cott, *The Bonds of Womanhood*.

109. McDuffie, " 'I Wanted a Communist Philosophy,' " 183.

110. Taylor, *Veiled Garvey*, 69.

111. Eva Aldred-Brooks, "An Appeal for Race Solidarity," *Negro World*, July 4, 1925.

112. Saydee E. Parham, "Women's Part in Nationhood," *Negro World*, November 22, 1924.

113. Louise J. Edwards, "The New Day Appears," *Negro World*, June 12, 1926.

114. Tera W. Hunter, "Feminist Consciousness and Black Nationalism: Amy Jacques Garvey and Women in the Universal Negro Improvement Association" (Unpublished paper presented at Women's History Research Seminar, Yale University, 1983).

115. Amy Jacques Garvey, "What Some Women of the Race Has Accomplished," *Negro World*, June 7, 1924.

116. Jacques Garvey, "What Some Women of the Race Has Accomplished."

117. Leadett, "The Negro Girl of Today."

118. Adler, "Always Leading Our Men in Service and Sacrifice," 358.

119. Amy Jacques Garvey to Richard Newman, January 31, 1972, Laura Adorkor Kofey Research Collection, 1926–1981, Box 1, Folder 8, New York Public Library at Schomburg Center for Research in Black Culture, New York, New York.

120. Bair, "'Ethiopia Shall Stretch Forth Her Hands unto God,'" 55.

121. Richard Newman, "'Warrior Mother of Africa's Warriors of the Most High God': Laura Adorkor Kofey and the African Universal Church," in *This Far by Faith: Readings in African-American Women's Religious Biography*, ed. Richard Newman and Judith Weisenfeld (New York: Routledge, 1996); Bair, "'Ethiopia Shall Stretch Forth Her Hands unto God'"; Natanya Duncan, "Princess Laura Kofey and the Reverse Atlantic Experience," in *The American South and the Atlantic World*, ed. Brian Ward, Martyn Bone, and William A. Link (Gainesville: University of Florida, 2013).

122. Quoted in Newman, "'Warrior Mother of Africa's Warriors of the Most High God,'" 113.

123. Bair, "'Ethiopia Shall Stretch Forth Her Hands unto God,'" 54–56.

124. Newman, "'Warrior Mother of Africa's Warriors of the Most High God,'" 111.

125. J. A. Craigen Western Union telegram to Marcus Garvey, September 20, 1927, Gershon E. Harris/Garvey Club Collection, Schomburg Center for Research in Black Culture, New York Public Library, New York, N.Y.

126. Quoted in Bair, "'Ethiopia Shall Stretch Forth Her Hands unto God,'" 56.

127. Newman, "'Warrior Mother of Africa's Warriors of the Most High God,'" 113.

128. Duncan, "Princess Laura Kofey and the Reverse Atlantic Experience," 221.

129. Bair, "'Ethiopia Shall Stretch Forth Her Hands unto God,'" 58.

130. Bair, "'Ethiopia Shall Stretch Forth Her Hands unto God,'" 58.

131. Hill, *Marcus Garvey and the UNIA Papers*, VII:10, 14.

132. Martin, *Race First*, 18.

133. Hill, *Marcus Garvey and the UNIA Papers*, VII:311–12.

134. Martin, *Race First*, 18; Wilson Jeremiah Moses, *Creative Conflict in African American Thought* (Cambridge: Cambridge University Press, 2004), 282.

135. Hill, *Marcus Garvey and the UNIA Papers*, VII:317, 342.

136. Hill, *Marcus Garvey and the UNIA Papers*, VII:317.

137. Seraile, "Henrietta Vinton Davis and the Garvey Movement," 19.

138. Established in 1921 by Antiguan George Alexander McGuire, the African Orthodox Church was an international religious order, which taught a blend of Pan-Africanism, Ethiopianism, and Garveyism. The church generally attracted West Indians who were sympathetic to Anglicanism and others who embraced Roman Catholicism and the teachings of the Episcopal Church. See Richard Newman, "The Origins of the African Orthodox Church," in *Black Power and Black Religion: Essays and Reviews* (West Cornwall: Locust Hill Press, 1987).

139. "Fred A. Toote Takes Stand in Convention," *Negro World*, September 7, 1929, in Hill, *Marcus Garvey and the UNIA Papers*, VII:327.

140. Hill, *Marcus Garvey and the UNIA Papers*, VII:315–17.

141. Kenneth Barnes, *Journey of Hope: The Back to Africa Movement in Arkansas in the Late 1880s* (Chapel Hill: University of North Carolina Press, 2004).

142. John McKivigan, *The War Against Proslavery Religion: Abolitionism and the Northern Churches, 1830–1865* (Ithaca, N.Y.: Cornell University Press, 1984), 34; Claude A. Clegg, *The Price of Liberty: African Americans and the Making of Liberia* (Chapel Hill: University of North

Carolina Press, 2004); Eric Burin, *Slavery and the Peculiar Solution: A History of the American Colonization Society* (Gainesville: University Press of Florida, 2005); Allan Yarema, *American Colonization Society: An Avenue to Freedom?* (Lanham, Md.: University Press of America, 2006).

143. Michele Mitchell, *Righteous Propagation: African Americans and the Politics of Racial Destiny After Reconstruction* (Chapel Hill: University of North Carolina Press, 2005), 21–22.

144. Barnes, *Journey of Hope*, 3–12; James T. Campbell, *Middle Passages: African American Journeys to Africa, 1787–2005* (New York: Penguin, 2006).

145. Barnes, *Journey of Hope*, 2.

146. Mary G. Rolinson, *Grassroots Garveyism: The Universal Negro Improvement Association in the Rural South, 1920–1927* (Chapel Hill: University of North Carolina Press, 2007), 24, 26. Also see Claudrena Harold, *The Rise and Fall of the Garvey Movement in the Urban South, 1918–1942* (New York: Routledge, 2007).

147. Mittie Maude Lena Gordon's Statement to Richard W. Axtell and James E. Conerty, September 21, 1942, Records of the Federal Bureau of Investigation (FBI), Investigative Files on the Peace Movement of Ethiopia, File No. 100-124410, RG 60, National Archives, Washington, D.C.

148. George McCray, *The Universal Negro Improvement Association: As an Expression of Caste and Class Relations in a Negro Community* (unpublished work), Box 57, St. Clair Drake Papers, 1935–1990, Schomburg Center for Black Research, New York, N.Y.

149. Statement from Mittie Maude Lena Gordon to Richard W. Axtell and James E. Conerty, September 21, 1942, Records of the FBI, Investigative Files on the Peace Movement of Ethiopia, File No. 100-124410, RG 60, National Archives, Washington, D.C.

150. Amy Jacques Garvey to Hilbert Keys, April 5, 1944, Amy Jacques Collection, Box 1, Charles Blockson Collection, Temple University, Philadelphia, Pa.

Chapter 2

1. Brief History of the Peace Movement of Ethiopia to President Roosevelt Pamphlet, March 1939, Reel 243, American Colonization Society Records, Library of Congress, Washington, D.C.

2. McCray, *The Universal Negro Improvement Association*.

3. Anonymous informant, June 19, 1942, Chicago, Ill., Records of the FBI, Investigative Files on the Peace Movement of Ethiopia, File No. 100-124410, RG 60, National Archives, Washington, D.C.

4. Taylor, "Street Strollers," 153–71. Taylor's conceptualization of "street scholar" mirrors an "organic intellectual." See Antonio Gramsci, "The Formation of the Intellectuals," in *Selections from the Prison Notebooks of Antonio Gramsci*, ed. Quintin Hoare and Geoffrey Nowell-Smith (London: Lawrence & Wishart, 1971), 134–47.

5. Taylor, "Street Strollers," 155.

6. Mittie Maude Lena Gordon to Earnest Sevier Cox, October 27, 1939, Box 5, Folder 2, Earnest Sevier Cox Papers, 1821–1973, Rare Book, Manuscript, and Special Collections Library, Duke University, Durham, N.C.

7. Gordon to Cox, October 27, 1939, Box 5, Folder 2, Cox Papers.

8. Katharine L. Dvorak, *An African-American Exodus: The Segregation of the Southern Churches* (Brooklyn, N.Y.: Carlson, 1991).

9. Gordon to Cox, October 27, 1939, Box 5, Folder 2, Cox Papers.

10. Tunde Adeleke, *UnAfrican Americans: Nineteenth-Century Black Nationalists and the Civilizing Mission* (Lexington: University Press of Kentucky, 1998), 92, 99.

11. Gordon to Cox, October 27, 1939, Box 5, Folder 2, Cox Papers.

12. Koritha Mitchell, *Living with Lynching: African American Lynching Plays, Performance, and Citizenship, 1890–1930* (Urbana: University of Illinois Press, 2011); Anne P. Rice, *Witnessing*

Lynching: American Writers Respond (New Brunswick, N.J.: Rutgers University Press, 2003); Kidada E. Williams, *They Left Great Marks on Me: African American Testimonies of Racial Violence from Emancipation to World War I* (New York: New York University Press, 2012).

13. *Twelfth Census of the United States, 1900* (Washington, D.C.: National Archives and Records Administration, 1900), Ancestry.com subscription database, http://www.ancestry.com (accessed April 24, 2012).

14. Gordon to Cox, October 27, 1939, Box 5, Folder 2, Cox Papers.

15. James Grossman, *Land of Hope: Chicago, Black Southerners, and the Great Migration* (Chicago: University of Chicago Press, 1989); Joe William Trotter Jr., *The Great Migration in Historical Perspective: New Dimensions on Race, Class, and Gender* (Bloomington: Indiana University Press, 1991). On African Americans' involvement in World War I, see Adriane Lentz-Smith, *Freedom Struggles: African Americans and World War I* (Cambridge, Mass.: Harvard University Press, 2009); Chad Williams, *Torchbearers of Democracy: African American Soldiers in the World War I Era* (Chapel Hill: University of North Carolina Press, 2010).

16. Gordon to Cox, October 27, 1939, Box 5, Folder 2, Cox Papers; Statement of Mittie Maude Lena Gordon, September 21, 1942, FBI Investigative File No. 100-124410, National Archives, Washington, D.C.

17. Harper Barnes, *Never Been a Time: The 1917 Race Riot That Sparked the Civil Rights Movement* (New York: Walker, 2008); Charles L. Lumpkins, *American* Pogrom: The East St. Louis Race Riot and Black Politics (Athens: Ohio University Press, 2008).

18. Cook County, Illinois Death Index, 1878–1922, Ancestry.com subscription database, http://www.ancestry.com (accessed October 28, 2011).

19. Marcus Garvey, "The Conspiracy of the East St. Louis Riots," in *Ain't but a Place: An Anthology of African American Writings About St. Louis*, ed. Gerald Lyn Early (St. Louis: Missouri Historical Society Press, 1998), 300–306.

20. Garvey, "The Conspiracy of the East St. Louis Riots," 300–301, 306.

21. Davarian Baldwin, "Making the Black Metropolis: African Americans in Chicago, 1910–1985," in *African American Communities* (London: Adam Matthew Digital Ltd., 2015).

22. Baldwin, "Making the Black Metropolis."

23. McDuffie, "Chicago, Garveyism, and the History of the Diasporic Midwest," 5; Wallace Best, *Passionately Human, No Less Divine: Religion and Culture in Black Chicago, 1915–1952* (Princeton, N.J.: Princeton University Press, 2005), 19.

24. Davarian L. Baldwin, *Chicago's New Negroes: Modernity, the Great Migration, and Black Urban Life* (Chapel Hill: University of North Carolina Press, 2007).

25. Gordon to Cox, October 27, 1939, Box 5, Folder 2, Cox Papers.

26. *United States of America v. Mittie Maud Lena Gordon*, Reply Brief for Appellants, Box 34, Cox Papers. On William Gordon's genealogy records, see 1920 U.S. Federal Census, Ward 6, Cook County, Chicago, Ill., Ancestry.com subscription database, http://www.ancestry.com (accessed October 28, 2011).

27. *United States of America v. Mittie Maud Lena Gordon*, United States Court of Appeals for the Seventh Circuit, Reply Brief for Appellants (Prepared by Attorney Lloyd Bailey), Box 34, Cox Papers. Statement of William Green Gordon, September 20, 1942, FBI Investigative File No. 100-124410, National Archives, Washington, D.C.

28. Gordon to Cox, October 27, 1939, Box 5, Folder 2, Cox Papers. On Moore, see McDuffie, "'I Wanted a Communist Philosophy,'" 181–95.

29. Bair, "'Ethiopia Shall Stretch Forth Her Hands unto God,'" 41, 45.

30. Some of the largest UNIA branches were located in Chicago. See Martin, *Race First*, 17.

31. Duncan, "Efficient Womanhood," 121–22.

32. *United States of America v. Mittie Maud Lena Gordon*, United States Court of Appeals for the Seventh Circuit, Reply Brief for Appellants (Prepared by Attorney Lloyd Bailey), Box 34, Cox Papers.

33. Robin D. G. Kelley, *Race Rebels: Culture, Politics and the Black Working Class* (New York: Free Press, 1996), 51.

34. Matera, *Black London*, 100–144.

35. Ernest Allen Jr., "When Japan Was Champion of the 'Darker Races': Satokata Takahashi and the Flowering of Black Messianic Nationalism," *Black Scholar* 24 (1994): 23–46.

36. Robert A. Hill, *The FBI's RACON: Racial Conditions in the United States During World War II* (Boston: Northeastern University Press, 1995), 517, 523–24.

37. Hill, *The FBI's RACON*, 523.

38. Hill, *The FBI's RACON*, 517; "Dayton, O. Div. Is Reorganized," *Negro World*, February 6, 1932; "Ethiopian Club," *Negro World*, January 2, 1932.

39. Erika Lee, "The 'Yellow Peril' and Asian Exclusion in the Americas," *Pacific Historical Review* 76 (2007): 537–62; Eiichiro Azuma, "Japanese Immigrant Settler Colonialism in the U.S.-Mexican Borderlands and the U.S. Racial-Imperialist Politics of the Hemispheric 'Yellow Peril,'" *Pacific Historical Review* 83 (2014): 255–76; Mae Ngai, *Impossible Subjects: Illegal Aliens and the Making of Modern America* (Princeton, N.J.: Princeton University Press, 2004).

40. Fred Ho and Bill V. Mullen, eds., *Afro Asia: Revolutionary Political and Cultural Connections Between African Americans and Asian Americans* (Durham, N.C.: Duke University Press, 2008), 3.

41. Walton Look Lai, *The Chinese in the West Indies 1806–1995: A Documentary History* (Kingston: University of the West Indies Press, 1998); Ho and Mullen, *Afro Asia*, 3.

42. Ho and Mullen, *Afro Asia*, 45; Also see Kathleen M. Lopez, *Chinese Cubans: A Transnational History* (Chapel Hill: University of North Carolina Press, 2013).

43. Reginald Kearney, *African American Views of the Japanese: Solidarity or Sedition?* (Albany: State University of New York Press, 1998), 72–75.

44. *United States of America v. Mittie Maud Lena Gordon*, United States Court of Appeals for the Seventh Circuit, Reply Brief for Appellants, Box 34, Cox Papers; Ernest Allen Jr., "Waiting for Tojo: The Pro-Japan Vigil of Black Missourians, 1932–1943," *Gateway Heritage* 15 (Fall 1994): 38–55.

45. *United States of America v. Mittie Maud Lena Gordon*, Reply Brief for Appellants, Box 34, Cox Papers.

46. Hill, *FBI's RACON*, 524.

47. *United States of America v. Mittie Maud Lena Gordon*, Reply Brief for Appellants, Box 34, Cox Papers.

48. Allen, "When Japan Was Champion of the 'Darker Races,'" 28–29; Kearney, *African American Views of the Japanese*, 18–30.

49. Peace Movement of Ethiopia Constitution, 14.

50. Gordon to Cox, October 27, 1939, Box 5, Folder 2, Cox Papers.

51. Peace Movement of Ethiopia Constitution, 2.

52. William L. Van Deburg, *Modern Black Nationalism* (New York: New York University Press, 1997), 24–29; "UNIA Declaration of Rights of the Negro Peoples of the World," New York, August 13, 1920, in Hill, *Marcus Garvey and UNIA Papers*, II:571–80.

53. Peace Movement of Ethiopia Constitution, 2–3.

54. Michael Gomez, *Black Crescent: The Experience and Legacy of African Muslims in the Americas* (Cambridge: Cambridge University Press, 2005), 212–13, 230.

55. Gomez, *Black Crescent*, 68, 72–73.

56. Newman, "The Origins of the African Orthodox Church."

57. Martin, *Race First*, 70. Garvey also drew some of his ideas from black Muslims. See Richard Brent Turner, *Islam in the African American Experience* (Bloomington: Indiana University Press, 2003), 81–86. On the religious dimensions of Garveyism, see Randall Burkett, *Garveyism as a Religious Movement: The Institutionalization of a Black Civil Religion* (Metuchen, N.J.:

Scarecrow Press, 1978); Burkett, *Black Redemption: Churchmen Speak for the Garvey Movement* (Philadelphia: Temple University Press, 1978).

58. Quoted in PME Report, May 28, 1942, Exhibit No. 53, FBI Investigative File No. 100-124410, National Archives, Washington, D.C. Also see D. S. Kemp Bey to Gordon, April 7, 1933, Exhibit No. 227, FBI Investigative File No. 100-124410, National Archives, Washington, D.C.

59. This biography of Ali is based on Moorish Science tradition. However, historian Judith Weisenfeld's research reveals that Ali's real name was likely Thomas (rather than Timothy), and he was likely born in Virginia and not in North Carolina. See Weisenfeld, *New World A-Coming: Black Religion and Racial Identity During the Great Migration* (New York: New York University Press, 2017), 46–47.

60. Ali initially established the Moorish Holy Temple of Science in 1923 and later renamed it the Moorish Science Temple of America in 1928.

61. Turner, *Islam in the African American Experience*, 92.

62. Turner, *Islam in the African American Experience*, 93.

63. Turner, *Islam in the African American Experience*, 93.

64. McDuffie, "Chicago, Garveyism, and the History of the Diasporic Midwest."

65. Edward E. Curtis IV, "Debating the Origins of the Moorish Science Temple: Toward a New Cultural History," in *The New Black Gods: Arthur Huff Fauset and the Study of African American Religions*, ed. Edward E. Curtis IV and Danielle Brune Sigler (Bloomington: Indiana University Press, 2009), 82. Michael Gomez points out that Ali may have also been a member of the UNIA. See Gomez, *Black Crescent*, 211.

66. Elijah Muhammad, who became one of the founders of the Nation of Islam, was one of Noble Drew Ali's followers. See Martha Simmons and Frank A. Thomas, eds., *Preaching with Sacred Fire: An Anthology of African American Sermons, 1750 to the Present* (New York: W. W. Norton, 2010), 378.

67. Charles Eric Lincoln, *The Black Muslims in America* (Trenton, N.J.: African World Press, 1994), 48.

68. Peace Movement of Ethiopia Constitution, 3.

69. Statement of William Gordon, September 20, 1942, FBI Investigative File No. 100-124410, National Archives, Washington, D.C.

70. Gomez, *Black Crescent*, 210, 213, 230. On Noble Drew Ali's teachings and links to mainstream Islam, see Curtis, "Debating the Origins of the Moorish Science Temple."

71. Peace Movement of Ethiopia Constitution, 12–13.

72. Turner, *Islam in the African American Experience*, 78; Weisenfeld, *New World A-Coming*, 19. For a gendered perspective on the MSTA, see Marcia Chatelain, *South Side Girls: Growing Up in the Great Migration* (Durham, N.C.: Duke University Press, 2015), chap. 2.

73. Gramsci, "The Formation of the Intellectuals."

74. Best, *Passionately Human, No Less Divine*, 19.

75. Douglass S. Massey and Nancy A. Denton, *American Apartheid: Segregation and the Making of the Underclass* (Cambridge, Mass.: Harvard University Press, 1993), 116.

76. Erik Gellman, *Death Blow to Jim Crow: The National Negro Congress and the Rise of Militant Black Civil Rights* (Chapel Hill: University of North Carolina Press, 2012), 21.

77. Other communist-affiliated radical groups attracted black men and women during this period. The most significant was the African Blood Brotherhood (ABB), a relatively small leftist group of black intellectuals and activists. Established in Harlem in 1919, the ABB had an estimated eight thousand members during its peak. See Minkah Makalani, *In the Cause of Freedom: Radical Black Internationalism from Harlem to London, 1917–1939* (Chapel Hill: University of North Carolina Press, 2011), 45.

78. Mark Naison, *Communists in Harlem During the Depression* (Urbana: University of Illinois Press, 1983); Robin D. G. Kelley, *Hammer and Hoe: Alabama Communists During the Great*

Depression (Chapel Hill: University of North Carolina Press, 1990); Mark Solomon, *The Cry Was Unity: Communists and African Americans, 1917–36* (Jackson: University Press of Mississippi, 1998); Carole Boyce Davies, *Left of Karl Marx: The Political Life of Black Communist Claudia Jones* (Durham, N.C.: Duke University Press, 2007); Erik S. McDuffie, *Sojourning for Freedom: Black Women, American Communism, and the Making of Black Left Feminism* (Durham, N.C.: Duke University Press, 2011); Dayo F. Gore, *Radicalism at the Crossroads: African American Women Activists in the Cold War* (New York: New York University Press, 2011); Glenda Gilmore, *Defying Dixie: The Radical Roots of Civil Rights, 1919–1950* (New York: W. W. Norton, 2008).

79. On communism in Chicago, see Randi Storch, *Red Chicago: American Communism at Its Grassroots, 1928–1935* (Urbana: University of Illinois Press, 2007).

80. McDuffie, *Sojourning for Freedom*, 3–4; Gore, *Radicalism at the Crossroads*, 12.

81. Kelley, *Hammer and Hoe*, 46.

82. McDuffie, *Sojourning for Freedom*, 21.

83. On Garvey's view on Marxism, see Marcus Garvey and Amy Jacques Garvey, *The Philosophy and Opinions of Marcus Garvey, or Africa for the Africans* (Dover, Mass.: Majority Press, 1986), 69–70.

84. A number of scholarly works have debunked the strict black communist/nationalist dichotomy, underscoring how activists often embraced both ideologies. These include Winston James, *Holding Aloft the Banner of Ethiopia: Caribbean Radicalism in Early Twentieth-Century America* (London: Verso, 1998); McDuffie, *Sojourning for Freedom*; Gore, *Radicalism at the Crossroads*.

85. Black women faced a number of reprisals for allying with communists. See LaShawn D. Harris, "Running with the Reds: African American Women and the Communist Party During the Great Depression," *Journal of African American History* 94 (2009): 21–43.

86. Peace Movement of Ethiopia Constitution, 4.

87. Indrias Getachew, *Beyond the Throne: The Enduring Legacy of Emperor Haile Selassie I* (Addis Ababa, Ethiopia: Shama Books, 2001); Harold G. Marcus, *Haile Selassie I: The Formative Years, 1892–1936* (Los Angeles: University of California Press, 1987); Theodore M. Vestal, *The Lion of Judah in the New World: Emperor Haile Selassie of Ethiopia and the Shaping of Americans' Attitudes Toward Africa* (Santa Barbara, Calif.: Praeger, 2011).

88. Gordon to Cox, May 22, 1938, Box 4, Folder 5, Cox Papers.

89. George Shepperson, "Ethiopianism and African Nationalism," *Phylon* 14, no. 1 (1953): 9–18; St. Clair Drake, *The Redemption of Africa and Black Religion* (Chicago: Third World Press, 1970); Wilson Jeremiah Moses, *Afrotopia: The Roots of African American Popular History* (New York: Cambridge University Press, 1998), 26–27.

90. PME Installation Ceremony, September 20, 1942, Exhibit No. 29, FBI Investigative Files, "Peace Movement of Ethiopia" (SAC, Chicago, 100-8932), File No. 100-124410, RG 60, National Archives, Washington, D.C.

91. Moses, *The Golden Age of Black Nationalism*, 156–57.

92. Melinda Plastas, *A Band of Noble Women: Racial Politics in the Women's Peace Movement* (Syracuse, N.Y.: Syracuse University Press, 2011).

93. On the women's peace movement, see Harriet Alonso, *Peace as a Women's Issue: A History of the U.S. Movement for World Peace and Women's Rights* (Syracuse, N.Y.: Syracuse University Press, 1993); Joyce Blackwell, *No Peace Without Freedom: Race and the Women's International League for Peace and Freedom, 1915–1975* (Carbondale: Southern Illinois University Press, 2004).

94. Jill Watts, *God, Harlem, USA: The Father Divine Story* (Berkeley: University of California Press, 1995); Beryl Satter, "Marcus Garvey, Father Divine and the Gender Politics of Race Difference and Race Neutrality," *American Quarterly* 48, no. 1 (March 1996): 43–76; Weisenfeld, *New World A-Coming*.

95. Statement of Sam Hawthorne, November 7, 1942, File No. 100-124410.

96. McCray, *The Universal Negro Improvement Association*.

97. Membership roll in the Peace Movement of Ethiopia Report, August 8, 1942, FBI File No. 100-124410-65, National Archives, Washington, D.C.

98. Hill, *FBI's RACON*, 93.

99. Peace Movement of Ethiopia Minutes, June 15, 1942, Exhibit No. 46, FBI Investigative Files, "Peace Movement of Ethiopia" (SAC, Chicago, 100-8932), File No. 100-124410, RG 60, National Archives, Washington, D.C.

100. Report of PME Meetings (Excerpts of Minutes), FBI Investigative Files, "Peace Movement of Ethiopia" (SAC, Chicago, 100-8932), File No. 100-124410, National Archives, Washington, D.C.

101. Report of PME Meetings (Excerpts of Minutes).

102. "Nation Stirred over Move to Colonize Race in Africa," *Chicago Defender*, March 7, 1936.

103. "Nation Stirred over Move to Colonize Race in Africa." "Better class" phrase comes from W. E. B. Du Bois, who used it to describe class divisions in *The Philadelphia Negro: A Social Study* (Philadelphia: Published for the University, 1899).

104. Quoted in Ibrahim Sundiata, *Brothers and Strangers: Black Zion, Black Slavery, 1914–1940* (Durham, N.C.: Duke University Press, 2003), 312. Such critiques were also reminiscent of the ones Garvey received from Du Bois and other race leaders during the 1920s. See Martin, *Race First*, 274–280; Grant, *Negro with a Hat*, 298–317.

105. Mitchell, *Righteous Propagation*, 20; Nell Irvin Painter, *Exodusters: Black Migration to Kansas After Reconstruction* (New York: W. W. Norton, 1986), 141–45. Steven Hahn makes a similar argument that emigrationism held greater currency for southern black laborers. See Hahn, *A Nation Under Our Feet: Black Political Struggles in the Rural South from Slavery to the Great Migration* (Cambridge, Mass.: Belknap Press of Harvard University Press, 2003), 318.

106. Hill, *FBI's RACON*, 528–29.

107. Kearney, *African American Views of the Japanese*, 99.

108. Organizational Records of the Peace Movement of Ethiopia, January 23, 1941, Exhibit No. 32, FBI Investigative Files, "Peace Movement of Ethiopia" (SAC, Chicago, 100-8932), File No. 100-124410, National Archives, Washington, D.C.

109. This is based on the author's calculations.

110. Peace Movement of Ethiopia Constitution, 12.

111. Peace Movement of Ethiopia Constitution, 7–8.

112. Organizational Records of the Peace Movement of Ethiopia, January 23, 1941, Exhibit No. 32, FBI Investigative Files, "Peace Movement of Ethiopia" (SAC, Chicago, 100-8932), File No. 100-124410, National Archives, Washington, D.C. 1940 Census records indicate that Jernigan was a housewife, although city records from 1926 have her listed as a "laborer." See United States of America, Bureau of the Census, Sixteenth Census of the United States, 1940, National Archives and Records Administration, Washington, D.C., 1940, Ancestry.com subscription database, http://www.ancestry.com (accessed February 5, 2013); U.S. City Directories, 1821–1989, Galesburg, Ill., City Directory, 1926, Ancestry.com subscription database, http://www.ancestry.com (accessed February 5, 2013).

113. United States of America, Bureau of the Census, Sixteenth Census of the United States, 1940, National Archives and Records Administration, Washington, D.C., 1940, Ancestry.com subscription database, http://www.ancestry.com (accessed February 5, 2013); United States of America, Bureau of the Census, Twelfth Census of the United States, 1900, National Archives and Records Administration, Washington, D.C., 1900, Ancestry.com subscription database, http://www.ancestry.com (accessed February 5, 2013).

114. 106th session of the Supreme Council of the Peace Movement of Ethiopia, December 5, 1941, Exhibit No. 35, FBI Investigative Files, "Peace Movement of Ethiopia" (SAC, Chicago, 100-8932), File No. 100-124410, National Archives, Washington, D.C.

115. Organizational Records of the Peace Movement of Ethiopia, January 23, 1941, Exhibit No. 32, FBI Investigative Files, "Peace Movement of Ethiopia" (SAC, Chicago, 100-8932), File No. 100-124410, National Archives, Washington, D.C.

116. Peace Movement of Ethiopia Constitution, 5.

117. Martin Summers, *Manliness and Its Discontents: The Black Middle Class and the Transformation of Black Masculinity, 1900–1930* (Chapel Hill: University of North Carolina Press, 2004), 93; Organizational Records of the Peace Movement of Ethiopia, 1942, Exhibit No. 38, FBI Investigative Files, "Peace Movement of Ethiopia" (SAC, Chicago, 100-8932), File No. 100-124410, National Archives, Washington, D.C.

118. 106th session of the Supreme Council of the Peace Movement of Ethiopia. On the Deacons for Defense and Justice, see Timothy Tyson, *Radio Free Dixie: Robert F. Williams and the Roots of Black Power* (Chapel Hill: University of North Carolina Press, 1999); Lance Hill, *The Deacons for Defense: Armed Resistance and the Civil Rights Movement* (Chapel Hill: University of North Carolina Press, 2004).

119. On armed self-defense, see Akinyele Umoja, *We Will Shoot Back: Armed Resistance in the Mississippi Freedom Struggle* (New York: New York University, 2013).

120. Stephen Ward Angell, *Bishop Henry McNeal Turner and African-American Religion in the South* (Knoxville: University of Tennessee Press, 1992), 138; Adeleke, *UnAfrican Americans*, 100.

121. Martin, *Race First*, 347.

122. On the New Deal, see William Leuchtenburg, *Franklin D. Roosevelt and the New Deal, 1932–1940* (New York: Harper and Row, 1963).

123. Kelley, *Hammer and Hoe*; Patricia Sullivan, *Days of Hope: Race and Democracy in the New Deal Era* (Chapel Hill: University of North Carolina Press, 1996).

124. Peace Movement of Ethiopia Constitution, 20.

125. Peace Movement of Ethiopia Constitution, 23.

126. Charles Spurgeon Johnson, *Bitter Canaan: The Story of the Negro Republic* (New Brunswick, N.J.: Transaction Books, 1987); Ibrahim K. Sundiata, *Brothers and Strangers: Black Zionism, Black Slavery, 1914–1940* (Durham, N.C.: Duke University Press, 2003); Emily S. Rosenberg, "The Invisible Protectorate: The United States, Liberia, and the Evolution of Neocolonialism, 1909–40," *Diplomatic History* 9 (Summer 1985): 191–205.

127. Peace Movement of Ethiopia Constitution, 4; *United States v. Mittie Maude Lena Gordon, et al.*, 138 F.2d 174 (7th Cir. October 9, 1943).

128. Peace Movement of Ethiopia Constitution, 15. By 1933, the organization's leaders decided on Liberia as the ideal location.

129. Brief History of the Peace Movement of Ethiopia to President Roosevelt Pamphlet, March 1939, Reel 243, American Colonization Society Records, Library of Congress, Washington, D.C.

130. Peace Movement of Ethiopia Constitution, 14–15, 19; Gunnar Myrdal, *An American Dilemma: The Negro Problem and Modern Democracy* (New York: Harper and Brothers, 1944), 813. This account is also described in Ralph J. Bunche and Gunnar Myrdal, *The Programs, Ideologies, Tactics and Achievements of Negro Betterment and Interracial Organizations* (New York: International Microfilm Press, 1945).

131. Peace Movement of Ethiopia Constitution, 22.

132. Pierrepont Moffat to Gordon, October 11, 1934, Box 4, Folder 1, Cox Papers.

133. Gordon to Cox, March 7, 1934, Box 4, Folder 1, Cox Papers.

Chapter 3

1. Long, Miss., is located between Greenville and Leland on the Washington County/Sunflower County line at the intersection of Longswitch and Bamboo Roads.

2. Neil R. McMillen, *Dark Journey: Black Mississippians in the Age of Jim Crow* (Urbana: University of Illinois Press, 1989), 229. In the postwar era, Mississippi witnessed a significant increase in lynching even as national trends revealed an overall decline in mob violence. See Jason Morgan Ward, *Hanging Bridge: Racial Violence and America's Civil Rights Century* (New York: Oxford University Press, 2016).

3. Rev. George Green to Theodore Bilbo, March 8, 1938, Box 340, Folder 1, Theodore G. Bilbo Papers, McCain Library, University of Southern Mississippi, Hattiesburg, Miss. On Green's living arrangements, see 1940 U.S. Federal Census, Washington County, Miss., Ancestry.com subscription database, http://www.ancestry.com (accessed May 10, 2013).

4. Statement of Thomas H. Bonner, November 18, 1942, Mobile, Ala., Records of the FBI, Investigative Files on the Peace Movement of Ethiopia, File No. 100-124410, RG 60, National Archives, Washington, D.C. For reflections on life in Matherville, see Gayle Graham Yates, *Life and Death in a Small Southern Town: Memories of Shubuta, Mississippi* (Baton Rouge: Louisiana State University Press, 2004), 181–200.

5. Peace Movement of Ethiopia Constitution, 29.

6. Celia Jane Allen to Theodore Bilbo, 1939 (no month or date listed), Box 1091, Folder 4, Bilbo Papers.

7. Allen to Bilbo, August 4, 1942, Box 1091, Folder 7, Bilbo Papers.

8. Charles Payne, *I've Got the Light of Freedom: The Organizing Tradition and the Mississippi Freedom Struggle* (Berkeley: University of California Press, 2007).

9. On scholarship on black women in the Jim Crow South, see Vicki L. Crawford, Jacqueline Anne Rouse, and Barbara Woods, eds., *Women in the Civil Rights Movement: Trailblazers and Torchbearers, 1941–1965* (Bloomington: Indiana University Press, 1990); Chana Kai Lee, *For Freedom's Sake: The Life of Fannie Lou Hamer* (Urbana: University of Illinois Press, 1999); Lynne Olson, *Freedom's Daughters: The Unsung Heroines of the Civil Rights Movement from 1830 to 1970* (New York: Scribner, 2001); Barbara Ransby, *Ella Baker and the Black Freedom Movement: A Radical Democratic Vision* (Chapel Hill: University of North Carolina Press, 2003); Shannon Frystak, *Our Minds on Freedom: Women and the Struggle for Black Equality in Louisiana, 1924–1967* (Baton Rouge: Louisiana State University Press, 2009).

10. Celia Jane Allen to Thomas Bernard, September 28, 1942, FBI File No. 100-124410-65, National Archives, Washington, D.C. Also see Celia Jane Allen to Theodore Bilbo, no date listed, Box 1091, Folder 4, Bilbo Papers; Allen to Bilbo, October 18, 1941, Box 1091, Folder 7, Bilbo Papers; Allen to Bilbo, August 4, 1942, Box 1091, Folder 7, Bilbo Papers.

11. Photograph of PME's Executive Council, Oversize Materials, Earnest Sevier Cox Papers, 1821–1973, Rare Book, Manuscript, and Special Collections Library, Duke University, Durham, N.C.

12. James Grossman, *Land of Hope: Chicago, Black Southerners, and the Great Migration* (Chicago: University of Chicago Press, 1989); Joe William Trotter Jr., *The Great Migration in Historical Perspective: New Dimensions on Race, Class, and Gender* (Bloomington: Indiana University Press, 1991).

13. 1930 U.S. Federal Census, Cook County, Chicago, Ill., Ancestry.com subscription database, http://www.ancestry.com (accessed May 7, 2013). On black women in domestic service, see Elizabeth Clark-Lewis, *Living In, Living Out: African American Domestics in Washington, D.C., 1910–1940* (Washington, D.C.: Smithsonian Institution Press, 1994); Phyllis Palmer, *Domesticity and Dirt: Housewives and Domestic Servants in the United States, 1920–1945* (Philadelphia: Temple University Press, 1989).

14. 1940 U.S. Federal Census, Ward 15, Cook County, Chicago, Ill., Ancestry.com subscription database, http://www.ancestry.com (accessed May 7, 2013).

15. Joe William Trotter Jr., *From a Raw Deal to a New Deal? Black Americans, 1929–1945* (New York: Oxford University Press, 1996); Harvard Sitkoff, *A New Deal for Blacks: The Emergence of Civil Rights as a National Issue* (New York: Oxford University Press, 1978).

16. Allen to Bilbo, August 4, 1942, Box 1091, Folder 7, Bilbo Papers.

17. Allen to Bilbo, June 9, 1938, Box 354, Folder 15, Bilbo Papers.

18. Allen to Bilbo, October 8, 1941?, Box 1091, Folder 8, Bilbo Papers. It is unclear if the five dollar payment was a one-time occurrence or recurring payment.

19. Allen to Bilbo, June 9, 1938, Box 354, Folder 15, Bilbo Papers.

20. McMillen, *Dark Journey*, 229–230. McMillen points out that the majority of lynchings (about 70 percent) occurred in Mississippi counties with the greatest density of black population.

21. McMillen, *Dark Journey*, 229, 335.

22. McMillen, *Dark Journey*, 335. Also see Ida B. Wells and Jacqueline Jones Royster, eds., *Southern Horrors and Other Writings: The Anti-Lynching Campaign of Ida B. Wells, 1892–1900* (Boston: Bedford, 1997); Mia Bay, *To Tell the Truth Freely: The Life of Ida B. Wells* (New York: Hill and Wang, 2010).

23. Crystal N. Feimster, *Southern Horrors: Women and the Politics of Rape and Lynching* (Cambridge, Mass.: Harvard University Press, 2009), 158–85.

24. Feimster, *Southern Horrors*, 159.

25. These statistics are based on recorded cases between 1890 and 1939. See Kerry Segrave, *Lynchings of Women in the United States: The Recorded Cases, 1851–1946* (Jefferson, N.C.: McFarland, 2010), 8. Neil McMillen cites fourteen lynch cases involving black women (after 1888). See McMillen, *Dark Journey*, 229.

26. Amy Louise Wood, *Lynching and Spectacle: Witnessing Racial Violence in America, 1890–1940* (Chapel Hill: University of North Carolina Press, 2009), 197; Jason Morgan Ward, *Defending White Democracy: The Making of a Segregationist Movement and the Remaking of Racial Politics, 1936–1965* (Chapel Hill: University of North Carolina Press, 2011), 22–23.

27. McMillen, *Dark Journey*, 252.

28. Nan Woodruff, *American Congo: The African American Freedom Struggle in the Delta* (Cambridge, Mass.: Harvard University Press, 2003), 38–73.

29. Crystal Sanders, *A Chance for Change: Head Start and Mississippi's Black Freedom Struggle* (Chapel Hill: University of North Carolina Press, 2016), 11–31; Tiyi M. Morris, *Womanpower Unlimited and the Black Freedom Struggle in Mississippi* (Athens: University of Georgia Press, 2015), 1–14.

30. Woodruff, *American Congo*, 152–90.

31. Mark Solomon, *The Cry Was Unity: Communists and African Americans, 1917–1936* (Jackson: University Press of Mississippi, 1998), 125.

32. Kelley, *Hammer and Hoe*, 132.

33. Kelley, *Hammer and Hoe*, 124.

34. 1940 U.S. Federal Census, Washington County, Miss., Ancestry.com subscription database, http://www.ancestry.com (accessed May 10, 2013).

35. Rev. George Green to Bilbo, March 8, 1938, Box 340, Folder 2, Bilbo Papers.

36. Statement of George G. Green, Matherville, Miss., November 5, 1942, FBI File No. 100-124410-65, National Archives, Washington, D.C. For an overview of federal surveillance of black radicals, see Theodore Kornweibel, *Seeing Red: Federal Campaigns Against Black Militancy, 1919–1925* (Indianapolis: Indiana University Press, 1991).

37. Eric Lincoln and Lawrence H. Mamiya, eds., *The Black Church in the African American Experience* (Durham, N.C.: Duke University Press, 1990); Steven Hahn, *A Nation Under Our Feet: Black Political Struggles in the Rural South from Slavery to the Great Migration* (Cambridge, Mass.: Belknap Press of Harvard University Press, 2003).

38. Robin D. G. Kelley, *Race Rebels: Culture, Politics and the Black Working Class* (New York: Free Press, 1996), 51.

39. Evelyn Brooks-Higginbotham, *Righteous Discontent: The Women's Movement in the Black Baptist Church, 1880–1920* (Cambridge, Mass.: Harvard University Press, 1993), 10.

40. Lincoln and Mamiya, *The Black Church in the African American Experience*; Cheryl Townsend Gilkes, " 'Together and in Harness': Women's Traditions in the Sanctified Church, *Signs* 10, no. 4 (Summer 1985): 678–99; Bair, " 'Ethiopia Shall Stretch Forth Her Hands unto God.' "

41. Tera W. Hunter, "Feminist Consciousness and Black Nationalism: Amy Jacques Garvey and Women in the Universal Negro Improvement Association" (unpublished paper presented at Women's History Research Seminar, Yale University, 1983); Bair, " 'Ethiopia Shall Stretch Forth Her Hands unto God' "; Bair, "True Women, Real Men"; Beryl Satter, "Marcus Garvey, Father Divine, and the Gender Politics of Race Difference and Race Neutrality," *American Quarterly* 48, no. 1 (March 1996): 43–76. Historian Claudrena Harold describes the New Orleans division of the UNIA as one notable exception in terms of gendered leadership, arguing that the division was "quite progressive with regards to the promotion of women to leadership positions." See Harold, *The Rise and Fall of the Garvey Movement*, 142, n. 102.

42. Taylor, *Veiled Garvey*, 2.

43. McDuffie, *Sojourning for Freedom*, 147. Also see Gore, *Radicalism at the Crossroads*; Harris, "Running with the Reds." On respectability, see Brooks-Higginbotham, *Righteous Discontent*; Cheryl Hicks, *Talk with You like a Woman: African American Women, Justice, and Reform in New York, 1890–1935* (Chapel Hill: University of North Carolina Press, 2010).

44. Statement of George Green, Matherville, Mississippi, November 5, 1942, FBI File No. 100-124410-65, National Archives, Washington, D.C.

45. World War I Selective Service System Draft Registration Cards, 1917–1918, National Archives and Records Administration, Washington, D.C., Ancestry.com subscription database, http://www.ancestry.com (accessed May 5, 2013).

46. Statement of Thomas H. Bonner (Bernard), November 18, 1942, Mobile, Ala., FBI File No. 100-124410-65, National Archives, Washington, D.C.

47. Statement of Thomas H. Bonner (Bernard), November 18, 1942. On black Americans and World War I, see Lentz-Smith, *Freedom Struggles*; Williams, *Torchbearers of Democracy*.

48. Benedict Anderson, *Imagined Communities: Reflections on the Origin and Spread of Nationalism*, rev. ed. (London: Verso, 1991); also see Sidney Lemelle and Robin D. G. Kelley, eds., *Imagining Home: Class, Culture, and Nationalism in the African Diaspora* (London: Verso, 1994).

49. Peace Movement of Ethiopia Constitution, 29–31.

50. See Wilson Jeremiah Moses, *Alexander Crummell: A Study of Civilization and Discontent* (New York: Oxford University Press, 1989).

51. Harold, *The Rise and Fall of the Garvey Movement*, 14.

52. Harold, *The Rise and Fall of the Garvey Movement*, 3, 27.

53. Rolinson, *Grassroots Garveyism*, 98–100.

54. Rolinson, *Grassroots Garveyism*, 122.

55. Harold, *The Rise and Fall of the Garvey Movement*.

56. Rolinson, *Grassroots Garveyism*, 182.

57. See Kenneth C. Barnes, *Journey of Hope: The Back-to-Africa Movement in Arkansas in the Late 1800s* (Chapel Hill: University of North Carolina Press, 2004); James T. Campbell, *Middle Passages: African American Journeys to Africa, 1787–2005* (New York: Penguin, 2006); Robert Johnson, *Returning Home: A Century of African-American Repatriation* (Trenton, N.J.: Africa World Press, 2005); Wilson Jeremiah Moses, *Liberian Dreams: Back-to-Africa Narratives from the 1850s* (University Park: Pennsylvania State University Press, 1998).

58. T. Elwood Davis to Gordon, April 24, 1936, Box 4, Folder 2, Cox Papers.

59. "Liberia Offers Haven to U.S. Colored People," *Chicago Tribune*, July 6, 1936.

60. See Adeleke, *UnAfrican Americans*; Moses, *The Golden Age of Black Nationalism*.

61. See Ibrahim K. Sundiata, *Brothers and Strangers: Black Zion, Black Slavery, 1914–1940* (Durham, N.C.: Duke University Press, 2003).

62. Hedlin, "Earnest Cox and Colonization," 135; Gordon to Cox, October 9, 1938, Box 5, Cox Papers.

63. Executive Mansion (Monrovia, Liberia) to Gordon, January 3, 1939, Box 5, Cox Papers.

64. Peace Movement of Ethiopia Constitution, 28.

65. Statement of Thomas H. Bonner, Mobile, Ala., November 18, 1942, FBI File No. 100-124410-65, National Archives, Washington, D.C.

66. Report of Special Agent John L. Sullivan, February 4, 1943, Jackson, Miss., FBI File No. 100-124410-65, National Archives, Washington, D.C. On canvassing, see Payne, *I've Got the Light of Freedom*, 250–56.

67. Report of Special Agent John L. Sullivan, February 4, 1943, FBI File No. 100-124410-65, National Archives, Washington, D.C. On armed self-defense, see Umoja, *We Will Shoot Back*.

68. Statement of Thomas H. Bonner, Mobile, Ala., November 18, 1942, File No. 100-124410-65.

69. Report of Special Agent John L. Sullivan, February 4, 1943, Jackson, Miss., FBI File No. 100-124410-65, National Archives, Washington, D.C.

70. Statement of William Butler, November 23, 1942, Palataka, Fla., FBI File No. 100-124410-65, National Archives, Washington, D.C.

71. Statement of Rosa Boyd, November 23, 1942, Palataka, Fla., FBI File No. 100-124410-65, National Archives, Washington, D.C.

72. Bettye Collier-Thomas, *Jesus, Jobs and Justice: African American Women and Religion* (New York: Knopf, 2010); Barbara Savage, *Your Spirit Walks Besides Us: The Politics of Black Religion* (Cambridge, Mass.: Harvard University Press, 2008); Elsa Barkley Brown, "Negotiating and Transforming the Public Sphere: African American Political Life in the Transition from Slavery to Freedom," *Public Culture* 7, no. 1 (Fall 1994): 107–46; Brooks-Higginbotham, *Righteous Discontent*.

73. Lincoln and Mamiya, *The Black Church in the African American Experience*, 277. Also see Levine, *Black Culture and Black Consciousness*.

74. Gordon to T. H. Bernard, August 20, 1942, FBI File No. 100-124410 (capitalizations in original text), National Archives, Washington, D.C.

75. Gordon to Tommie Thomas, August 28, 1942, Exhibit 125, FBI File No. 100-124410, National Archives, Washington, D.C. On African Americans' political engagement with India, see Gerald Horne, *The End of Empires: African Americans and Indians* (Philadelphia: Temple University Press, 2009); Nico Slate, *Colored Cosmopolitanism: The Shared Struggle for Freedom in the United States and India* (Cambridge, Mass.: Harvard University Press, 2012).

76. PME Installation Ceremony, September 20, 1942, Exhibit 29, FBI Investigative File No. 100-124410, National Archives, Washington, D.C.

77. See Slate, *Colored Cosmopolitanism*, 2, 7. Also see Horne, *The End of Empires*.

78. See Kornweibel, *Seeing Red*.

79. Peace Movement of Ethiopia Constitution, 3.

80. Gordon to Kenji Nakauchi, May 22, 1934, Exhibit 164a in Report by Special Agents Francis A. Regan, Aubrey Elliott Jr., and Richard W. Axtell, FBI Investigative File No. 100-124410, National Archives, Washington, D.C.

81. Gordon to Sadao Araki, n.d., Exhibit 160a in Report by Special Agents Francis A. Regan, Aubrey Elliott Jr., Andrew J. Rafferty, and Richard W. Axtell, FBI Investigative File No. 100-124410, National Archives, Washington, D.C.

82. Gordon to Sadao Araki, n.d., Exhibit 160a in Report by Special Agents Francis A. Regan, Aubrey Elliott Jr., Andrew J. Rafferty, and Richard W. Axtell, FBI Investigative File No. 100-124410, National Archives, Washington, D.C.

83. Marc Gallichio, *The African American Encounter with Japan and China: Black Internationalism in Asia, 1895–1945* (Chapel Hill: University of North Carolina Press, 2000), 121–25.

84. These figures are based on the author's calculations using PME membership data obtained by the Federal Bureau of Investigation in 1942. The author was unable to determine the sex of thirty-six individuals. It is unclear exactly why much of the organization's membership was concentrated in these three specific counties.

85. 1930 U.S. Federal Census, Beat 5, Washington, Miss., Ancestry.com subscription database, http://www.ancestry.com (accessed May 13, 2013); Mittie Maude Lena Gordon to Joella Johnson, January 15, 1942, FBI File No. 100-124410-65, National Archives, Washington, D.C.

86. Peace Movement of Ethiopia Constitution, 28–29; Program at the AME Zion Church, February 3, 1939 in Box 5, Folder 2, Cox Papers.

87. Peace Movement of Ethiopia Constitution, 28–29. Allen might have been referring to one of the PME's standard prayers that members recited during weekly meetings.

88. Peace Movement of Ethiopia Constitution, 28–29 (capitalizations included in the original text).

89. Leon Litwack, *Been in the Storm So Long: The Aftermath of Slavery* (New York: Knopf, 1979).

90. William Leuchtenburg, *Franklin D. Roosevelt and the New Deal, 1932–1940* (New York: Harper and Row, 1963).

91. Sitkoff, *A New Deal for Blacks*; Kelley, *Hammer and Hoe*; Zaragosa Vargas, *Labor Rights Are Civil Rights: Mexican American Workers in Twentieth-Century America* (Princeton, N.J.: Princeton University Press, 2007); Patricia Sullivan, *Days of Hope: Race and Democracy in the New Deal Era* (Chapel Hill: University of North Carolina Press, 1996).

92. Bruce Schulman, *From Cotton Belt to Sunbelt: Federal Policy, Economic Development, and the Transformation of the South, 1938–1980* (Durham, N.C.: Duke University Press, 1994).

93. Statement from Joella Johnson, Long, Miss., November 5, 1942, and November 6, 1942, FBI File No. 100-124410-65, National Archives, Washington, D.C.

94. Census records confirm the literacy of Joella Johnson, who was certainly able to read and write. 1930 U.S. Federal Census, Beat 5, Washington, Miss., Ancestry.com subscription database, http://www.ancestry.com (accessed May 13, 2013).

95. 1930 U.S. Federal Census, Beat 5, Washington, Miss.

96. Robin D. G. Kelley, "'We Are Not What We Seem': Rethinking Black Working-Class Opposition in the Jim Crow South," *Journal of American History* 80, no. 1 (June 1993): 75–112. Kelley draws on James C. Scott's theory of *infrapolitics*. See Scott, *Domination and the Arts of Resistance: Hidden Transcripts* (New Haven, Conn.: Yale University Press, 1990).

97. The FBI acknowledges that very few African Americans worked as agents during the early twentieth century. They can only confirm that four black agents worked with the agency prior to 1962, when Aubrey Lewis and James Barrow became the first African Americans admitted to the FBI academy. See "'A Byte Out of History': Early African-American Agents," Federal Bureau of Investigation, www.fbi.gov/news/stories/2011/february/history_021511 (accessed June 9, 2013).

98. Statement of George G. Green, Matherville, Mississippi, November 5, 1942, FBI File No. 100-124410-65, National Archives, Washington, D.C.; Organizational Records of the Peace Movement of Ethiopia, January 23, 1941, Exhibit No. 32, FBI File No. 100-124410-65, National Archives, Washington, D.C.

99. Statement of George G. Green, Matherville, Miss., November 5, 1942, FBI File No. 100-124410-65, National Archives, Washington, D.C.

100. List of Officers of Locals Number 10 and 11 in Report of Special Agent John Sullivan, February 4, 1943, Jackson, Mississippi, FBI File No. 100-124410-65, National Archives, Washington, D.C.

101. In Garvey's UNIA, the "lady president" was a title bestowed upon women leaders who were responsible for overseeing a woman's division. See Bair, "'Ethiopia Shall Stretch Forth Her Hands unto God,'" 41, 45.

102. Gordon to Johnson, January 15, 1942, FBI File No. 100-124410-65, National Archives, Washington, D.C.

103. Gordon to Johnson, January 15, 1942, FBI File No. 100-124410-65, National Archives, Washington, D.C. See Garvey and Jacques Garvey, *The Philosophy and Opinions of Marcus Garvey*.

104. Gordon to Green, July 22, 1941; enclosure in letter from A. H. Johnson to Director of the Federal Bureau of Investigation, October 29, 1942, FBI File No. 100-124410-65, National Archives, Washington, D.C.

105. Gordon to Hawthorne, April 15, 1942, FBI File No. 100-124410-65, National Archives, Washington, D.C.

106. Gordon to T. H. Bernard, July 29, 1942, enclosure in letter from A. H. Johnson to Director of the Federal Bureau of Investigation, October 29, 1942, FBI File No. 100-124410-65, National Archives, Washington, D.C.

107. Allen to Bilbo, August 4, 1942, Box 1091, Folder 7, Bilbo Papers.

108. Allen to Bilbo, 1939 (no month or date listed), Box 1091, Folder 4, Bilbo Papers.

109. Gordon to Bilbo, August 10, 1938, Box 1091, Folder 10, Bilbo Papers.

110. Allen to Bilbo, June 9, 1938, Box 354, Folder 15, Bilbo Papers.

111. Harold, *The Rise and Fall of the Garvey Movement*, 25.

112. On the roots of the southern segregationist movement, see Jason Ward, *Defending White Democracy: The Making of a Segregationist Movement and the Remaking of Racial Politics, 1939–1965* (Chapel Hill: University of North Carolina Press, 2011).

113. Robert L. Fleegler, "Theodore G. Bilbo and the Decline of Public Racism, 1938–1947," *Journal of Mississippi History* 68 (Spring 2006): 2; Dan T. Carter, *From George Wallace to Newt Gingrich: Race in the Conservative Counterrevolution, 1963–1994* (Baton Rouge: Louisiana State Press, 1996).

114. Michael Fitzgerald, "'We Have Found a Moses': Theodore Bilbo, Black Nationalism, and the Greater Liberia Bill of 1939," *Journal of Southern History* 63 (1997): 296.

115. Quoted in Chester Morgan, *Redneck Liberal: Theodore G. Bilbo and the New Deal* (Baton Rouge: Louisiana State University Press, 1985), 227.

116. Morgan, *Redneck Liberal*, 227.

117. Moses, *The Golden Age of Black Nationalism*; Pinkney, *Red, Black, and Green*.

118. While Delany and Turner received financial support from the ACS, they were also critical of the organization. See Eric Burin, *Slavery and the Peculiar Solution: A History of the American Colonization Society* (Gainesville: University of Florida Press, 2005).

119. Martin, *Race First*, 344–57; Fitzgerald, "We Have Found a Moses."

120. Michele Mitchell, *Righteous Propagation: African Americans and the Politics of Racial Destiny After Reconstruction* (Chapel Hill: University of North Carolina Press, 2004), 220.

121. Allen to Bilbo, June 9, 1938, Box 354, Folder 15, Bilbo Papers.

122. This was the case for several black nationalists including Marcus Garvey, Amy Jacques Garvey, Mittie Maude Lena Gordon, and, later, Malcolm X. See Martin, *Race First*, 344–57; Manning Marable, *Malcolm X: A Life of Reinvention* (New York: Viking, 2011), 178–79.

123. Morgan, *Redneck Liberal*; Fleegler, "Theodore G. Bilbo and the Decline of Public Racism."

124. Morgan, *Redneck Liberal*, 1.

125. Allen to Bilbo, August 4, 1942, Box 1091, Folder 7, Bilbo Papers.

126. Green to Bilbo, March 8, 1938, Box 340, Folder 1, Bilbo Papers.

127. Bilbo to Green, March 17, 1938, Box 341, Folder 12, Bilbo Papers.

128. Bilbo to Green, March 17, 1938, Box 341, Folder 12, Bilbo Papers.

129. Peace Movement of Ethiopia Constitution, 28.

130. Allen to Bilbo, August 4, 1942, Box 1091, Folder 7, Bilbo Papers.

131. The Bilbo Papers include hundreds of pages of signed petitions from the Peace Movement of Ethiopia emigration campaign, which began in 1933. The petitions are not dated, and thus it is impossible to determine exactly when signatures were obtained. See PME Petitions, Boxes 1186 and 1187, Bilbo Papers.

132. Glenda Gilmore argues that black women's invisibility during the Jim Crow era provided new avenues for their political participation. See Gilmore, *Gender and Jim Crow: Women and the Politics of White Supremacy in North Carolina, 1896–1920* (Chapel Hill: University of North Carolina Press, 1996).

133. Celia Jane Allen to Bernard, September 28, 1942, File No. 100-124410-65.

134. For example, Bernard, who helped establish two local PME chapters in Mississippi, went on to help establish a local chapter in Mobile, Ala., where he eventually relocated for work. Statement of Thomas H. Bonner, November 18, 1942, Mobile, Ala., File No. 100-124410-65.

Chapter 4

1. Florence Kenna to Theodore G. Bilbo, March 15, 1938, Box 341, Folder 1, Theodore G. Bilbo Papers, McCain Library and Archives, University of Southern Mississippi, Hattiesburg, Miss. (hereafter cited as Bilbo Papers).

2. Examples of these congratulatory letters include Ellen Johnson to Theodore Bilbo, March 15, 1938, Box 341, Folder 1, Bilbo Papers; George Calbert to Bilbo, March 15, 1938, Box 341, Folder 1; Emma Beal to Bilbo, March 13, 1938, Box 340, Folder 16, Bilbo Papers.

3. Fitzgerald, " 'We Have Found a Moses.' "

4. Du Bois, *Souls of Black Folk*; Marable and Agard-Jones, *Transnational Blackness*.

5. Martin, *Race First*, 344–57.

6. Paula Baker, "The Domestication of Politics: Women and American Political Society, 1790–1920," *American Historical Review* 89, no. 3 (1984): 622; Judith Butler, "Performative Acts and Gender Constitution: An Essay in Phenomenology and Feminist Theory," *Theatre Journal* 40, no. 4. (December 1988): 521.

7. Mittie Maude Lena Gordon to Earnest Sevier Cox, August 7, 1934, Box 4, Folder 1, Earnest Sevier Cox Papers, 1821–1973, Rare Book, Manuscript, and Special Collections Library, Duke University, Durham, N.C. (hereafter cited as Cox Papers). Capitalizations are included in the original text.

8. Watts, *God, Harlem, USA*; Satter, "Marcus Garvey, Father Divine."

9. "Greetings! Children of Ethiopia," *Ethiopian World*, May 26, 1934.

10. "Division of U.N.I.A., August 29, Is Active," *Ethiopian World*, May 26, 1934.

11. Ibrahim Sundiata, *Brothers and Strangers: Black Zion, Black Slavery, 1914–1940* (Durham, N.C.: Duke University Press, 2003), 79–96.

12. Ibrahim K. Sundiata, "Prelude to Scandal: Liberia and Fernando Po, 1880–1930," *Journal of African History* 15, no. 1 (1974): 97–112.

13. James Meriwether, *Proudly We Can Be Africans: Black Americans and Africa, 1935–1961* (Chapel Hill: University of North Carolina, 2002), 24.

14. Albert McCall, "Liberia," in Peace Movement of Ethiopia Constitution.

15. Peace Movement of Ethiopia Constitution, 35.

16. "Liberia Offers a Welcome," *Ethiopian World*, May 26, 1934.

17. "Liberia Needs U.N.I.A. Groups, Mitchell Says," *Ethiopian World*, May 26, 1934.

18. Letter from the African Reconstruction Association to W. E. B. Du Bois, June 15, 1934, W. E. B. Du Bois Papers, Special Collections and University Archives, University of Massachusetts Amherst Libraries (MS 312); Preamble of the Constitution of the African Reconstruction Association (enclosure), June 15, 1934, W. E. B. Du Bois Papers, Special Collections and University Archives, University of Massachusetts Amherst Libraries (MS 312).

19. Ethiopian World, May 26, 1934, vol. 1, no. 1.

20. Gaines, *Uplifting the Race*.

21. "Home Through Self-Help Is Negro's Need," *Ethiopian World*, May 26, 1934.

22. "A.R.A. Hears Liberian Tell of Possibilities," *Ethiopian World*, May 26, 1934.

23. Lloyd Graves, "Help Save Our Race," *Ethiopian World*, September 19, 1934.

24. "A Petition," March 9, 1938, Box 340, Folder 4, Bilbo Papers.

25. Cora Lee Frazier to Theodore Bilbo, March 14, 1938, Box 340, Folder 18, Bilbo Papers.

26. Anonymous letter to Bilbo, May 16, 1939, Box 1091, Folder 12, Bilbo Papers.

27. Albert McCall, "My Home," in Peace Movement of Ethiopia Constitution, 34.

28. W. E. Johnson, D.D.S. to Theodore Bilbo, February 2, 1939, Box 1091, Folder 1, Bilbo Papers.

29. Anderson, *Imagined Communities*; Lemelle and Kelley, *Imagining Home*.

30. James Ciment, *Another America: The Story of Liberia and the Former Slaves Who Ruled It* (New York: Hill and Wang, 2013), 188.

31. Mary Renda, *Taking Haiti: Military Occupation and the Culture of U.S. Imperialism, 1915–1940* (Chapel Hill: University of North Carolina Press, 2001); Brenda Gayle Plummer, *Haiti and the United States: The Psychological Moment* (Athens: University of Georgia Press, 1992).

32. Thomas Bender, *A Nation Among Nations: America's Place in World History* (New York: Hill and Wang, 2006).

33. W. E. B. Du Bois and Nahum Dimitri Chandle, *The Problem of the Color Line at the Turn of the Twentieth Century: The Essential Early Essays* (New York: Fordham University Press, 2015), 22.

34. For an excellent overview of the history of eugenicist ideas in the United States, see Ibram X. Kendi, *Stamped from the Beginning: The Definitive History of Racist Ideas in America* (New York: Nation Books, 2016).

35. Thomas Borstelmann, *The Cold War and the Color Line: American Race Relations in the Global Arena* (Cambridge, Mass.: Harvard University Press, 2003), 19.

36. Mia Bay, *The White Image in the Black Mind: African American Ideas About White People* (New York: Oxford University Press, 2000).

37. Reena N. Goldthree, "Amy Jacques, Theodore Bilbo, and the Paradoxes of Black Nationalism," in *Global Circuits of Blackness: Interrogating the African Diaspora*, ed. Jean Muteba Rahier, Percy C. Hintzen, and Felipe Smith (Urbana: University of Illinois Press, 2010), 156.

38. Ethel Wolfskill Hedlin, "Earnest Cox and Colonization: A White Racist's Response to Black Emigration, 1923–1966" (Ph.D. diss., Duke University, 1974), 23–27, 48.

39. Hedlin, "Earnest Cox and Colonization," 48, 86.

40. Gordon to Cox, March 7, 1934, Box 4, Folder 1, Cox Papers.

41. Cox to Gordon and the PME, March 10, 1934, Box 4, Folder 1, Cox Papers.

42. Gordon to Cox, March 15, 1934, Box 4, Folder 1, Cox Papers.

43. Gordon to Cox, September 19, 1934, Box 4, Folder 1, Cox Papers.

44. Elin Diamond, ed., *Performance and Cultural Politics* (London: Routledge, 1996), 1.

45. Hedlin, "Earnest Cox and Colonization," 117.

46. Gordon to Cox, September 19, 1934, Box 4, Folder 1, Cox Papers.

47. Hedlin, "Earnest Cox and Colonization," 120.

48. Gordon to Cox, February 27, 1936, Box 4, Folder 2, Cox Papers.

49. "Races: Mr. Bilbo's Afflatus," *Time*, May 8, 1939.

50. Gordon to Cox, February 3, 1937, Box 4, Folder 3, Cox Papers.

51. Grossman, *Land of Hope*; Trotter, *The Great Migration in Historical Perspective*.

52. 1930 U.S. Census, Ward 4, Cook County, Chicago, Ill., Ancestry.com subscription database, http://www.ancestry.com (accessed May 11, 2012); 1940 U.S. Census, Ward 2, Cook County, Chicago, Ill., Ancestry.com subscription database, http://www.ancestry.com (accessed May 11, 2012).

53. Gordon to Bilbo, March 15, 1938, Box 341, Folder 2, Bilbo Papers.

54. Gordon to Bilbo, March 15, 1938, Box 341, Folder 2, Bilbo Papers.

55. Waddell sued Gordon three times. After the initial lawsuit in January 1937, another injunction was brought against Gordon in February 1937. With both being dismissed for lack of evidence, Waddell filed a third lawsuit in 1938. Gordon filed a countercomplaint in March 1938. See Gordon to Cox, February 3, 1937, Box 4, Folder 3, Cox Papers. On the countercomplaint, see *The Peace Movement of Ethiopia, Inc. v. Mittie Maude Lena Gordon, William Gordon, William Merriweather, and Joseph Rockmore*, No. 37 S 1961, State of Illinois, Cook County in Box 1089, Folder 12, Bilbo Papers.

56. Hill, *Marcus Garvey and UNIA Papers*, VII:823.

57. Hedlin, "Earnest Cox and Colonization," 126.

58. Hedlin, "Earnest Cox and Colonization," 135; Gordon to Cox, October 9, 1938, Box 5, Folder 1, Cox Papers.

59. McCray, *The Universal Negro Improvement Association*.

60. Waddell and Watkins to Cox, March 4, 1938, Box 4, Cox Papers.

61. See Hill, *Marcus Garvey and UNIA Papers*, X:681, n. 6. Tony Martin, *Message to the People: The Course of African Philosophy* (Dover, Mass.: Majority Press, 1986), xv. There are significant parallels between the African School of Philosophy and the UNIA's Liberty University (est. 1926), which was geared toward younger Garveyites. See Barbara Bair, "Renegotiating Liberty: Garveyism, Women, and Grassroots Organizing in Virginia," in *Women of the American South: A Reader*, ed. Christie Farnham (New York: New York University Press, 1997).

62. Martin, *Message to the People*, x.

63. Waddell to Thomas Harvey, May 26, 1938, Box 2, Folder 7, Universal Negro Improvement Association Records, 1916, 1921–1989, Stuart A. Rose Manuscript Archives, and Rare Book Library, Emory University, Atlanta, Ga. (hereafter cited as UNIA Records).

64. Waddell and Watkins to Cox, March 4, 1938, Box 4, Folder 5, Cox Papers.

65. Gordon to Cox, February 3, 1937, Box 4, Folder 4, Cox Papers.

66. Waddell to Thomas Harvey, February 19, 1938, Box 2, Folder 6, UNIA Records.

67. Sitkoff, *A New Deal for Blacks*; Trotter, *From a Raw Deal to a New Deal?*

68. Gordon to Cox, June 26, 1936, Box 4, Folder 2, Cox Papers.

69. Gordon to Cox, June 26, 1936, Box 4, Folder 2, Cox Papers, 123, 138. See Gordon to Eleanor Roosevelt, December 17, 1938, Box 5, Folder 1, Cox Papers. Gordon wrote to Eleanor Roosevelt in 1938 after learning of the first lady's work with the NAACP.

70. Gordon to Cox, June 23, 1937, Box 4, Folder 3, Cox Papers.

71. Record of the 75th Congress, January 21, 1938, CR-1938-0121, 881, 883.

72. Hedlin, "Earnest Cox and Colonization," 129, 130.

73. Theodore Bilbo to Earnest Sevier Cox, February 17, 1938, Box 4, Folder 5, Cox Papers.

74. Bilbo to Cox, February 17, 1938, Box 4, Folder 5, Cox Papers.

75. Fitzgerald, " 'We Have Found a Moses.' "

76. Quoted in Fitzgerald, "We Have Found a Moses," 302.

77. Gordon to Cox, June 29, 1938, Box 5, Folder 1, Cox Papers.

78. Gordon to Cox, June 19, 1938, Box 5, Folder 1, Cox Papers.

79. Deborah G. Plant, *Zora Neale Hurston: A Biography of the Spirit* (Westport, Conn.: Greenwood Press, 2007), 125. Also see Lawrence Levine, *Black Culture and Black Consciousness: Afro-American Folk Thought from Slavery to Freedom* (New York: Oxford University Press, 1977); Vincent Wimbush, ed., *African Americans and the Bible: Sacred Texts and Social Textures* (New York: Continuum, 2000); Eddie S. Glaude Jr., *Exodus! Religion, Race, and Nation in Early Nineteenth-Century Black America* (Chicago: University of Chicago Press, 2000).

80. Diamond, *Performance and Cultural Politics*, 1.

81. Gordon to Cox, June 29, 1938, Box 5, Folder 1, Cox Papers.

82. U.S. Congressional Record, 76th Congress, First Session, 1939, 4659.

83. U.S. Congressional Record, 76th Congress, First Session, 1939, 4674.

84. Fitzgerald, "We Have Found a Moses," 307–8.

85. Peace Movement of Ethiopia to Bilbo, May 22, 1938, Box 353, Folder 14, Bilbo Papers.

86. U.S. Congressional Record, 76th Congress, First Session, 1939, 4673.

87. U.S. Congressional Record, 76th Congress, First Session, 1939, 4673.

88. Gordon to Bilbo, March 7, 1939, Cox Papers, Box 5, Folder 2.

89. Gordon to Bilbo, March 7, 1939, Cox Papers, Box 5, Folder 2.

90. Hedlin, "Earnest Cox and Colonization," 140–42.

91. Tunde Adeleke, *The Case Against Afrocentrism* (Jackson: University Press of Mississippi, 2009), 110.

92. Quoted in U.S. Congressional Record, 76th Congress, First Session, 1939, 4651.

93. Quoted in U.S. Congressional Record, 76th Congress, First Session, 1939, 4651.

94. Hill, *Marcus Garvey and UNIA Papers*, VII:851, 854–55.

95. Sundiata, *Brothers and Strangers*, 311.

96. Gordon to Cox, July 13, 1936, Box 4, Folder 3, Cox Papers.

97. "A Petition," March 9, 1938, Box 340, Folder 4, Bilbo Papers.

98. Waddell and Watkins to Bilbo, March 1, 1938, Box 339, Folder 2, Bilbo Papers.

99. Program at the AME Zion Church, February 3, 1939, Box 5, Folder 2, Cox Papers.

100. Allen to Bilbo, June 9, 1938, Box 354, Folder 15, Bilbo Papers.

101. Grace Elizabeth Hale, *Making Whiteness: The Culture of Segregation in the South, 1890–1940* (New York: Pantheon, 1998).

102. Allen to Bilbo, September 8, 1941?, Box 1091, Folder 8, Bilbo Papers.

103. PME to Bilbo, 1939 (no month or day listed), Box 1089, Folder 12, Bilbo Papers.

104. Quoted in Statement of William A. Fergerson, November 21, 1942, FBI File No. 100-6668, National Archives, Washington, D.C.

105. Gordon to Bilbo, August 5, 1939, Box 1090, Folder 8, Bilbo Papers.

106. "President of Liberia Encourages Migration of Select Race Groups," *Chicago Defender*, May 6, 1939.

107. "Senate Snubs Bilbo: 'African Plan' Flops," *Chicago Defender*, April 29, 1939; "Chicagoans Favor 'Back to Africa' Bill," *Chicago Defender*, April 29, 1939.

108. U.S. Congressional Record, 76th Congress, First Session, 1939, 4650, 4654.

109. "Senate Snubs Bilbo"; "Senator Bilbo's Repatriation Bill," *African Nationalist*, July 5, 1939, Albert Porte Papers, Roll 2.

110. U.S. Congressional Record, 76th Congress, First Session, 1939, 4659. On Senator James Davis, see Paul B. Beers, *Pennsylvania Politics Today and Yesterday: The Tolerable Accommodation* (University Park: Pennsylvania State University Press, 1980), 104–6.

111. "Senate Snubs Bilbo"; "Senator Bilbo's Repatriation Bill."

112. See "500 Want to Go Back to Africa," *Baltimore Afro-American*, April 29, 1939; Florence Murray, "Anything Except Mr. or Mrs. Bilbo's Policy," *Chicago Defender*, May 20, 1939; "Races: Mr. Bilbo's Afflatus," *Time*, May 8, 1939.

113. Ralph Matthews, "'Back to Africa' Pilgrimage Proves Barnum Was Right!" *Baltimore Afro-American*, April 29, 1939.

114. "500 Want to Go Back to Africa."

115. "500 Want to Go Back to Africa."

116. Fitzgerald, "We Have Found a Moses," 312.

117. These UNIA men included A. L. King and Thomas Harvey.

118. Quoted in Sudiata, *Brothers and Strangers*, 312.

119. See Randi Storch, *Working Hard for the American Dream: Workers and Their Unions, World War I to the Present* (Chichester: John Wiley, 2013).

120. Matthews, " 'Back to Africa' Pilgrimage Proves Barnum Was Right!"

121. "She's 1939 Moses," *Baltimore Afro-American*, April 29, 1939.

122. Sarah H. Bradford, *Harriet Tubman: The Moses of Her People* (Gloucester, Mass.: P. Smith, 1981); Rosemary Sadlier, *Harriet Tubman: Freedom Seeker, Freedom Leader* (Toronto: Dundurn Press, 2012).

123. Mrs. Jowers, "You Better Run," in Peace Movement of Ethiopia Constitution, 37.

124. Juanita Carter, "The Battle Hymn of the Peace Movement," in Peace Movement of Ethiopia Constitution, 27.

125. Best, *Passionately Human, No Less Divine*, 158.

126. McCray, *The Universal Negro Improvement Association*.

127. Juanita Carter, "The Land for Me," in Peace Movement of Ethiopia Constitution, 31.

128. Albert McCall, "My Home," in Peace Movement of Ethiopia Constitution, 34.

129. J. E. Hart, "Is My Name Down There?" in Peace Movement of Ethiopia Constitution, 36.

130. Fitzgerald, "We Have Found a Moses," 313; Hedlin, "Earnest Cox and Colonization," 147.

131. Henry L. West to Bilbo, September 23, 1939, Reel 246, American Colonization Society Records, Library of Congress, Washington, D.C.

132. Gordon to Bilbo, October 15, 1939, Box 1090, Folder 9, Bilbo Papers.

133. Richard Polenberg, *War and Society: The United States, 1941–1945* (Westport, Conn.: Greenwood, 1980).

134. Michael Carew, *Becoming the Arsenal: The American Industrial Mobilization for World War II, 1938–1942* (Lanham, Md.: University Press of America, 2010).

135. Gordon to Bilbo, October 15, 1939, Box 1090, Folder 9, Bilbo Papers.

136. Taylor, *Veiled Garvey*, 158–59.

Chapter 5

1. Amy Jacques Garvey to A. Balfour Linton, February 8, 1944, Box 1, Marcus Garvey Memorial Collection, Fisk University, Nashville, Tenn.

2. Hakim Adi and Marika Sherwood, eds., *Pan-African History: Political Figures from Africa and the Diaspora Since 1787* (New York: Routledge, 2003); Esedebe, P. Olisanwuche, *Pan-Africanism: The Idea and Movement, 1776–1991* (Washington, D.C.: Howard University Press, 1994).

3. Richard Polenberg, *War and Society: The United States, 1941–1945* (Westport, Conn.: Greenwood, 1980); Nat Brandt, *Harlem at War: The Black Experience in WWII* (Syracuse, N.Y.: Syracuse University Press, 1996); Neil A. Wynn, *The African American Experience During World War II* (Lanham, Md.: Rowman & Littlefield, 2010).

4. Penny Von Eschen, *Race Against Empire: Black Americans and Anticolonialism, 1937–1957* (Ithaca, N.Y.: Cornell University Press, 1997); James Meriwether, *Proudly We Can Be Africans: Black Americans and Africa, 1935–1961* (Chapel Hill: University of North Carolina Press, 2002);

Lindsey R. Swindall, *The Path to the Greater, Freer, Truer World: Southern Civil Rights and Anticolonialism, 1937–1955* (Gainesville: University of Florida, 2014); Carol Anderson, *Bourgeois Radicals: The NAACP and the Struggle for Colonial Liberation, 1941–1960* (New York: Cambridge University Press, 2015).

5. A. Philip Randolph was the president of the Brotherhood of Sleeping Car Porters (BSCP), the first black-led labor union. See Cornelius Bynum, *A. Philip Randolph and the Struggle for Civil Rights* (Urbana: University of Illinois Press, 2010). On the "Double V" campaign, see Rawn James Jr., *The Double V: How Wars, Protest, and Harry Truman Desegregated America's Military* (New York: Bloomsbury, 2013). On the March on Washington, see David Lucander, *Winning the War for Democracy: The March on Washington Movement, 1941–1946* (Urbana: University of Illinois Press, 2014).

6. Grossman, *Land of Hope*; Isabel Wilkerson, *The Warmth of Other Suns: The Epic Story of America's Great Migration* (New York: Random House, 2010). On CORE, see August Meier and Elliot Rudwick, *CORE: A Study in the Civil Rights Movement, 1942–1968* (New York: Oxford University Press, 1973).

7. Maureen Honey, ed., *Bitter Fruit: African American Women in World War II* (Columbia: University of Missouri Press, 1999), 2.

8. Honey, *Bitter Fruit*. On the WAC, see Mattie E. Treadwell, *The Women's Army Corps* (Washington, D.C.: Government Printing Office, 1954); Brenda L. Moore, *To Serve My Country, to Serve My Race: The Story of the Only African American WACS Stationed Overseas During World War II* (New York: New York University Press, 1996); Charity Adams Earley, *One Woman's Army: A Black Officer Remembers the WAC* (College Station: Texas A&M University Press, 1989); Charissa J. Threats, *Nursing and Civil Rights: Gender and Race in the Army Nurse Corps* (Urbana: University of Illinois Press, 2015).

9. Gail Lumet Buckley, *American Patriots: The Story of Blacks in the Military from the Revolution to Desert Storm* (New York: Random House, 2001), 295–304.

10. Karen Tucker Anderson, "Last Hired, First Fired: Black Women Workers During World War II," *Journal of American History* 69 (1982): 84.

11. Mittie Maude Lena Gordon to Earnest Sevier Cox, March 2, 1942, Exhibit 142 in Report by Special Agents Francis A. Regan, Aubrey Elliott Jr., and Richard W. Axtell, FBI Investigative File No. 100-124410, National Archives, Washington, D.C.

12. Gordon to Cox, December 31, 1941, Box 6, Cox Papers.

13. Gordon to Cox, April 1, 1941, Box 6, Cox Papers; "Education: Prince with a Purpose," *Time*, January 1, 1945.

14. Marika Sherwood, *Kwame Nkrumah: The Years Abroad, 1935–1947* (Legon, Ghana: Freedom Publications, 1996), 54 n.27; Sir Nwafor Orizu, *Liberty or Chains-Africa Must Be: An Authobiography* [sic] *of Akweke Abyssinia Nwafor Orizu* (Anambra State, Nigeria: Horizontal Publishers, 1994).

15. Orizu, *Liberty or Chains-Africa Must Be*, 193–220.

16. "African Students Urge Liberation for 'Fatherland,'" *Pittsburgh Courier*, September 26, 1942; Sherwood, *Kwame Nkrumah*, 90.

17. Adebayo Oyebade and Toyin Falola, "West Africa and the United States in Historical Perspectives," in *The United States and West Africa: Interactions and Relations*, ed. Alusine Jalloh and Toyin Falola (Rochester, N.Y.: University of Rochester Press, 2008), 26; Frank Furedi, *Colonial Wars and the Politics of Third World Nationalism* (New York: St. Martin's, 1994), 35.

18. Keisha N. Blain, "'We Want to Set the World on Fire': Black Nationalist Women and Diasporic Politics in the *New Negro World*, 1940–1944," *Journal of Social History* 49, no. 1 (Fall 2015): 194–212.

19. Huggins, *Harlem Renaissance*; Lewis, *When Harlem Was in Vogue*; Baker, *Modernism and the Harlem Renaissance*; Baldwin, *Chicago's New Negroes*; Baldwin and Makalani, *Escape from New York*.

20. Josephine Moody, "We Want to Set the World on Fire," *New Negro World*, January 1942.

21. Florine Wilkes, "My Race," *New Negro World*, February 1943.

22. Theresa E. Young, "The Real Solution," *New Negro World*, September 1943.

23. See Davies, *Left of Karl Marx*; McDuffie, *Sojourning for Freedom*; Gore, *Radicalism at the Crossroads*; Harris, "Running with the Reds."

24. McDuffie, *Sojourning for Freedom*, 115.

25. Erik S. McDuffie, " 'For the Full Freedom of . . . Colored Women in Africa, Asia, and in these United States . . . ': Black Women Radicals and the Practice of a Black Women's International," *Palimpsest: A Journal on Women, Gender and the Black International* 1 (2012): 8.

26. Rod Bush, *We Are Not What We Seem: Black Nationalism and Class Struggle in the American Century* (New York: New York University Press, 1998).

27. Peace Movement of Ethiopia Constitution, 33.

28. Ethel M. Collins, "Liberty," *New Negro World*, January 1942.

29. Eustance G. Campbell, "Wake Up Negro," *New Negro World*, July 1942.

30. Robert A. Hill, "Black Zionism: Marcus Garvey and the Jewish Question," in *African Americans and Jews in the Twentieth Century: Studies in Convergence and Conflict*, ed. V. P. Franklin (Columbia: University of Missouri Press, 1998).

31. Campbell, "Wake Up Negro" (capitalizations in the original text).

32. Lemelle and Kelley, *Imagining Home*, 7.

33. Frank Guridy, *Forging Diaspora: Afro-Cubans and African Americans in a World of Empire and Jim Crow* (Chapel Hill: University of North Carolina Press, 2010), 4.

34. Collins, "Liberty."

35. Collins, "Liberty."

36. Elaine Cooper, *New Negro World*, January 1942. On Garveyism in Canada, see Carla Marano, " 'Rising Strongly and Rapidly': The Universal Negro Improvement Association in Canada, 1919–1940," *Canadian Historical Review* 91 (2010): 233–59.

37. Theresa E. Young, "The Real Solution," *New Negro World*, September 1943.

38. Edith Allen, "Ga. Prisoner Chained to Tree," *New Negro World*, October 1941.

39. Collins, "Liberty."

40. Adeleke, *UnAfrican Americans*; Moses, *Alexander Crummell*.

41. E. Frances White, "Africa on My Mind: Gender, Counter Discourse and African-American Nationalism," *Journal of Women's History* 2 (1990): 73–97.

42. Barbara Bush, *Imperialism, Race, and Resistance: Africa and Britain, 1919–1945* (New York: Routledge, 1999), 14.

43. Florine Wilkes, "Our Condition," *New Negro World*, March 1943. Stephanie Batiste, *Darkening Mirrors: Imperial Representation in Depression-Era African American Performance* (Durham, N.C.: Duke University Press, 2011), 258.

44. Madhu Dubey, *Black Women Novelists and the Nationalist Aesthetic* (Bloomington: Indiana University Press, 1994), 25.

45. Adelia Ireland, "Arise," *New Negro World*, July 1942.

46. Ethel M. Collins, "A Tribute to the Late Marcus Garvey," *New Negro World*, July 1942.

47. Moses, *The Golden Age of Black Nationalism*, 156–57; George Shepperson, "Ethiopianism and African Nationalism," *Phylon* 14 (1953): 9–18; Drake, *The Redemption of Africa and Black Religion*; Moses, *Afrotopia*, 26–27.

48. J. P. Giddings, "Have I a Place in My Father's House?" *New Negro World*, March 1942.

49. Collins, "Liberty."

50. McDuffie, *Sojourning for Freedom*, 3–4.

51. Ireland, "Arise."

52. "Elinor White, State Commissioner of Illinois, Make Stiring [sic] Appeal to Black Women and Men All Over the World," *New Negro World*, May 1942.

53. Florine Wilkes, "To Black Men Everywhere," *New Negro World*, November 1944 (capitalizations in the original text).

54. James Stewart, "To the Officers, Members and Friends of the Association and of the Race," *New Negro World*, March 1943; Erik S. McDuffie, "Garveyism in Cleveland, Ohio and the History of the Diasporic Midwest, 1920–1975," *African Identities* 9, no. 2 (2011): 163–82.

55. McDuffie, "Garveyism in Cleveland, Ohio," 176.

56. Ethel Collins to Officers, Members and Friends of the UNIA and of the Race, August 15, 1943, Box 1, Marcus Garvey Memorial Collection, Fisk University, Nashville, Tenn.

57. See Robert Carr, *Black Nationalism in the New World: Reading the African American and West Indian Experience* (Durham, N.C.: Duke University Press, 2002).

58. Veronica Marie Gregg, " 'How with This Rage Shall Beauty Hold a plea': The Writings of Miss Amy Beckford Bailey as Moral Education in the Era of Jamaican Nation-Building," *Small Axe* 23 (June 2007): 16–33.

59. Jennifer Brown MacLeavy, "Amy Beckford Bailey: A Biography," *Jamaican Historical Review* 18 (1993): 31–39.

60. Paula Baker, "The Domestication of Politics: Women and American Political Society, 1790–1920," *American Historical Review* 89, no. 3 (1984): 622.

61. Amy Bailey, "Marcus Garvey," *Jamaica Gleaner*, October 21, 1978, 8.

62. Lara Putnam, *Radical Moves: Caribbean Migrants and the Politics of Race in the Jazz Age* (Chapel Hill: University of North Carolina Press, 2013).

63. Amy Bailey, "Are We Satisfied? (Part I)," *Public Opinion*, January 29, 1938, 10.

64. Jennifer Brown MacLeavy, "Amy Beckford Bailey: A Biography," *Jamaican Historical Review* 18 (1993): 31–39.

65. Amy Bailey, "Don't Shoot—Educate!" *Public Opinion*, July 2, 1938, 7, 11.

66. Amy Bailey, "Letter to the Editor: This Colour Question," *Daily Gleaner*, February 18, 1944.

67. Delia Jarret-Macauley, *The Life of Una Marson, 1905–1965* (Manchester: Manchester University Press, 1998), 37.

68. Quoted in Jarret-Macauley, *The Life of Una Marson*, 161.

69. Tiffany Ruby Patterson and Robin D. G. Kelley, "Unfinished Migrations: Reflections on the African Diaspora and the Making of the Modern World," *African Studies Review* 43, no. 1 (April 2000): 11–45; Lawrence Grossberg, "On Postmodernism and Articulation: An Interview with Stuart Hall," in *Stuart Hall: Critical Dialogues in Cultural Studies*, ed. David Morley and Kuan-Hsing Chen (New York: Routledge, 2005), 131–50.

70. Guridy, *Forging Diaspora*, 4.

71. Frederick Cooper, *Colonialism in Question: Theory, Knowledge, History* (Berkeley: University of California Press, 2005), 27.

72. Hakim Adi, *West Africans in Britain, 1900–1960: Nationalism, Pan-Africanism, and Communism* (London: Lawrence & Wishart, 1998); Bill Schwarz, ed., *West Indian Intellectuals in Britain* (Manchester: Manchester University Press, 2003).

73. Hakim Adi, "Amy Ashwood and the Nigerian Progress Union," in *Gendering the African Diaspora: Women, Culture, and Historical Change in the Caribbean and Nigerian Hinterland*, ed. Judith A. Byfield, LaRay Denzer, and Antea Morrison (Bloomington: Indiana University Press, 2010), 200.

74. Adi, "Amy Ashwood and the Nigerian Progress Union." Also see Minkah Makalani, *In the Cause of Freedom: Radical Black Internationalism from Harlem to London, 1917–1939* (Chapel Hill: University of North Carolina Press, 2011); Susan D. Pennybacker, *From Scottsboro to Munch: Race and Political Culture in 1930s Britain* (Princeton, N.J.: Princeton University Press, 2009).

75. Adi, "Amy Ashwood and the Nigerian Progress Union," 200.

76. "Amy Ashwood Garvey," *New York Amsterdam News*, October 20, 1926; Display ad for "Hey Hey," *New York Amsterdam News*, November 3, 1926; "Mme. Garvey's Show a Hit at the Lafayette," *New York Amsterdam News*, November 10, 1926.

77. Errol G. Hill and James V. Hatch, *A History of African American Theater* (New York: Cambridge University Press, 2003), 278.

78. Hill and Hatch, *A History of African American Theater*.

79. Makalani, *In the Cause of Freedom*, 196; Matera, *Black London*, 107.

80. The IASB was previously the International African Friends of Abyssinia (IAFA).

81. "Mrs. Garvey at Trafalgar Square," *Jamaican Gleaner*, September 11, 1935.

82. Quoted in Martin, *Amy Ashwood Garvey*, 143.

83. Quoted in Adi and Sherwood, *Pan-African History*, 72.

84. See Martin, *Race First*; Martin, *Amy Ashwood*.

85. On interracialism, see Lauren Kientz Anderson, "A Nauseating Sentiment, a Magical Device, or a Real Insight? Interracialism at Fisk University in 1930," *Perspectives on the History of Higher Education* 29 (2012): 75–112. My use of the term in this context does not imply that Ashwood advocated slow gradual change or accommodationism.

86. Fitzroy Andre Baptiste, "Amy Ashwood Garvey and Afro-West Indian Labor in the United States Emergency Farm and War Industries' Programs of World War II, 1943–1945," www.africamigration.com/archive_02/f_baptiste.htm (accessed October 10, 2013). On Smith, see Judith Stein, *The World of Marcus Garvey: Race and Class in Modern Society* (Baton Rouge: Louisiana State University Press), 260.

87. "Mrs. Garvey Still Alive with Crusade," *New York Amsterdam*, March 4, 1944.

88. Baptiste, "Amy Ashwood Garvey and Afro-West Indian Labor."

89. Constance Curtis, "Women's International Magazine Planned as One Avenue to Lead to World Unity," *New York Amsterdam News*, April 1, 1944.

90. Maymie De Mena Aiken to James R. Stewart, January 22, 1942, Hanif Wahab Collection (Unclassified), Charles H. Wright Museum of African American History, Detroit, Mich.

91. Nicole Bourbonnais, "Our Joan of Arc: Women, Gender, and Authority in the Harmony Division of the UNIA" (unpublished manuscript in author's possession).

92. Bourbonnais, "Our Joan of Arc."

93. Bourbonnais, "Our Joan of Arc."

94. Courtney Morris, "Becoming Creole, Becoming Black: Migration, Diasporic Self-Making, and the Many Lives of Madame Maymie Leona Turpeau de Mena," *Women, Gender and Families of Color* 4, no. 2 (Fall 2016): 171–95.

95. Taylor, *Veiled Garvey*, 119–24.

96. Adler, " 'Always Leading Our Men in Service and Sacrifice,' " 369; Taylor, *Veiled Garvey*, 143–74; Amy Jacques Garvey, *Garvey and Garveyism* (Kingston, Jamaica: A. J. Garvey, 1963).

97. George E.Eaton, *Alexander Bustamante and Modern Jamaica* (Kingston, Jamaica: LMH Publishers, 2000), 40–42.

98. Taylor, *Veiled Garvey*, 158–59.

99. *United States of America v. Mittie Maud Lena Gordon*, Reply Brief for Appellants, Box 34, Cox Papers.

100. "FBI Accuses 80 in Chicago of Part in Seditious Activities," *Baltimore Afro-American*, September 26, 1942. Several activist men were also charged with violating draft laws.

101. Hedlin, "Earnest Cox and Colonization," 154.

102. See *United States v. Gordon et al.*, 138 F.2d 174 (7th Cir. October 9, 1943).

103. Amy Jacques Garvey to Hilbert Keys, April 5, 1944, Amy Jacques Collection, Box 1, Charles Blockson Collection, Temple University, Philadelphia, Pa.

104. Jacques Garvey to Bilbo, March 26, 1944, Box 15, Folder 4, Marcus Garvey Memorial Collection, Fisk University, Nashville, Tenn.

105. Manning Marable, *Black Leadership* (New York: Columbia University Press, 1988), 106.

106. Jacques Garvey to Harold Moody, April 17, 1944, Box 2, Folder 10, Garvey Memorial Collection.

107. Jacques Garvey to Moody, April 17, 1944, Box 2, Folder 10, Garvey Memorial Collection.

108. Jacques Garvey to Jarrett, April 14, 1944, Box 2, Folder 5, Garvey Memorial Collection.

109. Douglas Brinkley and David R. Facey-Crowther, eds., *The Atlantic Charter* (New York: St. Martin's, 1994).

110. Anderson, *Eyes Off the Prize*, 17; Immanuel Geiss, *Pan African Movement: A History of Pan-Africanism in America, Europe, and Africa*, trans. Ann Keep (New York: Africana Publishing Company, 1974).

111. Anderson, *Eyes Off the Prize*, 17.

112. Von Eschen, *Race Against Empire*, 25–26.

113. Quoted in Anderson, *Eyes Off the Prize*, 17.

114. Jacques Garvey to James A. Blades Jr., February 14, 1944, Box 1, Folder 3, Garvey Memorial Collection.

115. Jacques Garvey to Father Divine, February 8, 1944, Box 1, Folder 7, Garvey Memorial Collection.

116. Jacques Garvey to Hilbert Keys, May 3, 1944, Box 2, Folder 7, Garvey Memorial Collection.

117. Amy Jacques Garvey to Hilbert Keys, June 30, 1944, Box 2, Folder 7, Garvey Memorial Collection; Amy Jacques Garvey to Hilbert Keys, June 30, 1944, Box 1, Folder 23, Amy Jacques Garvey Collection, Charles Blockson Collection, Temple University, Philadelphia.

118. Jacques Garvey to Keys, April 5, 1944, Box 2, Folder 7, Garvey Memorial Collection; Jacques Garvey to Keys, May 3, 1944, Box 2, Folder 7, Garvey Memorial Collection.

119. Jacques Garvey to Keys, April 5, 1944, Box 2, Folder 7, Garvey Memorial Collection.

120. James Blades to Jacques Garvey, August 7, 1944, Box 1, Folder 3, Garvey Memorial Collection.

121. Jacques Garvey to Blades, August 14, 1944, Box 1, Folder 3, Garvey Memorial Collection.

122. Jacques Garvey to Keys, March 11, 1944, Box 2, Folder 7, Garvey Memorial Collection.

123. Jacques Garvey to Keys, May 3, 1944, Box 2, Folder 7, Garvey Memorial Collection. On the women's page of the *Negro World*, see Taylor, *Veiled Garvey*, 64–90.

124. Jacques Garvey to Keys, May 3, 1944, Box 2, Folder 7, Garvey Memorial Collection; Jacques Garvey to Keys, June 30, 1944, Box 2, Folder 7, Garvey Memorial Collection.

125. Bilbo certainly received Jacques Garvey's letters. See two letters to Bilbo of the same date: Jacques Garvey to Bilbo, March 26, 1944, Box 1090, Folder 4, Bilbo Papers. On Bilbo's failing health, see Hedlin, "Earnest Cox and Colonization," 158.

126. Jacques Garvey to Keys, June 30, 1944, Box 2, Folder 7, Garvey Memorial Collection.

127. Jacques Garvey to Keys, June 30, 1944, Box 2, Folder 7, Garvey Memorial Collection.

128. Taylor, *Veiled Garvey*, 159–60. Jacques Garvey advised Keys to print copies of the UNIA aims and objectives instead of the bill. See Jacques Garvey to Keys, August 2, 1944, Box 2, Folder 7, Garvey Memorial Collection.

129. Geiss, *The Pan-African Movement*. There has been much scholarly debate concerning Nkrumah's role as well as Du Bois's role in organizing the conference. For these varying perspectives, see James R. Hooker, *Black Revolutionary: George Padmore's Path from Communism to Pan-Africanism* (New York: Praeger, 1970); David Levering Lewis, *W. E. B. Du Bois: The Fight for Equality and the American Century, 1919–1963* (New York: Henry Holt, 1995); Kwame Nkrumah, *Ghana: The Autobiography of Kwame Nkrumah* (New York: International Publishers, 1957); Marika Sherwood, *Kwame Nkrumah: The Years Abroad, 1935–1947* (Legon: Freedom Publications, 1996).

130. Taylor, *Veiled Garvey*, 165–70.

131. Amy Ashwood Garvey, speech given to the Manchester Pan-African Congress, October 19, 1945, in *History of the Pan-African Congress: Colonial and Coloured Unity, a Programme of Action*, ed. George Padmore (Manchester: Pan-African Federation, 1945).

132. Amy Jacques Garvey to George Padmore, September 22, 1945, Box 2, File 11, Marcus Garvey Memorial Collection, Fisk University, Nashville, Tenn.

133. Hillina Seife, "A New Generation of Ethiopianists: The Universal Ethiopian Students Association and *The African: Journal of African Affairs*, 1937–1948," *African and Black Diaspora: An International Journal* (2010) 3, no. 2: 197–209.

134. John Munro, "Ethiopia Stretches Forth Across the Atlantic: African American Anticolonialism During the Interwar Period," *Left History* 13, no. 2 (Fall–Winter 2008): 37–68.

135. See Seife, "A New Generation of Ethiopianists."

136. Clare Courbould, *Becoming African Americans: Black Public Life in Harlem, 1919–1939* (Cambridge, Mass.: Harvard University Press, 2009), 207.

137. Clare Courbould, *Becoming African Americans*, 207; George S. Schuyler, *Ethiopian Stories* (Boston: Northeastern University Press, 1994), 20.

138. See Seife, "A New Generation of Ethiopianists."

139. Stanley Davis, Letter to the Editor, *African*, September 1946.

140. Seife, "A New Generation of Ethiopianists," 198, 200. See "The African Magazine Banned in Kongo," *African*, September 1946.

141. Erez Manela, *A Wilsonian Moment: Self-Determination and the International Origins of Anticolonial Nationalism* (New York: Oxford University Press, 2007).

142. Amy Jacques Garvey, "Africans at Home and Abroad," *African*, October 1945.

143. Jacques Garvey, "The Coming Era," *African*, August 1944.

144. Gordon was released from prison several months early after making several requests because of failing health. Gordon to Cox, August 11, 1945, Box 6, Folder 3.

145. Jacques Garvey, "Be Prepared," *African*, May 1946.

146. Jacques Garvey, "Adversity + Courage = Advantages," *African*, November–December 1944.

147. Garvey, "Adversity + Courage = Advantages."

148. Jacques Garvey, "The Language of Freedom," *African*, May–June 1945.

149. Jacques Garvey, "Where Are My Children," *African*, June 1946.

150. Amy Jacques Garvey, "Is Yours a Home," *African*, April 1945.

151. "Mrs. Victoria Schaack Points to Liberia as Land of Opportunity," *Afro-American*, April 27, 1946.

152. Hill, *Marcus Garvey and the Universal Negro Improvement Association Papers*, II:431.

153. "Mrs. Victoria Schaack Points to Liberia as Land of Opportunity."

154. "Reclaim the Home and African Family," *African*, August 1946.

155. Victoria J. Schaack, "Home and Family Life," *African*, September 1946.

156. Joy James, "Radicalizing Feminism," in *The Black Feminist Reader*, ed. Joy James and T. Denean Sharpley-Whiting (Malden, Mass.: Blackwell, 2000), 246.

Chapter 6

1. Mittie Maude Lena Gordon to Earnest Sevier Cox, August 13, 1956, Box 11, Folder 3, Earnest Sevier Cox Papers, 1821–1973, Rare Book, Manuscript, and Special Collections Library, Duke University, Durham, N.C.

2. The literature on the Civil Rights–Black Power era is extensive. Key works include Clayborne Carson, *In Struggle: SNCC and the Black Awakening of the 1960s* (Cambridge, Mass.:

Harvard University Press, 1981); Aldon D. Morris, *The Origins of the Civil Rights Movement: Black Communities Organizing for Change* (New York: Free Press, 1984); Barbara Ransby, *Ella Baker and the Black Freedom Movement: A Radical Democratic Vision* (Chapel Hill: University of North Carolina Press, 2003); William L. Van Deburg, *New Day in Babylon: The Black Power Movement and the American Culture* (Chicago: University of Chicago Press, 1992); Lance Hill, *Deacons of Defense: Armed Resistance and the Civil Rights Movement* (Chapel Hill: University of North Carolina Press, 2004); Nikhil Pal Singh, *Black Is a Country: Race and the Unfinished Struggle for Democracy* (Cambridge, Mass.: Harvard University Press, 2005); Jeffrey O. G. Ogbar, *Black Power: Radical Politics and African American Identity* (Baltimore: Johns Hopkins University Press, 2004); Peniel Joseph, *Waiting 'Til the Midnight Hour: A Narrative History of Black Power* (New York: Henry Holt, 2006).

3. Peniel Joseph, "The Black Power Movement: A State of the Field," *Journal of American History* 96, no. 3 (December 2009): 752; Ransby, *Ella Baker and the Black Freedom Movement*; Tim Tyson, *Radio Free Dixie: Robert F. Williams and the Roots of Black Power* (Chapel Hill: University of North Carolina Press, 1999); Pero Dagbovie, " 'God Has Spared Me to Tell My Story': Mabel Robinson Williams and the Civil Rights–Black Power Movement," *Black Scholar* 43: 1–2, 69–88.

4. Clifton E. Marsh, *The Lost-Found Nation of Islam in America* (Lanham, Md.: Scarecrow Press, 2000), 11. Also see Edward E. Curtis, *Black Muslim Religion in the Nation of Islam, 1960–1975* (Chapel Hill: University of North Carolina Press, 2006); Dan Berger, "The Malcolm X Doctrine, The Republic of New Afrika and National Liberation on U.S. Soil," in *New World Coming: The Sixties and the Shaping of Global Consciousness*, ed. Karen Dubinsky (Toronto: Between the Lines, 2009).

5. Scott Brown, *Fighting for US: Maulana Karenga, the US Organization, and Black Cultural Nationalism* (New York: New York University Press, 2003); Joshua Bloom and Waldo E. Martin, *Black Against Empire: The History and Politics of the Black Panther Party* (Berkeley: University of California Press, 2013).

6. Joseph, *Waiting 'Til the Midnight Hour*, 3.

7. Earnest Sevier Cox to Benjamin Jones, October 9, 1950, Box 8, Folder 1, Cox Papers.

8. Cox references this card in a 1948 letter. See Earnest Sevier Cox to Mittie Maude Lena Gordon, December 18, 1948, Box 7, Folder 1, Cox Papers.

9. Earnest Sevier Cox to Rosie Lee Gearring, April 4, 1944, Box 6, Folder 2; Mittie Maude Lena Gordon to Earnest Sevier Cox, January 28, 1947, Box 6, Folder 5, Cox Papers.

10. Mittie Maude Lena Gordon and Alberta Spain to Earnest Sevier Cox, June 18, 1953, Box 9, Folder 4, Cox Papers.

11. Mittie Maude Lena Gordon to Earnest Sevier Cox, November 14, 1949, Box 7, Folder 5, Cox Papers.

12. Indiana State Board of Health, Birth Certificates, 1907–40, Indiana Archives and Records Administration, Indianapolis, Ind., Ancestry.com subscription database, http://www.ancestry.com (accessed July 10, 2016).

13. Report of Special Agent Harry B. Behrmann, March 27, 1944, Indianapolis, Ind., FBI File No. 100-V24410-166, National Archives, Washington, D.C.

14. Rosie Lee Gearring to Earnest Sevier Cox, May 31, 1944, Box 6, Folder 2, Cox Papers.

15. Marriage Announcement of John and Rosa Lee Gearring, *Indianapolis Recorder*, August 17, 1940, 4.

16. Report of Special Agent Harry B. Behrmann, March 27, 1944, Indianapolis, Indiana, FBI File No. 100-V24410-166, National Archives, Washington, D.C.

17. Report of Special Agent Harry B. Behrmann, March 27, 1944, Indianapolis, Indiana, FBI File No. 100-V24410-166, National Archives, Washington, D.C.

18. Rosie Lee Gearring to Earnest Sevier Cox, January 22, 1944, Box 6, Folder 2, Cox Papers.

19. Rosie Lee Gearring to Earnest Sevier Cox, June 6, 1944, Box 6, Folder 2, Cox Papers.

20. Rosie Lee Gearring to Earnest Sevier Cox, January 22, 1944, Box 6, Folder 2, Cox Papers.

21. Rosie Lee Gearring to Earnest Sevier Cox, April 21, 1944, Box 6, Folder 2, Cox Papers.

22. Rosie Lee Gearring to Earnest Sevier Cox, January 5, 1945, Box 6, Folder 3, Cox Papers.

23. Peace Movement of Ethiopia Constitution, 12.

24. Program for the Memorial Service of William Gordon, Box 7, Folder 2, Cox Papers.

25. Alberta Spain to Earnest Sevier Cox, September 10, 1962, Box 14, Folder 6, Cox Papers.

26. Seminal works on Black Power include Joseph, *Waiting 'Til the Midnight Hour*; Quito Swan, *Black Power in Bermuda: The Struggle for Decolonization* (New York: Palgrave Macmillan, 2009); Nico Slate, ed., *Black Power Beyond Borders: The Global Dimensions of the Black Power Movement* (New York: Palgrave Macmillan, 2012); Kate Quinn, ed., *Black Power in the Caribbean* (Gainesville: University Press of Florida, 2014); Russell Rickford, *We Are an African People: Independent Education, Black Power and the Radical Imagination* (Oxford: Oxford University Press, 2016); Rhonda Williams, *Concrete Demands: The Search for Black Power in the 20th Century* (New York: Routledge, 2015).

27. Erik S. McDuffie, "A New Day Has Dawned for the UNIA: Garveyism, the Diasporic Midwest and West Africa, 1920–1980," *Journal of West African History* 2, no. 1 (Spring 2016): 74.

28. Adeleke, *UnAfrican Americans.*

29. Mittie Maude Lena Gordon and Alberta Spain to Earnest Sevier Cox, January 17, 1955, Box 10, Folder 2, Cox Papers.

30. Earnest Sevier Cox to Mittie Maude Lena Gordon, April 10, 1946, Box 6, Folder 4, Cox Papers. On the NAACP's quest for UN intervention, see Anderson, *Eyes Off the Prize.*

31. Mittie Maude Lena Gordon to Earnest Sevier Cox, September 8, 1948, Box 7, Folder 1, Cox Papers.

32. Mittie Maude Lena Gordon to Earnest Sevier Cox, October 26, 1948, Box 7, Folder 1, Cox Papers.

33. Earnest Sevier Cox to Mittie Maude Lena Gordon, May 22, 1949, Box 7, Folder 1, Cox Papers.

34. Benjamin Gibbons to Earnest Sevier Cox, December 24, 1947, Box 6, Folder 5, Cox Papers.

35. Benjamin Gibbons to Jacques Garvey, June 23, 1944, Box 1, Folder 12, Marcus Garvey Memorial Collection, Fisk University, Nashville, Tenn.

36. Benjamin Gibbons, "Letter to the Editor: UNIA Backs Legislation for Migration to Liberia," *Philadelphia Tribune*, April 19, 1958.

37. Hedlin, "Earnest Cox and Colonization," 178.

38. Hedlin, "Earnest Cox and Colonization," 177.

39. Hedlin, "Earnest Cox and Colonization," 177–82.

40. Mittie Maude Lena Gordon to Earnest Sevier Cox, January 25, 1950, Box 7, Folder 6, Cox Papers; Mittie Maude Lena Gordon to Earnest Sevier Cox, January 17, 1950, Box 7, Folder 6, Cox Papers.

41. Mittie Maude Lena Gordon to Earnest Sevier Cox, July 2, 1949, Box 7, Folder 3, Cox Papers.

42. Mittie Maude Lena Gordon to Earnest Sevier Cox, July 2, 1949, Box 7, Folder 3, Cox Papers.

43. McDuffie, "A New Day Has Dawned for the UNIA," 88.

44. "Back-to-Africa Slayer Is Held to Grand Jury," *Chicago Defender*, June 21, 1941.

45. "Back-to-Africa Slayer Is Held to Grand Jury."

46. Lucreacy Rockmore to Earnest Sevier Cox, August 17, 1949, Cox Papers, Box 7, Folder 4.

47. Amy Jacques Garvey to Earnest Sevier Cox, October 31, 1947, Box 1, Folder 5, Marcus Garvey Memorial Collection, Fisk University, Nashville, Tenn.

48. Amy Jacques Garvey to Earnest Sevier Cox, January 5, 1948, Box 1, Folder 5, Garvey Memorial.

49. Tony Martin, *Amy Ashwood Garvey: Pan-Africanist, Feminist, and Mrs. Garvey No. 1* (Dover, Mass.: Majority Press, 2007), 208.

50. Amy Ashwood Garvey to William V. S. Tubman, May 26, 1946, William V. S. Tubman Papers, 1904–1992 (Record Group: Tubman Personal Papers), Liberian Collections Project, Indiana University Library, Bloomington, Ind.

51. Amy Ashwood Garvey to William V. S. Tubman, May 26, 1946, Tubman Papers.

52. Amy Ashwood to William V. S. Tubman, May 26, 1946, Tubman Papers.

53. On racial uplift politics, see Gaines, *Uplifting the Race.*

54. Chandra Talpade Mohanty, "Under Western Eyes: Feminist Scholarship and Colonial Discourses," in *Feminism Without Borders: Decolonizing Theory, Practicing Solidarity* (Durham, N.C.: Duke University Press, 2003).

55. Paul Robeson, *Here I Stand* (Boston: Beacon, 1958), 33–35. See also Penny Von Eschen, *Race Against Empire: Black Americans and Colonialism, 1937–1957* (Ithaca, N.Y.: Cornell University Press, 1997).

56. Adi and Sherwood, *Pan-African History*, 73.

57. Nydia Swaby, "Women Radical, Woman Intellectual, Woman Activist: The Political Life of Pan-African Feminist Amy Ashwood Garvey" (M.A. thesis, Sarah Lawrence College, 2011), 72.

58. McDuffie, "A New Day Has Dawned for the UNIA," 91.

59. McDuffie, "A New Day Has Dawned for the UNIA," 78.

60. Mittie Maude Lena Gordon to Earnest Sevier Cox, January 4, 1957, Box 12, Folder 1, Cox Papers.

61. West, "'Like a River.'"

62. Mittie Maude Lena Gordon and Alberta Spain to Earnest Sevier Cox, January 17, 1955, Box 10, Folder 2, Cox Papers.

63. Alberta Spain and Josie Love to George W. Armstrong, November 14, 1949, Box 7, Folder 5, Cox Papers.

64. Mittie Maude Lena Gordon to Earnest Sevier Cox, November 14, 1949, Box 7, Folder 5, Cox Papers.

65. Mittie Maude Lena Gordon to Earnest Sevier Cox, March 27, 1956, Box 11, Folder 2, Cox Papers.

66. Mittie Maude Lena Gordon to Earnest Sevier Cox, January 4, 1957, Box 12, Folder 1, Cox Papers.

67. Mittie Maude Lena Gordon to Earnest Sevier Cox, September 2, 1952, Box 9, Folder 3, Cox Papers.

68. Mittie Maude Lena Gordon to Earnest Sevier Cox, February 18, 1953, Box 9, Folder 4, Cox Papers.

69. Mittie Maude Lena Gordon and Alberta Spain to Earnest Sevier Cox, June 29, 1953, Box 9, Folder 4, Cox Papers.

70. Mittie Maude Lena Gordon to Earnest Sevier Cox, September 2, 1952, Box 9, Folder 3, Cox Papers.

71. Mittie Maude Lena Gordon to Earnest Sevier Cox, November 19, 1956, Box 11, Folder 4, Cox Papers.

72. Mittie Maude Lena Gordon to Earnest Sevier Cox, August 2, 1954, Box 10, Folder 1, Cox Papers.

73. Mittie Maude Lena Gordon to Earnest Sevier Cox, March 3, 1961, Cox Papers, Box 14, Folder 3, Cox Papers.

74. James Meriwether, *Proudly We Can Be Africans: Black Americans and Africa, 1935–1961* (Chapel Hill: University of North Carolina Press, 2002).

75. Benjamin Gibbons to Earnest Sevier Cox, January 7, 1960, Box 14, Folder 1, Cox Papers.

76. Mittie Maude Lena Gordon to Earnest Sevier Cox, March 3, 1961, Box 14, Folder 3, Cox Papers.

77. Meriwether, *Proudly We Can Be Africans.*

78. Kevin Gaines, *African Americans in Ghana: Black Expatriates and the Civil Rights Movement* (Chapel Hill: University of North Carolina Press, 2007).

79. See Gaines, *African Americans in Ghana.* I have opted not to describe Ghana as *the first* nation to break free of European colonialism in recognition of Sudan's earlier victory in 1956.

80. Allison Paige Sellers, "The 'Black Man's Bible': The *Holy Piby*, Garveyism, and Black Supremacy in the Interwar Years," *Journal of Africana Religions* 3, no. 3 (2015): 325–42; Robert A. Hill, *Dread History: Leonard P. Howell and Millenarian Visions in the Early Rastafarian Religion* (Kingston: Miguel Lorne Publishers, 2001); Horace Campbell, *Rasta and Resistance: From Marcus Garvey to Walter Rodney* (Trenton, N.J.: Africa World Press, 1987); Rupert Lewis, "Marcus Garvey and the Early Rastafarians," in *Rastafari: A Universal Philosophy in the Third Millennium*, ed. Werner Zips (Kingston: Ian Randle, 2006), 42–58.

81. Maymie De Mena Aiken to Thomas Harvey, March 11, 1953, Box 4, Folder 1, Universal Negro Improvement Association (UNIA) Records, Stuart A. Rose Manuscript, Archives, and Rare Book Library (MARBL), Emory University, Atlanta, Ga.

82. Maymie De Mena Aiken to Thomas Harvey, November 25, 1952, Box 3, Folder 9, UNIA Collection.

83. Taylor, *Veiled Garvey*, 208.

84. Taylor, *Veiled Garvey*, 209.

85. Maymie De Mena Aiken to Thomas Harvey, November 25, 1952, Box 3, Folder 9, UNIA Collection.

86. Maymie De Mena Aiken to Thomas Harvey, November 25, 1952, Box 3, Folder 9, UNIA Collection.

87. Eugenie Bailey to Thomas Harvey, 1951 (no month or date listed), Box 3, Folder 4, UNIA Collection.

88. Eugenie Bailey to Thomas Harvey, 1951 (no month or date listed), Box 3, Folder 4, UNIA Collection.

89. Courtney Desiree Morris, "Becoming Creole, Becoming Black: Migration, Diasporic Self-Making, and the Many Lives of Madame Maymie Leona Turpeau de Mena," *Women, Gender, and Families of Color* 4, no. 2 (Fall 2016): 171–95.

90. "A Personality," *Daily Gleaner*, October 27, 1953.

91. Amy Jacques Garvey to William Sherrill, December 17, 1953, Box 1, Folder 3, UNIA Collection.

92. Amy Jacques Garvey to William Sherrill, December 17, 1953, Box 1, Folder 3, UNIA Collection.

93. Memorial Service Flier for Ethel Collins, Box 22, UNIA Collection.

94. Death Certificate of Mittie Gibson, File No. 41729, Cook County Genealogy Records Office, Chicago, Ill.

95. Alberta Spain to Earnest Sevier Cox, June 19, 1961, Box 14, Folder 3, Cox Papers.

96. David Garrow, *Bearing the Cross: Martin Luther King, Jr. and the Southern Christian Leadership Conference* (New York: W. Murrow, 1986).

97. Tyson, *Radio Free Dixie.*

98. See Dagbovie, "'God Has Spared Me to Tell My Story.'"

99. Tyson, *Radio Free Dixie*, 28.

100. Ashley Farmer, *Remaking Black Power: How Black Women Transformed an Era* (Chapel Hill: University of North Carolina Press, 2017).

101. Ashley Farmer, "Reframing African American Women's Grassroots Organizing: Audley Moore and the Universal Association of Ethiopian Women, 1957–1963," *Journal of African American History* 101, nos. 1–2 (Winter–Spring 2016): 69–96.

102. McDuffie, "'I Wanted a Communist Philosophy,'" 186, 189.

103. Farmer, *Remaking Black Power*.

104. Farmer, "Reframing African American Women's Grassroots Organizing."

105. Farmer, "Reframing African American Women's Grassroots Organizing."

106. Robert Trent Vinson, *The Americans Are Coming! Dreams of African American Liberation in Segregationist South Africa* (Athens: Ohio University Press, 2012), 20–21.

107. Farmer, "Reframing African American Women's Grassroots Organizing."

108. Quoted in Ashley Farmer, "Mothers of the Movement: Audley Moore and Dara Abubakari," *Women, Gender, and Families of Color* 4, no. 2 (Fall 2016): 274–95.

109. "Women's Group Seeks to Save 2 from 'Hot Seat,'" *Louisiana Weekly*, September 14, 1957.

110. Carole Elkins, *Imperial Reckoning: The Untold Story of Britain's Gulag in Kenya* (New York: Henry Holt, 2006).

111. Frank Guridy, *Forging Diaspora: Afro-Cubans and African Americans in a World of Empire and Jim Crow* (Chapel Hill: University of North Carolina Press, 2010).

112. Alberta Spain and Edmond Holiday to Earnest Sevier Cox, August 27, 1962, Box 14, Folder 6, Cox Papers.

113. Charise Cheney, *Brothers Gonna Work It Out: Sexual Politics in the Golden Age of Nationalism* (New York: New York University Press, 2005).

114. Alberta Spain to Senator of the United States of America, March 12, 1962, Box 14, Folder 6, Cox Papers.

115. Benjamin Gibbons to Earnest Sevier Cox, September 11, 1962, Box 14, Folder 6, Cox Papers.

116. Edward E. Curtis IV, *Black Muslim Religion in the Nation of Islam, 1960–1975* (Chapel Hill: University of North Carolina Press, 2006).

117. Erik S. McDuffie, "The Diasporic Journeys of Louise Little: Grassroots Garveyism, the Midwest, and Community Feminism," *Women, Gender, and Families of Color* 4, no. 2 (Fall 2016): 146–70.

118. Elijah Muhammad, *Message to the Blackman* (Phoenix, Ariz.: Sectarius MEMPS, 1973), 161.

119. Muhammad, *Message to the Blackman*, 161.

120. "It Is Time to Get a Divorce: Black Muslims Call for Separate U.S. Negro States," *Globe and Mail*, February 28, 1963.

121. Earnest Sevier Cox to Peace Movement of Ethiopia, September 1, 1962, Box 14, Folder 6, Cox Papers.

122. Mittie Maude Lena Gordon to Earnest Sevier Cox, October 10, 1947, Box 6, Folder 5, Cox Papers.

123. Alberta Spain to Earnest Sevier Cox, September 10, 1962, Box 14, Folder 6, Cox Papers.

124. Alberta Spain to Earnest Sevier Cox, September 10, 1962, Box 14, Folder 6, Cox Papers.

125. Alberta Spain to Earnest Sevier Cox, September 10, 1962, Box 14, Folder 6, Cox Papers.

126. Ross Valentine, "The Back to Africa Movement," *Richmond Times–Dispatch*, September 19, 1965.

127. Henry F. Cauthen and W. D. Workman Jr., "Resettlement Revived," *State*, September 21, 1965.

128. Cauthen and Workman, "Resettlement Revived."

129. Author's interviews with Mwariama Dhoruba Kamau, January 16, 2013, and July 28, 2013.

130. Michael O. West, "Garveyism Root and Branch: From the Age of Revolution to the Age of Black Power" (unpublished paper in author's possession).

131. A. Jacques Garvey, "The Source and Course of Black Power in America: The Dynamic Leadership of Garvey," *Star* (Kingston), October 4, 1966.

Epilogue

1. Gordon to Cox, September 17, 1951, Box 8, Folder 4, Cox Papers.

2. Cox to Gordon, August 18, 1951, Box 8, Folder 5, Cox Papers.

3. West, "'Like a River,'" 81–100; Wilson Jeremiah Moses, *The Golden Age of Black Nationalism* (New York: Oxford University Press, 1978).

4. McDuffie, "Garveyism in Cleveland."

5. McDuffie, "'A New Day Has Dawned for the UNIA.'"

6. Jakobi Williams, *From the Bullet to the Ballot: The Illinois Chapter of the Black Panther Party and Racial Coalition Politics in Chicago* (Chapel Hill: University of North Carolina Press, 2013).

7. The literature on the Black Panther Party is extensive. Some of the most important works include Joshua Bloom and Waldo E. Martin, *Black Against Empire: The History and Politics of the Black Panther Party* (Berkeley: University of California Press, 2013); Donna Murch, *Living for the City: Migration, Education, and the Rise of the Black Panther Party in Oakland, California* (Chapel Hill: University of North Carolina Press, 2010); Yohuru Williams, *Black Politics, White Power: Civil Rights, Black Power, and the Black Panthers in New Haven* (Malden, Mass.: Blackwell, 2008); Alondra Nelson, *Body and Soul: The Black Panther Party and the Fight Against Medical Discrimination* (Minneapolis: University of Minnesota Press, 2011; Robyn Spencer, *The Revolution Has Come: Black Power, Gender, and the Black Panther Party in Oakland* (Durham, N.C.: Duke University Press, 2016).

8. Robin D. G. Kelley, *Freedom Dreams: The Black Radical Imagination* (Boston: Beacon, 2002), ix.

INDEX

꠸

Page numbers in italics indicate illustrations.

ACKNOWLEDGMENTS

꙳

I am grateful to God for helping me finish this book. The journey from start to finish has not been easy, but at every step of the process, he placed the right people in my path to provide the support and guidance I needed to navigate a myriad of challenges.

I dedicate this book to my mom, who made so many sacrifices to ensure that I would have all the opportunities she desired for me. "Your gifts will make room for you," she assured me daily. I am thankful to her for being my greatest cheerleader and teaching me very early that I needed to blaze my own trail and not be preoccupied with what others were doing (or even with what they expected of me). Through her example, she taught me the importance of faith, the value of hard work, and the strength of humility.

My husband and best friend, Jay, has been an unwavering source of love and support, encouraging my research, writing, teaching, and public engagement in every possible way. He has had to endure all the challenges that come with being married to an (untenured) academic (including the constant moves across country!). I am thankful for his understanding and flexibility. My brother and sister helped me stay grounded throughout this journey, and for that I am most grateful. Lisa has been like a second mom, stepping in on numerous occasions to offer invaluable help and support. I owe a special thank you to my in-laws and the rest of my family who provided kind support and words of encouragement along the way.

In so many ways, this book began in Michael O. West's class, "Global Black Social Movements," at Binghamton University (SUNY). I am eternally grateful to West for sparking my interest in global black history and for providing unwavering support and encouragement—combined with honest, rigorous, and constructive feedback—from day one of this academic journey. At Binghamton, other wonderful scholars fed my intellectual curiosities and pushed me to reach my greatest potential. I am especially indebted to Thomas Dublin and Kathryn Kish Sklar, who enthusiastically supported my work.

At Princeton, Tera W. Hunter served as a model and a source of inspiration for me. When I doubted my ability to complete this project, she assured me that I could (and would) do it—and do it well. Her excitement for this project and unwavering faith in my ability to write this book encouraged and motivated me from start to finish.

So many scholars I deeply admire offered assistance during the writing process at various stages. Ula Y. Taylor provided unwavering support and advice throughout the past several years. I am grateful too for the kind support and assistance I received from Joshua B. Guild and Rebecca Rix.

No doubt the book is better because of the critical feedback and questions I received from a vast community of scholars. I would especially like to thank Carol Anderson, Kenneth Barnes, E. Tsekani Browne, Pero Dagbovie, Stephen G. Hall, LaShawn Harris, Shannon King, Minkah Makalani, Erik S. McDuffie, Lara Putnam, Mary Rolinson, Barbara Savage, Richard Brent Turner, Wilson Jeremiah Moses, Jason Morgan Ward, and Judith Weisenfeld. I owe gratitude to Mwariama Kamau for providing key research leads and connecting me with several veteran UNIA activists. I am also indebted to Michael Fitzgerald, who can best be described as an angel in disguise. It is no exaggeration to say that I could not have written this book without his willingness to assist me.

I cannot imagine what it would have been like to complete this book without having the support of my friends and colleagues in the African American Intellectual History Society (AAIHS). During each stage of the writing process, they jumped in to assist me in a myriad of ways and cheered me on toward the finish line. I would especially like to thank Christopher Cameron, Ashley Farmer, Ibram X. Kendi, Brandon Byrd, Greg Childs, Garrett Felber, Annette Joseph-Gabriel, Russell Rickford, Melissa Shaw, Quito Swan, and Phillip Luke Sinitiere.

At the University of Iowa, several colleagues offered support, including Ariana Ruiz, Lisa Heineman, Michaela Moore, Leslie Schwalm, and Jacki Rand. Two research assistants—Lori Megaro and Caroline Garske—provided invaluable help with the book, especially in the last few months. Mark Speltz, LaShawn Harris, and Clare Corbould extended help with securing copyright permissions and locating pictures for the book. My colleagues at the University of Pittsburgh have also been incredibly supportive. I am inspired by their innovative work and moved by their kindness and generosity. I owe special thanks to Lara Putnam, Larry Glasco, Liann Tsoukas, Mari Webel, and Pernille Roege.

Over the last few years, several organizations and institutions financially supported this project. Many thanks to Princeton University, the Pennsylvania State University, the University of Iowa, the University of Pittsburgh, the Organization of American Historians (OAH), the Society for Historians of American Foreign Relations (SHAFR), and the American Association of University of Women (AAUW). A research leave fellowship from AAUW made it possible for me to finish the remaining revisions for the book. During my fellowship year, the Department of Africana Studies at the University of Pennsylvania provided a quiet and supportive space for me to write.

Last, but certainly not least, I would like to thank everyone at the University of Pennsylvania Press for making the process of publishing this book such a smooth and enjoyable one. I am grateful to my amazing editor, Bob Lockhart, for his support and careful guidance during this process. Working with him has been an absolute pleasure—he has not only met but also exceeded all of my expectations. I am grateful for his sharp editorial eye, his excitement for this project, and his gentle nudge every now and then, which always kept me on track. I also want to extend my sincere appreciation to series editor Glenda Gilmore for her constructive feedback on the manuscript and for her kind prodding and encouragement toward the finish line.

In the process of writing this book, I racked up so many debts and owe thanks to so many people that I could not possibly mention everyone in these acknowledgments. Please know that I appreciate every kind word and gesture. I am grateful to all of you.